Immediate Fiction

Immediate Fiction

A COMPLETE WRITING COURSE

Jerry Cleaver

ST. MARTIN'S GRIFFIN
NEW YORK

"Homely Girl" by Elizabeth Brown reprinted by permission of author.
"Do Spiders Worry About Sex?" by Hugh Schulze reprinted by permission
of author.

IMMEDIATE FICTION: A COMPLETE WRITING COURSE. Copyright © 2002
by Jerry Cleaver. All rights reserved. Printed in the United States of
America. For information, address St. Martin's Press, 175 Fifth Avenue,
New York, N.Y. 10010.

www.stmartins.com

Library of Congress Cataloging-in-Publication Data
Cleaver, Jerry.
        Immediate fiction : a complete writing course / Jerry Cleaver.
            p. cm.
        ISBN 0-312-28716-X (hc)
        ISBN 0-312-30276-2 (pbk)
        EAN 978-0312-30276-4
        1. Fiction—Authorship.   I. Title.

    PN3355.C55 2002
    808.3—dc21   2001048868

10   9   8   7   6   5

DEDICATION

To Barney Sabath, the best mentor
and dearest friend anyone could ever have.

ACKNOWLEDGMENTS

Thanks to:
Frank Anselmo, my partner in crime.
Joe Hanley, catalyst, supersalesman.
Stanley Majka, editor, friend.
My wife, Leslie, my son, Matthew,
and my students.

Special thanks to:
Susan Reich, Hugh Schulze,
Elizabeth Brown, Helen Valenta, and my
editor, Michael Denneny, and Christina Prestia.

Contents

Introduction   *ix*

1. Rules of the Page   1

2. Theory   7

3. Story   19

4. Fine-Tuning   43

5. Use or Abuse—*Self-Editing*   64

6. The Active Ingredient—*Emotion*   72

7. Showing   100

8. The Second Time Around—*Rewriting*   110

9. Method—*How To. How Not To.*   138

10. Under the Sun—*Uniqueness. Universal Plots.*   146

11. Point of View   152

12. The Ticking Clock—*Fitting It In*   161

13. Dead Weight—*What You Can Ignore* 186

14. The Long and the Short of It—*From Short Story to Novel* 191

15. Hitting the Wall—*Blocking and Unblocking* 211

16. Stage and Screen 248

17. To Market to Market—*When to Submit, How, and Why* 260

Conclusion 273

Index 279

Introduction

A good story cannot be denied. Like falling in love, it's irresistible. It hits you before you have time to think. It touches your heart before it reaches your head. You're drawn in—whether you want to be or not. And you don't stand around asking, "Is it good?" or "Is it real?" These questions don't even come up. I've been walking through a room where a dramatic scene is playing on the TV, and been struck by a single line, a line that pulled me into the story. I have to stop and see what is happening. That's the kind of story you'll learn to write in this course.

The craft and techniques of *Immediate Fiction* are those used by all great writers. Whether a story is true or not doesn't matter. The craft is identical. A good story creates an experience and puts you in it, living and feeling it as if you were there.

All of this we're calling *Immediate Fiction*, because good stories are immediate. They're happening here and now, around you and in you, in the moment. But this is also about crafting and creating stories and about how to get yourself to sit down and do it. With *Immediate Fiction*, you will begin writing immediately, the moment you sit down. There are even techniques to help you sit down. And don't think getting yourself there and sitting down can't be a problem—even for the best of writers. "Ninety percent of life is showing up," the saying goes. *Immediate Fiction* will make it easy to show up.

After you do sit down, you won't be wasting time wondering what to do or where to start or how to get in the mood. You don't have to be in the mood or wait for inspiration or the Muse to strike, because with this method *the Muse is you.* You'll learn how to become your own Muse and not waste time looking for magic to come from somewhere outside yourself.

Immediate Fiction is the craft of story, but it's also *the craft of self*—finding what you have and making it work for you. So, it's immediate in two ways. *What* you create is immediate, and *how* you create is immediate. You're creating immediate fiction immediately.

One thing it's important to be aware of at the outset is that no problem is too small to paralyze you, and none is too big to be conquered. Problems are as big or as small as you make them. Writers have a knack for magnifying tiny troubles into great obstacles. So, if you've been doing that, don't worry. You'll learn how to get out of it.

This course is laid out with first things first. Follow it straight through, and you'll do fine. Each part starts with the theory behind what we're setting out to accomplish. The theory gives you a deeper sense of how things work. The first chapter covers the creative process—what to keep in mind to stay out of trouble. Chapter 2 is a short exploration of stories (the *why* of story—why every reader reads, why every writer writes). That flows right into chapter 3, the actual craft and technique of creating stories—how to do it—*how, what, when,* and *where.* You start writing at the end of chapter 3, with exercises designed to uncover what you have and tap into the drama in your ideas. Each chapter has its own set of writing exercises at the end.

Since each chapter flows into the next, you don't need to skip around, *but* if you're dying to get into the heart of putting a story together, go straight to chapter 3. Chapter 4 refines the story elements more precisely, making it even easier to breathe life into your story. Chapter 5 covers self-editing, staying on track, avoiding pitfalls—figuring out what you have and what to do with it. Capturing emotion on the page, and evoking it in the character and the reader, are covered in chapter 6. Chapter 7 covers the basic technique for creating the experience on the page in full scenes. Chapter 8 moves into expanded *re*writing techniques—what to do when you go back over your work. Work methods, different ways of approaching your story, are covered in chapter 9. Originality (what is it? how do you achieve it?) is covered in chapter 10. That chapter also explores universal plot forms. Chapter 11 covers point of view. If you feel you have no time to write, chapter 12 will show you how to get going in just minutes a day. Chapter 13 covers extraneous concepts and methods that often confuse the issue—what you can do without. Chapter 14 explores the difference between a short story and a novel and how you can turn any short story into a novel. If you're seriously blocked, go straight to chapter 15. Chapter 16 shows you how to turn your story into a stage play or screenplay if either is your goal. Chapter 17 covers what you need to know to market your work—how to submit, where to submit, agents, publishers. Even though the chapters are arranged in a specific order, each stands alone and deals with its topic completely.

THE ROAD TO HERE

I'd like to tell you how I got here. It's important because I *did* get here and even more important because *many don't*—many who could and should, but don't through no fault of their own. It's a trip along a tangled path, one you may be on already, one that may have led you to this very course. It's one you will avoid if you haven't set out upon it already. My journey isn't about me as much as it is about the world of writing and the teaching and learning of writing.

I took my first writing course at night at a junior college in Chicago. I took it just to pick up a few credits while I was working and saving money to go back to college full-time. I had no idea what I was doing in the writing class, but I had a lot of energy, and I had no conceptions or misconceptions because I had almost no literary background. The teacher and the class liked my writing. I was thrilled and started thinking that maybe, someday, after I got a degree in a sensible subject, I would do some writing. Our night class produced the first literary magazine in the Chicago junior college system.

I went back to school full-time at the University of Illinois, majoring in psychology but writing in my spare time. After a year, I took another writing class, taught by a professor who was a well-known author. I was excited and eager, a serious student ready to be molded into a successful writer by this literary expert. Now that I'd been writing awhile, I was full of questions: Why was it I kept starting stories I couldn't finish? Why did my clear ideas so often drift off into tangled messes? What should I do when a story I was writing that was full of energy and drama suddenly shut down and stopped dead before my eyes, never to rise again?

Unfortunately, the professor had few answers. He told us little about how stories work. "Write a twenty-five-hundred-word story for next week," he said. The following week he proceeded to take our writing apart, telling us what was wrong with it, but little about how to fix it. At the end of the course I had more questions than I had when I started, including: Was it beyond me? Was I just too dense?

The next time I had an elective, I took another writing course from a different professor. By now I had formulated my confusion a touch more. I kept wondering, "Does it have to be this hard, this vague, this disorganized?" I couldn't figure out if the problem was I just wasn't getting it or they just weren't giving it. It seemed like guesswork, trial and error, hit or miss, with no real guiding principles or techniques. "Does everybody do it this way?" I asked in class one day.

"How else could you do it?" the professor said.

"I don't know. I'm not very clear on exactly how this works."

"Look," he said. "It's art, not science. It doesn't come easy. If you want me to make it easy, maybe you shouldn't be here."

What was he saying? Do it his way or get out? "I'm not trying to be lazy. I just wish I knew a little more about what I'm supposed to be doing," I said.

"You work and work and work, and eventually you start to get a feel for it. It takes years."

Here I was again with more questions. Years? How many? When did you start to get a feel for it? What was *it* anyway? Did it hit you all at once, or did you get it little by little? What did the *feel* feel like, exactly? How did you know if the *feel* you were feeling was the *real feel?* I didn't ask any more questions, because I didn't want to get kicked out. After all, what did I know? Put in my years and wait for the *feel*—if that was what it took, I'd do it. Still, it seemed there should be a better way.

The more I wrote, the more possibilities I could see. My big fear was that I would follow the wrong one and drift off in a direction that would take me nowhere. If my aim was off just a fraction at the start, I might miss the mark by a mile.

Next, I took what I call the shit course. It was at one of Chicago's most famous universities, and it was taught by another well-known author. The first day, he swaggered in, looked at us with contempt, and said, "What makes you think the shit you write is worth reading? What makes you think the world needs to hear anything you have to say?"

Uh oh! Here was something else to worry about. Was my writing *worth* reading? Did the world *need* it? How could I know that? I was here because I liked writing. I just wanted to learn to be a good storyteller. I wasn't trying to tell the world anything.

It turned out that this teaching style was common at that university. "We know everything. You know nothing" was their motto, and this professor and author could have been their poster boy. He told us we were shit and then proceeded to shit on us and our writing throughout the entire course. He was scary, but I held on, clinging to the hope that he was wrong. It turned out that he *was* wrong—totally wrong. Neither concern—whether your writing is *worth reading* and whether the world *needs* to hear it—has anything to do with being a successful writer. Writers have enough to do without having to wrestle with such intangible issues.

This professor was also totally wrong about how to help writers develop. He was a successful writer, but a lousy teacher (a frequent combination). (My hunch is that this kind of high-handed cruelty is a cover-up for not knowing how to help writers develop.) Teaching and coaching writers are a specialty in themselves. It's taken me as long to become a good coach as it took me to become a good writer. Some great writers are lousy teachers, and some mediocre writers and nonwriters are great teachers. The two need not go hand in hand.

Maxwell Perkins was a great editor who coached Hemingway, Fitzgerald, Thomas Wolfe, James Jones *(From Here to Eternity),* and Marjorie Rawlings *(The Yearling),* but never wrote a word of fiction in his life. Picasso would not talk about his painting, saying, "If I could put it into words, I wouldn't paint it." Klee, on the other hand, was not only a great painter but a great teacher. He taught and wrote and spoke volumes about how he painted and what he was trying to do in his paintings.

My belief is that being able to teach well has a lot to do with how you learn. When I learn anything, I make every mistake possible before I catch on. I suffer, but when I get there, I've got it. I know what I've learned and how it relates to the rest of what I know. More importantly, for teaching, I know *how* I've learned. So, I've written fiction every *wrong* way imaginable.

I've had every writer's affliction known to man, and I've made every storytelling mistake possible—and some that are supposed to be impossible. In addition, all the bad guidance lured me off into areas I might not have gone into on my own. I've learned from that also. I've learned how to do it, but, just as importantly, I've learned **how not to do it, what not to waste time on.**

After I took my lumps in the shit course, I looked around for where to go next. My choice was made for me by the U.S. Army. I was drafted. The Vietnam War was raging, and I was lucky or unlucky enough to escape combat. I was stationed in a research post on the East Coast that was largely run by civilians. I spent two years producing, directing, and acting in plays for the few soldiers and the large civilian population. It was a cushy job that gave me time to do a fair amount of writing. I put together in a notebook what I'd learned in all the writing classes and set to applying it as best I could. I began writing and submitting stories.

Harper's magazine sent me a personal letter saying, "We enjoyed reading your story. It doesn't come together, somehow, but it does ring true, and we'd like to see more of your work." That was a real boost, but what did "doesn't come together" mean? And then there was the issue of "somehow." Somehow how? And "ring true"—how did that work?

"Sorry, and thanks. Try us again," the *New Yorker* said. "Keep trying. Sooner or later we'll click on something," came from the *Atlantic Monthly*. It seemed I was on the threshold. Maybe. Maybe not. I was flattered by the personal letters from senior editors and dying to publish, but I had only the vaguest notion of what I was doing or how I was doing it. If I ever did write a story that sold, could I do it again? Something was missing. It had to be, but I had no idea what it was.

When I got out of the army, I enrolled in a fiction night course at Northwestern University. I'd been writing and taking writing workshops for eight years now. This course was taught by Bernard Sabath, a man who regularly published fiction in the major national magazines (over one hundred stories in all) and was a successful playwright. One of his plays, *The Boys in Autumn,* starred Kirk Douglas and Burt Lancaster on the West Coast, ran on Broadway with George C. Scott and John Cullum and is still touring Europe and the United States.

I didn't know about his successes then, because Barney's course wasn't about him, but about his students and what he could help them become. It had a different tone from the other courses I had taken. He wasn't out to get us, but to help us. In his class, Barney gave me what I'd been asking for all these years. He defined story and story technique in clear, concrete, usable terms. And what happened?

I missed it. Because the brainwashing I'd been through over the years had convinced me, in spite of myself, of how hard and complicated it had to be, Barney's teaching went right past me. Thank God I wrote it down, even though it seemed too simple, too easy, too straightforward to be true. I wrote it down the way I wrote down everything.

What Barney gave us was a neat, simple little package—a story model with a few rules—complete, flexible, easy. Because it was new and because I couldn't see around the tangle of concepts that was already littering my mind, I couldn't see how it could work. No, this model was just too neat and too pat to work.

I worked on my own that summer, not sure if I was going back to the Northwestern workshop. Barney was by far the most specific, direct, and sensible writing coach I'd had. I had his simple, fundamental approach in my notebook, but I didn't look at it for most of the summer—until I was stumped by a story I was working on. It was driving me nuts. I had no idea where I was or how to find my way back to where I was supposed to be—wherever that was. Then, while poring over the first page of the story, something Barney said popped into my mind. I tried it, and it worked.

I got out my notes from his class, reviewed them, then started going over my story, line by line, page by page, using what Barney had given us. As I did, a new dimension in my story began opening up. It was Barney's model, his method, but it was my imagination, my characters, my story that were coming to life. I was able to see more revealing ways for the characters to act and more exciting ways to turn the story. There it was! All I had to do was use it. For the first time, I felt I'd really connected. I'd found what was missing—the full use of myself and my imagination in a scheme that shaped my ideas into a complete, meaningful story. It was his method, but it put me in touch with what I had. It drew me out onto the page in a new and exciting way. Plus, I could see how it worked. For the very first time, I knew what I was doing and why.

I was so thrilled, I called Barney and told him I wanted more than his class lectures and would pay him for his time. "No. No," he said. "Come in on Monday at seven o'clock."

Monday, I went over the whole thing with him. Damn, if I didn't have it right. I'd found **it**—finally—and I knew it. "It seems so simple," I said.

"Simple, yes, but you still have to perfect your craft," he said.

"But for once I'll know what I'm doing—I'll be working on the right things."

"Exactly," he said, smiling. "And that makes it happen all the faster."

It did happen. And it happened fast. At that time *Playboy* was printing some of the highest-quality fiction around (Updike, Algren,

Mailer). They were one of the toughest magazines to break into, but they were the highest paying. They bought the second story I wrote with the new model and paid me the highest price they would pay an unknown author at that time.

I was thrilled at what I'd discovered, but I was also furious that it had taken so long and that I'd been misled and stifled so often along the way. There was no need for any of it. Of all the arts, writing is taught in the vaguest and most inconsistent and disorganized way. My friends who were painters were given all kinds of guidelines and principles (line, composition, color theory, sketch classes). Art classes went way beyond the draw-a-picture-and-we'll-tell-you-what's-wrong-with-it approach, which was what my writing classes had amounted to.

Because of my *Playboy* success other writers began approaching me for help. In addition to doing my own writing, I became intrigued with the challenge of how to teach, coach, and help others learn what I'd learned and learn it in a way that wouldn't put them through all the confusion, false starts, and wasted effort I'd been through. Learning to coach others has turned out to be an even more formidable task than learning to write and just as exciting and fulfilling.

I stayed in the workshop at Northwestern with Barney Sabath, the man who had become my mentor. I wanted to learn what he knew and know it as well as he did, if that was possible. He coached me as I coached others. Eventually, I mastered his approach and went on to teach it myself. After ten years, I left Northwestern and created The Writer's Loft in Chicago, where I've spent the last twenty years perfecting the techniques in this course.

There's no need for anyone to have to go through what I went through. There's no need for it to take that long. My personal estimate, after writing and working with writers for over twenty years, is that a good writing coach can speed a writer's development by a factor of ten. This means that, with good guidance, you'll develop ten times faster than you would working on your own or with bad coaching. The reason why 99 percent of all writers never publish, why people write for a lifetime and get nowhere, isn't because they don't try or don't work hard or don't write their hearts out or do what the "experts" tell them. The reason they don't make it is because they haven't been given the right tools. The tools they need to teach themselves to write. In the end, you must teach yourself, but there are a lot of ways to teach yourself. Some are quick and effective, and some take forever.

The reason I can make such definite statements is that writing stories is different from the other arts. In music or painting, for example, you need some inborn talent to be successful, whereas no special talent is needed to write successful stories. The reason is that your life experience and life skills are also writing skills. You have a full set of emotions and enough dramatic experiences to draw on. You know how you work and how the world works. If you didn't, you wouldn't have survived this long. You don't have to know how to play the piano or paint a picture to get along in the world, but if you want to get by, you'd better know how people behave and how you should behave.

So, the ability to write successful stories is an **acquired skill,** not an inborn talent. For purposes of writing and selling your stories, talent is irrelevant. Don't let yourself use lack of talent or lack of ability as an excuse.

That's not to say that talent or personal brilliance doesn't exist or that they don't figure in at some point. If you're talking about the National Book Award or the Pulitzer Prize or the Nobel Prize, then talent makes a difference. But you don't need that level of ability to write successful stories. What you have is plenty.

If you read at all, you should have noticed that plenty of talentless writers are making fortunes. The success of some published writing seems to defy explanation, but in most cases what makes the difference is the ability to tell a strong story. If you can do that, any mistakes you make otherwise will not hurt you. A number of well-known novelists require heavy editing to make their stories readable. But the story is there, and that's what counts.

So what are the important points in all of this? There are two important messages to keep in mind. First, **you can do this.** Showing you how is what this course is all about. Second, **for every writing problem, there is a simple solution.**

Although the story is the thing, before you get to the story, you must first get to yourself, to what you have inside you. That's not always easy. Sometimes you stall out before you get going. Getting past yourself, your doubt and anxiety, is often the first hurdle. Helping you over that hurdle, helping you anticipate and avoid that kind of trouble, are what the first chapter is about.

1

Rules of the Page

Creativity obeys an unusual and contrary set of laws. If you violate them, you will expend enormous amounts of energy and get nowhere—just as you would if you pressed the gas and the brake to the floor of your car at the same time. Many writers give up, feeling they're incapable, when the only problem is that they're unwittingly violating these natural laws. To put it simply, they're **trying to do the impossible.** Trying to do the impossible is the major cause of frustration, discouragement, and failure for writers.

All of this trouble stems from misconceptions about how the process is *supposed* to work. It's the result of trying to impose normal, everyday, noncreative standards upon a process that isn't normal. That's right. **Creating isn't normal reality.**

THE RULES

You will make a mess. Creating stories is never a neat, orderly, or predictable process. Mess is inevitable. You make a mess. You clean it up.

You lose your way. You find it again. Your writing veers away from the story. You rein it in, or you follow it to see where it takes you. You do this many times until you get where you want to go. So, accept the mess as inevitable and good, let it happen, work with it, and you will get there a lot faster.

You must write badly first. Trying to get it perfect right away will only get you blocked, because the bad comes first. No one does it on the first draft. Writers write many drafts to get it right. Hemingway, in typical macho style, said, "The first draft is always shit." If Hemingway's first draft was shit, why should you expect more? Once again, bad is good. Believe it or not, you'll do better if you *lower your expectations*. By not expecting so much, you'll give yourself the space, the slop you need, to work. So, don't hold back. Gag the critic in you, and dare to write badly. It's the only way.

Mistakes lead to discovery. This is a game of mistakes. Art begins in error. Mistakes and uncertainty are good. They create new combinations and possibilities. Penicillin, the lightbulb, the Slinky were all the result of mistakes. Creative people have a lot more good ideas than other people do, and they have a lot more bad ideas. They have a lot more ideas because they *let everything out*. They know the good and the bad go hand in hand and that **letting yourself be bad is the best way to become good.**

Here's an old writing anecdote that expresses this well: The beginning writer writes his first draft, reads it, and says, "This is awful. I'm screwed." The experienced writer writes his first draft, reads it, and says, "This is awful. I'm on my way!"

THE FIX

Writing badly may not be fun (although it can be once you stop worrying about it), but the great thing about writing is **everything can be fixed.** And fixing makes exciting things happen. Writing is rewriting. Everything can work, because you can add, subtract, make changes and adjustments until your story comes alive. There's always a way. The way is *technique*—story *craft*.

In all of this, a relaxed, unhurried attitude will get you there faster. But that's hard to achieve when it's so important to you, which brings us to the next point.

THE UNIMPORTANCE OF IMPORTANCE

What I'm saying is, **The less you care, the better you write.** But how can you make yourself *not* care about something you're pouring your heart into? Well, it can be done. *Practice* is always the first step—*writing* and *writing* and *writing* until you let go of the tension and relax, until you no longer have the strength to be uptight. When you just dash it off to get it over with is when the best things happen.

Another thing to keep in mind is, **Everything that happens is OK.** No matter what problem you have (confusion, worry, self-doubt, panic, emptiness, paralysis), it's OK. It's no reflection on you or your ability. It's all a *natural part of the process*—what *every* writer must face. You're not the only writer who's ever had these problems. You'll *feel* you're the only one, but I can tell you that you won't be inventing any new writing miseries. They've all been experienced before—and dealt with successfully. So, try not to blame yourself or punish yourself. And keep the following examples in mind.

The famous French writer Gustave Flaubert *(Madame Bovary)*

struggled for three days, threw a monumental tantrum, rolled on the floor, chewed the rug, and bashed his head against the wall to get eight sentences on the page. Oscar Wilde *(The Importance of Being Earnest, The Picture of Dorian Gray)* said, "I spent the morning putting in a comma and the afternoon taking it out." All writers are susceptible to such misery. So, when you get into this kind of a jam, remind yourself that *you're in good company*. Then get your mind back on the craft and technique you're going to learn, and you'll get out of your funk.

THE JAGGED SLOPE

Progress is never even. In everything you do, some days you're a whiz, and other days you're a dud. Writing is no different. It's like everything else in life. So, when you have a bad day, don't despair. Just keep plugging away, because how you handle your slumps is what makes you or breaks you. And it's not all bleak because **it will get good again—always.** *You will bounce back.* I guarantee it. Not only will you rise out of your slump, but you will reach your best level of writing, and you will *exceed* it—if you keep at it. Then you will dip down—and rise again. You will always lose it, *and* you will always get it back—*and then some*. Think of writing as a relationship with another person. It's at least as *thrilling*—and at least as *miserable*. You don't get one (thrill) without the other (misery). But in writing, the thrills make up for the misery.

Speaking of misery: Some writers take years to write a novel. Joseph Heller took 10 years to write *Catch-22*. Tom Wolfe took 10 years to write *A Man in Full*. That's one end of the spectrum. At the other end is Nabokov, who wrote *Lolita* in three months. James Hilton wrote *Goodbye, Mr. Chips* in four days. Now, *Goodbye, Mr.*

Chips was a slim little novel, but at the rate Hilton took to write it, Heller would have finished *Catch-22* in a month or two.

So, what accounts for the difference between the 10-year novel and the four-day, four-month, or 1-year novel? Well, I can tell you that Heller and Wolfe were not banging away eight hours a day, five days a week, on their novels for 10 years. No—they were struggling, straining, spinning their wheels, doing all kinds of things *other than writing*. The difference between them and the writers who do it in days, weeks, or months is not how much time they *spend writing*, but how much time they *waste trying to write*.

Wasting time and energy is what you're going to learn to avoid. The point is: *it's easier than we make it*. But *it's hard to make it easy*— unless you know how.

Of all the advice writers give out, there is only one thing they all agree on. They all say: Stick to it. Don't quit. Don't give up. **Keep writing no matter how awful it feels.** Do your daily writing. Remember, it's no different from the rest of your life, with its ups and the downs.

A professional writer is an amateur who didn't quit. Not quitting is vital. The other equally important factor is *guidance*. Sadly, 99 percent of all writers never publish. It's not that they quit or don't try or don't write their hearts out or don't do what the writing books and courses tell them. They don't make it because they have *no guidance* or *poor guidance*. Sadder still, they could publish—*if* only they learned their craft. Craft is the key, but you can't learn it on your own. You can teach yourself golf, tennis, or basketball—up to a point. On your own, you can learn enough to get around eighteen holes, hit a ball over the net, or make a basket, but how many successful athletes learn on their own without lessons or coaching? How many teams play without a coach? None. Professional athletes are on teams getting coaching and lessons for years before they make it.

For writing, guidance and coaching are just as important. As in any discipline (sports, music, dance, painting), you need to practice until it's a part of you, until it's reflex, until you perform without thinking. Again, my personal estimate is, the right guidance will get you there at least *ten times* faster. Guiding you and giving you *the tools to guide yourself* are the goals. This course is designed to make a short trip out of what can otherwise be an endless journey.

What you'll learn is technique—*how* to do it. Technique is neutral. You can use it to write any kind of story you choose (science fiction, romance, adventure, fable, fantasy, mystery, crime, literary). With proper technique, whatever you write can be shaped into a complete story. The *complete* story is what all great story writers write (Shakespeare, Hemingway, Steinbeck, Fitzgerald). A complete story is the most fulfilling, because it has **the shape of our most meaningful experience.** Whether it's comedy or tragedy, it gives us what we need from experience. What we need from experience and stories, along with how to put together a story that fulfills that need, is what the next three chapters are about.

2

Theory

What is a story, and how does it work? That's where we're headed. If you're in a hurry to get there, to get the tools so you can jump in and get started immediately (this is *Immediate Fiction*, after all), then skip ahead to chapter 3. Come back when you have time. But if you want a fuller sense of why we have stories and what they do for us before you start, then stick around. The deeper your understanding, the better you'll write.

Stories happen not only in movies and books and on TV. Stories are playing out in us and through us continually. And they didn't arise because someone sat down one day and said, "OK, everybody, we're going to have stories. This is how we're going to do it." No, stories were here at the beginning. They were here when the caveman started scratching pictures on the walls of his cave. They evolved right along with us. More than anything else, they're an expression of who we are and how we work. They're our way of keeping in touch, of finding meaning and understanding. That goes for all genres—tragedy, adventure, mystery, fantasy, science fiction, comedy.

PROCESS

A story is not just a thing, but a process—a process that connects us to each other. If someone you work with sat down across from you and said, "I brushed my teeth this morning," you'd look at him waiting for more, for the connection. "So?" you'd say. "What's the point?" Even if he embellished his story with, "I got this great new curved bristle brush and mint-flavored, baking soda and peroxide toothpaste. I really got in there. My mouth has never been so clean," you still wouldn't be related or connected—unless you were wondering, "Why's he telling me this? Is he losing it?" You wouldn't be relating, because his story didn't *get to you*. Stories are about what gets to us. A good story is like falling in love. You don't think, "How do I really feel about this person? Do I love her or him or not?" No, you're bowled over, swept away, knocked out. Good stories involve the same process. It's chemistry. It goes straight to the heart. You respond whether you want to or not. Stories are the most personal and fundamental form of communication we have.

Now, if the same guy came in, breathless, and said, "I just got mugged in the elevator," he'd *get to you* instantly. You'd be totally related and certainly wouldn't be asking, "What's the point?" And on his end, he would be eloquent, dramatic, compelling. No one would say, "Too wordy," or "No passion," or "Lacks detail." He'd tell his story, and he'd know how to tell it, because it's who he is.

The difference between the two examples is story—THE STORY PROCESS. There's a story reason, a craft reason, why one left you cold and the other got to you.

Your coworker has his stories, and you have yours. We all have our stories. That's what's nice about this art. In order to survive in life, you must have skills—life skills. And LIFE SKILLS ARE STORY SKILLS. They both come from the same place. As I said earlier, that's the big difference between this art and others such as music or painting. You don't have to know how to play the piano or paint a portrait in order to survive on the street, but you damn well better be aware of what's going on around you and how you feel about it and what to do to protect yourself. It's not just on the street. You have to have the same kind of social skills and awareness to get along in any personal relationship. So, with stories YOU HAVE EVERYTHING YOU NEED ALREADY.

Now, that's good, but it's also bad. Good because with determination anyone can master this craft, since most of it is mastering yourself and using what you already have. Bad because it's so familiar. You've been there, so you may feel you know more than you do. In the midst of a compelling story, you may often feel so connected that you think, *Ah. This is how it works.* You feel so strongly that you think there's nothing to it, that writing a story is just like life. Like life, yes. But not life itself.

Creating stories is a special craft—a special way of capturing reality on the page. It feels real, but it isn't. You can't just break off a piece of reality and stick it on the page. It won't work. It won't work because fiction is concentrated, heightened, intensified reality. It's the essence of reality. All reality doesn't contain such essence or truth, but all fiction must. You, the author, must create it. So even though you already have everything you need, you have to learn how to use it. That's craft. That's technique. That's what you get from this course. That's where we're going, after the theory.

STORY AS NEED

We don't just happen to have stories. We *need* them. The story process involves the kinds of experiences we *must* talk about, experiences we can't wait to tell someone, experiences we can't stand *not* to talk about.

If a man comes home from work, flops into a chair, and says to his wife, "I almost didn't make it home tonight," he's had the kind of experience he *needs* to talk about and his wife now *needs* to hear. "Some idiot," he says, "cut me off on the expressway. When I blew my horn, he gave me the finger, so I gave it back to him." "No!" she says. "Yeah, and the crazy bastard pulled alongside and fired three shots into our engine." Now, can you imagine having had such an experience and keeping it to yourself? Or being the wife and not wanting to know what happened? No. Stories are how we live, how we relate—how we *need* to live and relate. The story process.

This need isn't limited to our own experiences. It reaches beyond us to the experiences of others several times removed—experiences we haven't witnessed, experiences that will not affect us in any way. Often, experiences that we only hear about, and that we're dying to pass along to someone else.

Suppose the same guy comes home from work and says to his wife, "Wait till you hear what this guy at work told me his buddy pulled on his wife."

Now, that's not his experience or the experience of the guy who told him, but the experience of another person he's never met. Yet he can't wait to tell his wife about what this other guy pulled on his wife. And, again, she wants to hear—and I'll bet you do too.

"He told his wife he was going on a business trip, withdrew twenty thousand dollars, and went to Vegas. He ran it up to eighty thousand dollars—then, guess what." "No!" she says. "Yep. Lost every penny."

Now a common, but curious, thing happens. They're into this other guy's story, relating and connecting, but that's not enough. They want more, to go farther, to go the limit. That's what stories are about—getting the maximum, that concentrated, intensified dose of reality. So he says, "What would you do if I did that?" And how does she respond? She might say, "Wait a minute. That's not our experience. We can't go into that," which might make sense in some way. But no, this is story. This is how we live. She doesn't miss a beat. "Castration followed by divorce," she says.

STORIES ARE US
(The story connection)

We live by stories—our own and those of others, real and imagined. It's how we relate and stay connected on the most personal and intimate level. We *need* stories, the story process, to maintain our balance and our identity. We don't think of it this way because we don't have to. We just do it. Story, the story process, is the active ingredient in all meaningful social interaction. Believe it or not, it's one of our deepest social needs.

HOW DEEP?

OK, it's a need, but exactly how deep a need is it? How far will we go to satisfy it? How much of an influence does it have on us, and can we find a way to measure it? Yes, we can.

I take you to the world of crime for the answer—heist crimes (banks, Brinks, famous jewels). Let's say three guys pull off the perfect Brinks robbery, except for killing a resistant guard in the process. Nobody knows a thing—no clues, no evidence. There's no chance they can get caught if they play it safe. They each take four million dollars and split for different parts of the country.

We'll go along with Eddie to California, where he hooks up with a woman and moves in with her. Everything is fine. No money problems. Life is great.

Except, after a while, something starts eating at Eddie. He's pulled this great robbery. It's part of his identity. But he's getting no recognition. He can't pull his money out of hiding, or it'll raise suspicion. So, he's got to walk around, feeling like all the other suckers who don't have the brains or guts to pull off a brilliant heist.

Sooner or later, he can't stand it. "C'mere, babe," he says, patting his knee. "What?" his girlfriend says, settling into his lap. "I got something to tell you." "OK," she says, wrapping her arms around his neck. "Something big," he says. "What?" "Real big," he says. "All right. Come on." "First, you have to promise, swear on your life, you won't tell another living soul as long as you live." "I won't. Never." "Well," he says, smiling. "Know that Brinks job in Arkansas?" "The twelve million?" she says. "The twelve million," he says, pointing to his chest. "What?" "I'm the guy." "What guy?" she says. "I did it—masterminded the whole damn job." "No!" she squeals. "Yep," he says, pushing out his chest. "Wow!" "Tell anyone, angel," he says, stroking her neck, "and I'll have to wring this pretty neck." "Hey, what do you take me for?"

He tells his story. He has to, even though he could get the chair if they caught him. It's who he is. But he's safe as long as his girlfriend keeps her mouth shut. And she does—for a while. Until it starts eating at her. "Listen," she says to her best friend. "I'm going to tell you something, but you've got to promise on the soul of your kid, you won't tell a single person as long as you live." "I swear." "If this gets out, I'm dead meat." "I swear." "Between you and me—take it to the grave." "Sure." "Guess what my boyfriend, the one who can't live without me, the one I have to do everything for, guess what the wonderful son of a bitch did." "What?" "Pulled that big Brinks job in Arkansas." "No!" "Yep." "Wow!" "You can't tell." "Never."

And he's still safe—until the secret starts eating at the girlfriend's friend, and she has to tell someone—someone who'll keep his or her mouth shut just the way she did. And so it goes until word gets out and someone turns him in.

One thing that stands out in these heist crimes is: These guys always get caught. Why? Because they can't keep their mouths shut. None of us can. We have to tell our stories. We *need* to tell them. Stories are who we are. They're how we live. Without stories, we have no identity. We don't exist.

A perfect real-life example of this is a recent (1998) high-profile case. A fugitive, subject of a nationwide manhunt for over ten years, sent his story to the newspapers to be printed nationally. Even after it was printed, no one knew who he was—until his brother recognized the writing and turned him in. Ted Kazinski, the Unabomber. He had to *tell his story*—give his manifesto—to the newspapers. Why? One theory was that the Oklahoma City bombing was taking away his publicity and he was jealous and wanted to recapture the spotlight. Someone else's story was overshadowing his story, and this recluse *needed* to tell his story so badly that he risked life in prison to do so.

Most crimes aren't solved by detective work, but by someone tipping off the cops—passing on the story they *need* to tell. So, at the risk of his life, the Brinks robber tells his story: "Hey, look at me. I'm the guy who . . ."

So, why do we have stories? Because we need them to maintain our identity, to express who we are. That's the *why* of it. The *how* of it, *how* stories fulfill our need, is what the craft is all about.

CRAFT

Craft is neutral. In chapter 1 I said that craft and technique can be used to write any kind of story—science fiction, fantasy, adventure, romance, mystery. It's worth saying twice. It's also important to realize that all genres can be literary. Here are examples of great books in different genres: Science fiction: *Brave New World*. Fantasy: *Ani-*

mal Farm and *Watership Down*. Adventure: *Moby Dick*. Romance: *Madame Bovary*. Mystery: *The Brothers Karamazov*.

Whatever the genre, the story must be *complete*, or it won't get to us, won't give us what we want and need. Craft is what we use to create a *complete* story. The complete story is the most satisfying, not only for the reader, but for the author. It's the natural form, the most compelling, because it has the shape of our most meaningful experiences. We recognize and relate to it instantly. It reaches us before we have time to think. We connect whether we want to or not. It's impossible to sit and watch a good movie and not be drawn into it.

The complete story gives us what we seek in trivial experience and what we need to manage painful experience. It's easiest to see in extreme cases. (Fiction is about the extreme case—extreme love story: *Romeo and Juliet;* extreme fish story: *Moby-Dick*.) What we seek and need from experience is what the survivors and relatives of TWA Flight 800, the Oklahoma City bombing, the Columbine massacre wanted and needed. What they had to have to manage the experience. Know what it was? You hear the word on the news all the time: *closure*.

And what is closure? Ever heard it defined? No. No newscaster has to tell us what it means. We all know in our hearts. That's fine—for life, but for fiction we have to pin it and everything else down as much as possible. After all, that's what fiction is about—pinning it down, going as deeply into it as possible.

What is this closure that we all need? It's a coming to terms, a final outcome, a putting to rest (as best we can). It's a way of dealing with a divorce, a death, a rape, a broken heart—a way of making sense of it, of finding a meaningful outcome—a way of living with it or dying because of it. It's not necessarily a happy ending. Some only find closure in the grave. And **it's the same in comedy as in tragedy.** Both must complete, finish, fulfill the promise of the story. Whether our tears are from laughter or sadness, the complete story must give us a sense of completion in ourselves—for the moment. Then we go in search of another connection—the story connection.

THE COMPLETE STORY

So, what is this complete story, and how does it work? A good way to get a feel for it is to take a look at what happens when a story works— what does it do to us and for us? What happens, for example, when you see a terrific movie? What takes place between you and that story and you and those characters that makes you feel it's a terrific movie?

THE BIG "I"

Typical answers to that question are: It's escapism. It takes me away from my troubles. It tells me something about life. I relate to the characters.

Well, only one of those answers is true in all cases. Stories can be escapism, but what about *Schindler's List*? It helps you escape into the Holocaust. Would you like those troubles in place of your own? Stories can tell you something about life, but so does a sociology book. Which excites you more? You *relate to the characters*. That's the answer, and it's what makes a story real. Relating to the characters, OK, but how does that work? In what way do we relate to the characters? What form does this relating take?

Stories are like falling in love. Love is an emotion. That's what it's about—relating, connecting, *emotionally*. That's an answer. We're getting there, but it's not the final answer. Now we need to ask, Whose emotions are we experiencing? The emotions are in us, so they're our own in that sense, but they're coming from somewhere else. We're not the only one having them. The emotions we're feeling are the emotions of the characters. What they feel, we feel. The better the story, the more we lose ourselves in the characters, the more we become them. If they're excited, we're excited. If they're sad, we're sad. We jump or cry out in fright when they're threatened.

This becoming the character is called **identification.** That's our technical term. It can be called empathy, sympathy, vicariousness, but our term, our technical/craft term, for becoming the character is **identification.** And identification is what this whole game is about. **Identification is why the reader reads and why the writer writes.**

THE PAYOFF

That's an answer, but still not a final answer. We can push it to a deeper level—to its limit, to its emotional extreme—to where we need to go *always*. We become the characters. We feel what they feel. OK, but if we're going to understand this story stuff, this story process, fully, we need to know why we are drawn to that. What does it do for us? What are we getting out of it?

We go to stories for this emotional connection, but why? Don't we have enough emotions of our own? Is there something missing in us? Are we deficient or incomplete? Why can't we just sit at home and experience our own emotions without going through all the effort it takes to see a movie? Wouldn't staying home with your emotions be easier than getting in the car, driving to the theater, paying to park, waiting in line for a ticket, waiting to be seated—just so that you can go in and sit in a room with a bunch of other people and feel the emotions of characters who never existed and never will, acting out a story that never happened? Make-believe! Is that anything for responsible adults to be doing? Indulging in fantasy—what good is that going to do us? What does that have to do with reality?

Yes, what does it have to do with reality? What relevance does it have to the real world? What do we get out of it that we couldn't get if we stayed home alone with our feelings? First, we need to answer a question I raised earlier: are we incomplete, lacking, deficient? I'll answer that with another question: Do you have yourself all figured out? Do you know yourself so well that you'll never do anything stupid or make a fool of yourself again? Is your self-knowledge so complete? When it comes to knowing ourselves, we *are* incomplete, lacking, deficient. Each of us is our own ongoing problem until the day we die.

When we go to a movie and experience the emotions of the characters (identify), we're experiencing ourselves in a way we couldn't if we stayed at home. Experiencing their emotions puts us in touch with ourselves, expands us, in a way we can't achieve on our own. When we feel what the characters feel, we feel more of ourselves. In becoming them, we become more of who we are. So the complete story fulfills us, gives us a sense of closure—completes us, for the moment.

CAUSE AND EFFECT

So, where are we? What have I given you so far? I've given you an understanding of what stories do. But have I given you anything you can actually use to put together a story? I have not. I've given you theory, and I've talked about the *effect* of the story, but I haven't given you one thing that you can actually use to put together a story—haven't given you the first step to actually make it happen. Identification is what the story does—the *effect*, what it makes happen, but not *how* it makes it happen. *How*—that's the *cause*. And that's what writers work with—

causes. It's important to understand the difference and to keep the two separate.

How do we put together a story that creates identification? Well, that's what this craft is all about, and that's the subject of the next chapter. There will be exercises within and at the end of that chapter and each chapter that follows. It's a good idea to be ready with what you need to write (notebook, laptop, tape recorder, etc.) so you can get right into it without hunting around for tools.

3

Story

How do we do it—put together a story that gets to the reader, one that causes him or her to live and feel the experiences of the characters, to **identify?** Well, it can be done in a couple of ways. I can give you a definition, a concept, or a model. But stories aren't ideas. They're not concepts or definitions. They're experience. So, rather than tell you how a story works, I'm going to show you—show you by giving you a little story to see how much of an experience I can cause you to have, how much I can get you to **identify,** to live through the characters. Here's the story:

My wife and I have a friend named Larry who is going through a nasty divorce. His wife wants it. He doesn't. My wife ran into him at the mall. He looked terrible—sad and despondent. He sounded worse than he looked, so she invited him over for dinner to try to cheer him up.

Larry's an old friend, so we know what he likes. I bought a bottle of his favorite Scotch and some fancy cigars he likes after dinner. We had a few drinks and were feeling pretty good. We let

Larry know we would be there for him whenever he needed us. He could call anytime night or day. We renewed our friendship. Larry felt better. We felt better. He went home happy. We went to bed happy. It was a great night, all around, for everybody.

That's the end. How was it? Moving? Compelling? Dramatic? Did you identify? Were you gripped? Did you have the kind of experience you want from a story?

The answer, of course, is NO. You did not have an experience. You did not connect. You did not identify. You could not. The reason you could not was: I purposely beat the life out of it.

So, the effect was boredom and maybe irritation. The cause was a dead story. I presented you with an experience that left you cold, with a mistake. Why? Because mistakes are what we start with. We make mistakes constantly. First drafts are loaded with them. Remember Hemingway: "The first draft is shit." Expecting too much is the surest way to become blocked. The other reason I started with a mistake is: We learn more from our mistakes than from our successes—not from the mistakes themselves, but from correcting them.

So, if I'm right, if I know what I'm doing, I should be able to show you how to turn this mistake into an involving story. But before I do, consider what's needed to make it happen.

MAKING IT WORK

What's needed to turn this dead story into something with some energy, some drama? Detail, dialogue, emotion, conflict? Well, I could give you reams of detail and keep the story as dull as it is. Dialogue? I could have the characters talking all night and far into the next day, and you would be even more bored than you were. Emotion? Well, the story has emotion. The characters are happy, satisfied, fulfilled. How much more could you stand of happy, happy, happy? That leaves conflict. Conflict? Now, why would we mess up a perfectly enjoyable dinner by stirring up trouble?

TEN-MINUTE EXERCISE

Before I give you my answer, why don't you work on one of your own. See what you can do to give this dead story some energy. Take ten minutes to rewrite it (more if you get rolling). You can do it two ways. You can write it all out the way it needs to be. Or you can write some general, summary statements about how it should go—plan it out without doing it word for word.

You've done yours. Now I'll do mine. Here's another version of the same story. See if I can get you more involved.

In this version, I've got a touch of bronchitis or flu the day Larry is coming for dinner. I'm not feeling great, but I'm still up for dinner with Larry. Now, the flu is a minor detail, but I want you to decide whether you want it in or out. You don't have to have a reason—just a feeling. Most people, nine out of ten, prefer the flu in. Remember, this is not flu we're talking about. This is story, and in story, *everything counts*. Nothing is along for the ride.

So, the flu is in. Larry comes over. We have a few drinks. He and my wife are both smokers. Before we get to dinner, they run out of cigarettes. "I'll go get them," I say. "I want to get out of this haze and clear my lungs." I head out for the corner store to get their smokes.

It's a nice walk. I get their cigarettes and head back, but instead of walking up the front walk, I decide to take the shortcut down the alley. OK, point two: alley in or out? Like the flu, most people go for the alley. Flu and alley. Why? The answer to that is at the very heart of successful storytelling. It's not flu. It's not alley. It's story.

So, I'm walking down the alley, relaxing, breathing fresh air, looking at the yards. Now, our kitchen sticks out from the back of the house and is all windows along the side. I can see Larry and my wife in the kitchen. As I come through the yard, I see they're having a rather intense conversation. My wife is especially lively. I haven't seen her that spirited in months.

OK, what's on your mind right now? What are you thinking? Let me guess. You're thinking, hanky-panky, fooling around, touching, embracing, kissing, etc. Not only are you *thinking* it, but you're *wanting* it. Oh, yes. Not only do you give me the flu and make me walk down the alley, but you throw my marriage into crisis by making my wife unfaithful. Maybe not in reality, but in story, we prefer cheating to loyalty—always. We want chemistry, passion, fireworks! You don't go to the amusement park to ride the merry-go-round. You go to ride the roller-coaster.

THE ACTIVE INGREDIENT

I knew what you were thinking, not because I read your mind, but because I led you there—with story. I gave you an experience that hooked you in. Fine, so far, but where do we go from here? We left me standing there, watching my wife talking to Larry. What's next? Well, I've raised your expectations, so I have to give you what you want—or something better. Let's go with the kiss. My wife says something. Larry laughs, opening his arms. They embrace and have a nice long kiss.

What now? She kisses Larry. End of story. Yes? No? Why not? I'm sure you know in your heart that it's not over. Your heart is a good guide. It might be enough for an obvious example like this—might be. But when it's not obvious, when the problem gets subtle and tricky, when you get lost, it's not enough. To be a successful storyteller, you have to know in story terms why a story's not over. So, what has to happen to complete this story, to give it a bang-up ending? How about this:

I figure, *Heck with it. What do I care? Everybody cheats. Look at Clinton.* Then I go in, we have a nice dinner, smoke cigars, renew our friendship, and wind up good friends just like before. A satisfying ending? Maybe the characters are satisfied, but we are not, and no reader will be either.

What I'm doing is playing around with the active ingredient, the one I'm trying to get you to see by putting it in and taking it out, by connecting you and disconnecting you—something you'll be able to do by the end of this chapter.

All right. If this story is going to hold anyone, I have to care, to feel betrayed and go in and *do* something about it. It could go like this:

"Hi, guys," I say happily as I come in. "Here're the smokes."

They thank me and both light up. Larry pours himself some Scotch.

"How'd it go while I was gone?" I say, flopping into a kitchen chair.

"Fine," my wife says.

"How about you, Lar? Enjoy yourself in my absence?"

He glances at my wife quickly. "I did," he says.

"Good. I was worried you might get lonely. But when I saw you through the window, I could see you didn't need me to entertain you."

"Well," Larry says. "We both missed you, and we're glad you're back."

"That's right, honey," my wife says. "It's not the same without you."

"Of course not," I say. "Say, hand me the butcher knife, darling."

"Butcher knife, what for?"

"No reason. I just feel like holding it."

"Don't be silly," she says.

"No, really. Indulge me."

"Will you stop?" she says.

"Stop what? You don't trust me with a knife? What is this: no sharp objects for the lunatic?"

"Very funny," she says.

Larry stares at me, smiling weakly.

"Afraid I'll hurt myself—slit my wrists—or my throat? What do you think, Lar? Can I be trusted with a knife in my own kitchen with my best friend and my loyal wife?"

"Of course you can," Larry says flatly, then downs his Scotch.

"Damn right. Hear that, angel? Larry trusts me. He trusts you. We all trust each other. So pass me the knife, sweets."

THE CRUCIAL DIFFERENCE
(Lifeblood of every story—and every writer)

All right, let's stop. The story's not over yet. (How we know it's not over, and what's needed to bring it to a satisfying ending, we'll get to later.) It can go in many directions. Each writer will do it his or her own way. The possibilities are endless. But no matter which way it goes, it must fulfill the basic story requirements, or it will fail.

For now, the question is: what's the difference between this last version and the first. It's not details. It's not dialogue. It's not emotion. It's something else, something I mentioned earlier, but sidestepped so you could experience it first. The first version—happy, happy, happy—left us cold. The last—trouble, trouble, trouble—got to us. What does that tell us?

FICTION IS A DIRTY GAME
(No conflict = No story)

The difference between the first, dead version and this version is **conflict. Conflict** made the difference, but conflict isn't important so much for what it *is* as for what it *does*—what it makes happen. So, what did conflict make happen? What did conflict do? What difference did it make in the story? Can you tell? The answer is at the very heart of storytelling, and it's what makes or breaks every story. What conflict does is make the characters *act*. It forces them to *use themselves*—to act in a way that *reveals who they are*. Nothing tells us more about characters than how they deal with their troubles. **Action is character.** Whether they want it to or not, conflict draws them out. And that draws us in.

All right, it's time to pin it down, to give you a working model you can use **to shape any idea into a story.** This is what I was talking about in chapter 1, what I've spent years distilling into this simple, complete form—a form that's important not just for *what it includes,* but for *what it excludes*—for what's left out, for what you *don't* have to bother with.

In its purest form a story is just three elements: **conflict, action, resolution.** Someone is faced with a problem (conflict) he must struggle with (action), and he wins or loses (resolution). From climbing Mount Everest to asking for a date, from Romeo to Ahab to Scarlett O'Hara, the story form is the same. Romeo loves Juliet, but their families are enemies (conflict). They marry secretly and try to find a way to unite (action). Each commits suicide, thinking the other is dead (resolution). Ahab is obsessed with avenging himself against the whale. He must overcome his own madness and the sea (conflict). He sets out across the sea to find the whale (action). When he finds the whale, he loses the battle (resolution). Scarlett loves Ashley Wilkes, but he marries Melanie (conflict). Scarlett pursues Ashley anyway (action). When she realizes she cannot have Ashley and that she loves Rhett, it's too late (resolution).

These story elements are what you will spend your writing life working to master:

CONFLICT + ACTION + RESOLUTION = STORY

All right, how about an ending to the scene with Larry. Is it hard to figure an ending? No. It's clear what has to happen. That's because the story has a real beginning, a dramatic beginning—a conflict. So, how are we going to end it? The first thing we need is a scene ending (resolution). How are the characters going to get through dinner—assuming they do. Then, after Larry leaves, the husband (me) has to hash it all out with his wife. That can be a scene resolution or the final resolution if it's the end of the story. How I work it out with my wife in the long run or fail to is the story ending (resolution). The story ends when the problem is solved, when the conflict is resolved. It ends with closure.

When you're having trouble ending a story, it's because you don't have a real beginning, a true conflict. The secret to endings is: **The end is in the beginning.** If the ending is your problem, look at your beginning. If the beginning is set up right, the characters propel the story to the end.

So, stories are about adversity (flu, alleys, cheating, knives)—always. Happiness is not dramatic. It never was. It never will be. Happy lives make lousy novels. Dealing with happiness is not the issue in life. Achieving happiness is, but not happiness itself. No one goes to a shrink because he's too happy. Happiness can be the resolution to a story, but not the story itself. When happiness does show up, we don't need much of it. How much happiness is in *Cinderella*? A bit at the ball (with the stroke of midnight looming on the horizon), and the moment when the slipper slides on, then cut to "And they lived happily ever after." That's enough. We don't care where they lived happily. We don't care how. Happiness takes care of itself. There is little room for happiness in stories.

So if a woman says, "My husband is totally loyal. He never flirts. He never looks at other women. He never has an unfaithful thought. Even in his dreams, he dreams of me. I never have to worry about him. He'd never cheat on me in a million years," what does that tell us the story *must* be about? His cheating. He has to—and he has to get caught. Otherwise, what's the point? You have a devoted husband? Fine. Good for you. We're not interested, because we want some action, and that requires conflict. Trouble, adversity, crisis get us every time. When happiness shows up, don't dwell on it. Remember: **If the characters are having a good time, the reader is not. If it's going well, it's going nowhere.**

To create conflict, the kind that's needed to move a story, you must have two elements—a **want** and an **obstacle.** Someone must want something and there must be an obstacle to be overcome to satisfy that want. Scarlett *wants* Ashely. Ashley is marrying Melanie *(obstacle)*. Romeo and Juliet *want* to unite. Their families are enemies *(obstacle)*. Ahab *wants* to kill the whale. The whale and the sea *(obstacles)* must be overcome. Both want and obstacle must be determined to overcome the other. If one is weak, you have no conflict. If Ahab got lucky and came upon the whale napping in shallow waters and harpooned him to death before he knew what hit him, no obstacle, no conflict, no story. Or if Ahab wised up and realized it was crazy to be risking his neck chasing the whale all over the sea (he's already lost one leg—did he want to lose another or worse?), again, no want, no conflict, no story. If Romeo decided Juliet was a fabulous girl, but not worth risking his neck for, no want, no conflict, no story. So, it's want + obstacle = conflict. You must have both, and both must be strong. These are obvious examples. It's not always so clear. One of the elements can be present but weak. When that happens, you will be straining and struggling to keep things going and never get there. The story must be driven by the energy and determination of the characters, not the author. The author creates the want and the obstacle and they do the job.

Conflict, action, resolution make up the story form. Someone said, "The form is the killer." It can be, but it doesn't have to be. For sure, it will be if you don't take time to learn the craft.

The craft includes two other basic elements:

Emotion: Since this is where the ultimate connection is made, the pay-off, where we become the character (feel what he or she feels), we must know at all times what the character is feeling. If we don't know what the character is feeling, we won't know what *we're* feeling. The emotion can be suggested or implied. It doesn't have to be spelled out, but we must know what it is at all times. Now, the character may not know what he is feeling, may be trying to figure out how he really feels. Confusion. That's fine. That's where the character is, and we're there also. But if we don't know, the character's not there, and neither are we. Emotion is the most complicated part of stories. We'll come back to it for a full treatment later (chapter 6).

Showing: If I wanted to give you the definition of *homely,* I could go to the dictionary and find a definition. "Homely, adj. Lacking in elegance or refinement. Not attractive or good-looking." That's the *idea* of homely. Not particularly moving, is it? If I wanted to give you an *experience* of homely, to *show* it, I would have to put it in personal terms, to give you a specific person's experience of it. For example:

"She's a homely girl. I don't know where she gets it," my six-year-old ears overhear my mother saying to my Aunt Beth. I don't know what "homely" means, but I know it's bad. I run to my room, bury my head in my pillow, and cry. Eventually, I learn what homely really means. It means to be taken to the dentist for my buckteeth: "Can you make them straighter?" To the plastic surgeon for my nose: "Can you make it smaller?" It means I am dragged to walking classes, talking classes, and posture classes: "Chin up. Shoulders back. Enunciate. Smile." Homely means that everything I put in my mouth is carefully weighed, measured, and calculated beforehand so I don't take up more space than I already do. "Will she ever lose weight, Doctor?" my mother asks. "She's just a big girl," says Doctor Chen. Homely means that you see a look of disdain on the face of a mother who wishes her daughter could be a beauty queen. You see that look every day of your life.

—Elizabeth Brown

There you have it. Which hits home? The idea or the experience?

If I say, "It was the worst day of George's life. He was so miserable, he went home and blew his brains out," do you feel for George? No you don't. Not because you're unfeeling, but because I haven't given you enough of George to make you feel. I've generalized George—given him to you in the abstract. I've given you the idea of George, but not George himself. I've told you *about* him instead of making him live, instead of making him happen before your eyes. I *told* you he was miserable. I *told* you he killed himself. But saying it doesn't make it so. *The reader will take your word for nothing.* You can't simply tell the reader. You have to **show** him.

If we're going to connect (identify) with George, I have to give you the experience of George. **Show** you what he's going through—how he's mistreated by his boss, by his friends, by himself. **Show** you how he struggles to have a life. I have to take you through his day so you can live it with him and think his thoughts and feel his misery. Only then can you become him, only then, when he puts the gun to his head, can you feel, *No, George, don't,* and shed a tear for George. Giving you the full story of George would take too much time here, but you should get the idea. We'll have more examples and exercises throughout the course, and chapter 7 is devoted to showing.

So, these are the five critical elements of storytelling: CONFLICT, ACTION, RESOLUTION, EMOTION, SHOWING. The first three define the shape of a complete story. Emotion is the critical ingredient. Showing is your basic technique to make your story come alive.

OK, let's see how it works. How we can use it to figure out what's working and what's not. We're going to go through three pieces of writing and see how to use these tools. As you read, relax and pay attention to your reactions, your emotions. That's your best guide always. Here's the first one:

Do spiders worry about sex?

A man on the television was talking about the way the world watches us, about how paintings are sizing us up, examining the brushstrokes on our souls. This may be why, in the presence of great beauty, we feel a vividness, a clarity, a recognition—because the beauty has found us, discovered who we truly are.

All right, stop for a moment. What's your level of involvement, from 1 to 10? How moved are you? Most people are on the low end at this point, at 3 to 5. Why would that be? Why isn't it at 8 to 10? From what we've gone over, can you tell what the issue is—what's not there and what needs to be there to get you hooked in a major way? What single writing technique might turn this piece into a gripping one? Remember *telling* versus *showing?* Ideas versus experience? These are ideas. Unless you really love these particular ideas, you're neither here nor there about them. You're neutral, and that's not high involvement. Of course, if they rub you the wrong way, you're set against them already. So, this is a good example of *telling* and not *showing*. Let's see where you go with the rest of it.

You notice her hair first. Not that you wouldn't want to spend hours in the warm lagoon of her eyes or learn the future by tracing her delicate hands. But it is her brown hair that men might spend hours devising ways to touch. A shade of brown that makes you long to be buried in leaves. An exquisite scent that forces you, against better judgment, to shut your eyes and savor. Hair that can keep a man from waxing the car, juggling, or building cathedrals. Your hands want nothing more than to touch it. But the beauty finds you first.

Do spiders worry about sex? Not yet. Not so far as anyone can tell.

Too bad.

—Hugh Schulze

That's all of it. How did the second part go? Did it get to you? If so, what did and where? Most people connect more with this second part. Why? Can you tell? First, because a person appears. We experience best through a person (even animal characters or Martians are personifications of ourselves). Also, there are a few striking images—"buried in leaves" and "waxing the car, juggling, or building cathedrals." Those are striking images for most people. They're real and visible. That brings us to another important point. **The written story is a visual medium.** Yes, good fiction is just as visual as film. Anytime you don't have a picture in your head, you're in trouble or will be soon. Stories are about the specifics of experience that we can see and touch. That doesn't mean you have to be highly descriptive or describe everything. You just have to give the reader enough so he can picture it. If done well, a few choice details can create a whole scene.

This short piece, as much a poem as a scene, is a good example of the difference between telling and showing. But what about the spider stuff? How does that tie in, or does it? Most people don't relate to it. It doesn't really tie in closely to the rest. It's a provocative idea and might go somewhere in its own right or be made to work if it were woven through the piece. If that were done, some literature professor might be assigning a paper on the meaning of the spider and how it relates to the rest of the piece (the black widow who devours the male after mating?).

This piece was written as a short exercise piece in one of my seminars. This writer had a knack for images and liked spiders. Another sample of his work is at the very end of this chapter.

Here's the next piece to examine, written by A. C. Paterson:

Big Daddy

Sex had never been Francesca's forte. In fact, she had to admit to her rather drab reflection in the bathroom mirror as she stood brushing her teeth, sex wasn't ever her mediumte—if that were a word. No.

All right, are you there? Most of us would be. You wouldn't put it down and say, "She's upset about no being good at sex. Sounds boring." "Had to admit" tells us she's not happy with it (emotion) and it's a problem (obstacle) and that she wishes it were different (want). So we have Want + Obstacle (conflict) and emotion—in just two sentences.

She paused in her brushing, listening for the sound of Jack's snoring, hoping for the snoring, waiting for the snoring.

No snoring.

Enter Jack and his snoring. Does that increase your interest? Yes it does. The plot is thickening, a term we've heard many times. But exactly what does this mean in a story? When something thickens it usually moves more slowly. No so in a story. In a story, thickening means getting worse, which is pressure to act. Worse almost always comes in the form of a person, Jack, in this case. She's hoping Jack is snoring and no one has to spell it out for us. We can put two and two together. She's thinking about sex and hoping Jack is asleep already. If he's awake, it's a problem (conflict) that she's going to have to face and deal with (action).

Francesca began brushing again. No. The fact was, she wasn't good at sex at all. Never had been. And, she looked again at her reflection—gray hair mixed freely with the brown, lines fanning out from the corners for her eyes, the sag underneath her chin— she realized now that she was forty-three, she was never going to get good at it. E

She spilt in the sink and listened again for the sound of snoring. In vain. o

It wasn't that she wanted it to be this way. A

And hadn't she enjoyed Jack—his kisses, the warm feel of his body in bed, the simple touch of his hand with the swirled scar from the time he went over the handlebars of his bike at twelve and landed with a stick piercing his palm?

Yes, she had enjoyed Jack, at one time at least. But that had been, what? A year ago? Two? Maybe two and a half.

Maybe she just needed to adjust her attitude.

"Hey, what's going on in there? Did you drown yourself?" Jack called.

Yes, adjust her attitude—be positive. Maybe sex would be . . . nice for a change.

"Did you flush yourself down the toilet?" Jack called again. "I Sure hope not 'cause big daddy is out here waiting for you."

Positive attitude. Francesca smiled to the mirror, flicked off the bathroom lights, and stepped into the bedroom.

"There you are," he said, looking up from the *Outdoor Sportsman* magazine he had in his hand.

"Here I am." Francesca kept smiling. He had already pushed all the covers down to the foot of the bed—the way she hated— and was lying on top of the top sheet in nothing but his boxers and round-framed glasses.

"Big daddy's ready for some fun." He smiled and wiggled his thin hips on the bed.

"I've told you I don't like it when you say that."

"Say what?" he grinned

"That."

"What?" He patted the side of bed next to him.

"Big daddy," Francesca said through her teeth. "It's really not a turn on." She walked around his scattered clothes—shirt, pants, half curled-up belt—on the floor.

"Big daddy," he said, smiling.

by A. C. Patterson

OK, that's it, did you have an experience? Is the character revealed so that you could identify? How is she revealed? She's revealed by the way she acts. She is forced to act by a conflict that she must face and struggle to overcome. Did that happen here? A good exercise would be to go through the story again (before reading on) and mark every place the character's want expresses itself and every place the obstacle threatens, and every place she acts to overcome or deal with the problem, and where and how her emotion is revealed.

What did you find? There's lots of conflict, action, and emotion.

Francesca isn't good at sex (obstacle) but she wants (want) to be. Also, she's hoping Jack is asleep (want) but Jack is wide-awake and hollering to her from the bed (obstacle). Also, she's struggling with herself (action). She's dealing with her feeling of not being good at sex and not wanting to have sex tonight by trying to change her feelings, adjusting her attitude, which is action. The mind is a dramatic place and lots of struggles go on there. A character's struggle with herself or himself is what gives us the deepest sense of the character.

When Francesca enters the room, she is hit with a number of things (obstacles), which upset her (emotion) and each one gives us more of her character. The covers pushed down the way she hates, the clothes strewn on the floor, and especially the "Big Daddy" comment, which she tells him she doesn't like (action). How much stronger is it when she voices her objection? And how much stronger is it that he doesn't get the message? The plot thickens.

The worse it gets the better it is. The pattern of a story is want, obstacle, action. Want, obstacle, action over and over as things get worse and worse until the end when they get better, end in disaster, or a combination of both. This is not only the pattern of a story but life itself—what we're all faced with over and over and over until we die. In a story, once the trouble starts there is no let up, no one gets time out to take a break and relax. Ahab never sat back and relaxed and sunned himself on the deck of his boat. Hamlet didn't get a moment's peace once his father's ghost bade him to avenge his murder. The old saying, "There's no rest for the wicked" may be true or not, but in a story there is not rest for the hero until the very end when there may or may not be.

Here's the beginning of the last piece:

Ever since I told her I was a lesbian, my mother has taken to talking about me in the past tense.

How are you with this piece? A provocative opening? Most people are with it with this first sentence. Why? Because there are a want and an obstacle—a mother who is not pleased with her daughter. Here's the rest:

"You were such a beautiful baby," she says, her large, sea green eyes filling up with a lethal mixture of nostalgia and longing.

I groan.

"You were the very essence of femininity." Her voice trails off dramatically. I begin to tap the toe of my cowboy boot very lightly on the tile floor beneath the kitchen table, bracing for the assault.

She shrugs, and in the sagging folds of her Eastern European face I see a ragtag clutter of disappointment and despair. Her mouth, which is usually bow shaped and generous, tightens slightly as she looks at me.

"Your walk, your voice, your body . . . everything about you was perfectly feminine." She shakes her head as she ponders this and the tap tap tap of the tip of my cowboy boot begins to pick up speed.

"For God's sake, mother, this is an absolutely ridiculous theory—and it's easily the third time you've presented it this month."

"Please hear me out," she says and I sag under the intensity of her conviction.

As I lean back in my chair, she leans forward and puts her hand—a smaller, more time worn version of my own—on my arm.

"I believe *we*—your father and I, that is—gave *you* a perfectly healthy endocrine system."

I can feel the slight pressure of her hand on my arm as I close my eyes. Through clenched teeth, I give her one last chance to explain her "theory" of my lesbianism before I explode. "What's that supposed to mean, 'a perfectly healthy endocrine system'?"

"Well, it means, it's not our fault," she says, letting her hand slide off my arm and hit the table with a small thud. She shrugs again, heaving her bosom. "So, the warp must be in your psyche. It's the only possible explanation."

That's it. How did it go? Whatever problems you might have with it, it's a strong piece that takes hold of most readers and hangs onto them as these two characters struggle with each other.

Let's look at it from the story angle. Who wants what? The daughter wants to be accepted as she is. The mother wants a straight daughter, ideally, but short of that, the mother's going for something else. What is it? She wants to be guiltless and to blame the daughter, the daughter whom she's trying to convince (action) has a "warp" in her "psyche." The daughter is putting up with her, for exactly what reasons we don't know. So we have want, obstacle, action. There is no resolution yet—neither scene resolution nor story resolution. Can you figure out where this is going? You should be able to, since it's already going in that direction. Victory, defeat, mixed victory.

So, that's the story form and technique. Conflict (want + obstacle), action, resolution, emotion, showing. Just five elements. If you stay focused on these five elements and don't let yourself get distracted or sidetracked, if you master these five, no matter what else you do wrong, you will succeed. You will succeed, because you'll be creating strong stories. The world—agents, publishers, editors—will bend over backwards for a strong story. Stephen King, for example, can be a sloppy writer (he himself says that his writing is like a Big Mac and an order of French fries), but he's one hell of a good storyteller.

All right. This has been a long stint. I've hit you with a lot. Conflict is tricky and elusive, so we'll revisit it and its finer points in the next chapter. For now, you need only be *aware* of these elements, to understand how they work and relate. But remember, awareness and understanding aren't mastery. Mastery takes practice. It'll come soon enough *if* you stay focused. The main thing is, don't expect too much. Just write and let whatever comes flow onto the page. You're just creating some raw material to work with, to turn into a compelling story—eventually, once you master the craft. For now, it's just practice.

So, it's time to try it, get loose, let go, warm up a bit. I want you to put something (anything) down, throw some words onto the page. But I'm not going to desert you. I'm going to give you some scene setups to help you get going.

Now, if you have something you're working on and want to use that, do so. The main thing is to write for 30 minutes. If you don't have 30 minutes, or you run out of energy, do what you can (5 minutes, 10, 15). When you have time or you feel up to it, come back and do some more until you've written for a total of 30 minutes. **If you have no time and you're not going to have any time,** go to chapter 12 and find the time plan that's workable. Use that plan to do these exercises or something from chapter 12 if you like that better.

EXERCISES

Here are a few scene ideas. Pick one and see what you can do with it.

- Blind date. First is getting set up, including the character's worries, fears, and hopes. Then the first contact on the telephone, which needs to raise both anxiety and hopes. The **want** is to have a wonderful lover. The **obstacle** is having to go through the anxiety and sense of humiliation to find out if this person is the one or is even worth the effort. E +S
- Going home to visit family (parents, siblings, etc.) for a holiday

visit or after having been away for an extended time. Now, if it's a wonderful family, don't bother. It has to be difficult. The character needs to be anticipating trouble and trying to figure out how to avoid it. The **want** is to get through the visit avoiding trouble/pain. The **obstacle** is the difficult family, who are going to give the character a hard time about as much as possible.

· Trapped on a ski lift, on an airplane, or in a taxi with someone who starts talking or acting strange. The **want** is to be left alone, to be at peace, to be safe. The **obstacle** is this weird person who is acting strange and maybe is dangerous.

Now, if none of those grab you, here's a much looser exercise. I'm going to give you three sets of unrelated words. You'll pick one set of the three and write a scene using the three-word set you pick. Here they are:

· Buddha, loveseat, belch.
· Albino, pistol, strawberry.
· Muzzle, telescope, nude.

The thing to do is to just hang loose and let the words stimulate you. Here's another exercise to do if you don't want to do any of the above. In this, I'll give you a list of settings. You pick a setting that strikes your fancy. Then I'll give you a list of characters. You pick two or more of the characters and have them interact in the setting.

· Settings: Cemetery, gas station, pawnshop, porn shop, porn theater, tavern, ballpark, church, train, doctor's office, dentist's office, airplane.
· Characters: Priest, cop, prostitute, nurse, vampire, doctor, burglar, tramp, cab driver, baby, mayor, gangster.

Don't worry about the story form, unless you feel like trying it. It's new, so it's not going to (and is not supposed to) feel comfortable. If you want to try it, see if you can establish a *want* and an *obstacle* (or *obstacle* first, then *want,* as in the Larry scene) and an initial *action.* But the main thing is to write. If trying to create want and obstacle gets in the way, forget it and just write. If you're using your own project and you feel up to it, work to create a want and an obstacle. On the other hand, if it takes off, after you create a want and an obstacle, go on and have your character take **action,** confront the problem, and push it through to a **resolution** (victory or defeat).

Here's the piece, from the writer who wrote the spider piece that appeared earlier.

As near as Clayton could recall, they had been talking about God when he mentioned the spider, no larger than an infant's thumbnail, that lives in mid-air at altitudes as high as 12,000 feet. This particular type of spider, in spite of the extreme cold and buffeting of air currents, is able to stride in the thin atmosphere like a pond insect using the water's surface tension, and even weaves webs, using water droplets or crystals of ice as anchors for the mooring threads. These free-floating webs, wet with woven rain or white with frost, have been known to dance across the windshields of airplanes, like handkerchiefs dropped by flirtatious angels—there and gone so quickly that pilots often never even noticed them.

Not until the dawn of aviation was there any record of these spiders (the first recorded sighting being that of a balloonist who had gone far too high and encountered what he called "a bright cathedral window in the air." Reaching out to touch it, his fingertips broke the tenuous film of water in the interstices of the web and he came away with only a few thin strands on his dampened fingertips). Not until the early 1920s was the first specimen captured. Clayton remembered that a controversy still surrounded the origins of the spiders: How had they come to live at those altitudes? Had a few daring arachnids stepped off a Himalayan mountainside thousands of years ago? How did they live? Did they draw nourishment from the air as some orchids did?

Clayton's point had been that until the advent of a particular type of technology, any knowledge of these spiders or their webs had been the subject of myth or superstition. Every so often, these webs slipped through a trough in the atmosphere, perhaps down through an eddy of air current. At sunset or sunrise, especially in the Western states, you may catch a glimpse of a web spiraling down to the earth, glittering at all its dewy points. The Navaho and Sioux told tales of Grandmother Spider.

As usual, her response to his argument had been unexpected. The thought that there was a type of spider that could, at any moment, fall upon her, web and all, kept her in the house for days. When he suggested that she might be overreacting, she answered: "You *know* I hate spiders. Why did you ever tell me about that one?" In some odd way, he felt she was right. He knew she was afraid of spiders and snakes and fiberglass insulation and empty metal boxes.

So, there's the spider again. When I read this, I asked this author if there was such a spider. He said, "Hell no. I made it up." Not only was the image of this spider vivid and real, but the author turned it into a bone of contention between the narrator and his wife. The image, as striking as it is, is not enough to make a story. For that we must have want, obstacle, and action. The author went on to raise the tension and drama with the following:

Tonight, he had planned on telling her about the place where people fear the rain (who knows what effect that might have had on her), but when he drove up the driveway, he found the house dark. When he entered the house, he found that she had not gone to bed early. And when he went into the kitchen to have a beer and call her mother, he found the note written on a piece of brown paper shopping bag, secured with two red magnetic letters to the freezer.

I can't take it any longer. I'm sorry.
I'm taking the baby with me.

—Hugh Schulze

You should know that this author had been writing for years. Don't get intimidated by someone else's writing. You can do this. The next chapter gets into the finer points of how it's done.

4

Fine-Tuning

After a Bulls game, a reporter asked Michael Jordan how one of the new players, Luke Longley, was doing. Jordan said that Longley was doing fine, but that he had to learn their system. The Bulls have a plan, Michael said. Everyone who comes to the Bulls must learn their plan, their system. Every player has to know the plan inside and out, forward and backward so it becomes part of him and he doesn't have to think about it. When the team is winning, they just play basketball. They don't worry about the plan or anything else. They just go. But when they're losing, when they're in trouble, they switch to the plan immediately. Everyone knows where to go and what to do. Everyone focuses on doing his job. Then, when they're back on track, they just play basketball again.

All right, why do I tell you this anecdote, and what does it have to do with writing? First of all, what I gave you in the last chapter, which is also what I'm refining in this chapter, is your plan—a plan you will use for the rest of your writing life. When things are going well, when you're writing and loving it, don't bother with the plan. Just go. But when you get into trouble (and you'll get into trouble a lot, as did the

Bulls), go to it immediately. Go to *want, obstacle, action* first—always. If those elements aren't in place, aren't set up and working properly, nothing else you do can make up for it. If you don't attend to them first, you will waste an enormous amount of energy working on something that will not fix the problem, and your story will shut down no matter how hard you work to keep it going.

So, when things aren't going right, do not let yourself get distracted by anything else—go to your plan (want, obstacle, action) immediately. Ask first, "Who wants what?" If no one wants anything, that's your problem. Nothing can happen without that. You'll be wasting your time if you work elsewhere. Once you have the character's want established, ask, "What's the obstacle?" If there is no obstacle, you have no conflict and no dramatic tension to move the story. After you've created a threatening obstacle, ask, "What's the character doing (action) to overcome the obstacle and fulfill his want?"

If you have these three story elements working, your story will be moving, and you won't be wondering what's wrong. I've never seen a story that was failing where the problem wasn't in one of these three story elements. They are the one, two, three of dramatic movement.

Getting into trouble is inevitable. The important thing is how quickly you get out of it. How fast you get out of trouble and back on track determines whether you spend a month to a year writing a novel or whether you spend three to five to ten years doing it. The difference between writers who write novels quickly and those who take years and years isn't how much time they *spend* writing, but how much time they *waste trying* to write. Your greatest weapon is understanding the story form and the story elements—mastering the plan.

In order to master the plan, we need to revisit the theory, to take another look at it from a couple of other perspectives, then define the story elements more precisely. Normally, the stricter a definition, the more limiting and restrictive it is. In this case, it's the opposite. The

more specific the definition, the more clearly you understand each element, the more choices you'll have, and the easier it'll be to get to the
energy and drama of your characters and your story. Understanding
the tools and how they work is the key to using them successfully.

In the last chapter, we examined identification—what it is and
what part it plays in stories and in life. Identification is the goal not
only of every story but of every life. It's our deepest social need. It's at
the heart of all meaningful social interaction. It's what makes life
worthwhile. It's what we're all after. We don't think of it that way. We
don't say, "I'm going out tonight to find someone to identify with,"
but that's what we're doing.

But why? Why do we need it? Remember, in stories we ask *why* of
everything to push it to the deepest level, to find the root cause, to get
to the very bottom of it. *It* being the character. That's what stories
do—get to the bottom, reach the limit, of the characters. We get to
the limit of Ahab and Gatsby and Scarlett and Romeo and Hamlet.
No one ever accused any of them (or the authors) of not going all the
way. No one ever accused Romeo of not loving and pursuing Juliet
with all his heart or Hamlet of not agonizing enough over his problems or Ahab of not going all-out to get *Moby-Dick*. If you want your
characters and your stories to go all the way, you, the author, must do
the same. You must push them as far as you can at every chance. One
way of going all the way is to ask why, why, and why of everything.

So, why do we need to identify? What does it do for us? A good
way to see what something does is to see what happens when we take
it away. It's always easiest to see things in the extreme. Stories are
about the extremes, always. Even if it's about an old lady fussing at
her dog to be more polite and considerate of her, it needs to be extreme in terms of who she and her dog are.

So, an extreme case of taking away identification can be reached by
asking: what's the worst punishment we can legally give someone in

prison, short of execution? Got the answer? Of course. You know instantly. We all do. Solitary confinement. We don't have to have been there to know. Imagining is enough.

But *why?* What's so bad about it? Why is it painful? It's painful because you're alone, because you have no contact with others. OK, but what's bad about that? What happens when we have no contact with others? Well, we get nutty. Stir-crazy. We flip out. We lose our emotional balance. If we're not connected to others, we lose our connection to ourselves.

Psychologists have done isolation studies in which they put people in special tanks—each person in a separate tank. Their hands were padded so that the sense of touch was cut off and they floated in a special heavy liquid so they were as weightless as possible. They were cut off from everything except their own minds What happened to them? In short order, everyone, even those with the strongest character, began hallucinating. They deteriorated. They lost touch with reality—with themselves. They couldn't tell the difference between fantasy and reality, where they began and where they ended.

So, if you're not in touch with others, you're not in touch with yourself. The purpose of stories, of identification, is to put us (and keep us) in touch with ourselves. Identification is what must happen before you can like someone, form a friendship, or fall in love. It's what holds the world together. Civilization could not survive without it. Lofty stuff? Well, it's still theory, so you don't have to swallow it all to write a strong story—as long as you understand the importance of identification.

Connecting with others is connecting with ourselves. The purpose of stories is to make this connection—to create identification. Identification is how we experience characters, how we feel what they feel, how we become them and, in doing so, experience more of ourselves. But we cannot identify unless the character is *revealed*. *Revealing character* is a new phrase. It's what leads to identification. REVEALING CHARAC-TER IS YOUR ONGOING PURPOSE AT ALL TIMES. You make all story choices based on this rule. When faced with a choice, ask yourself: Which way reveals more character? If it reveals more character, do it.

As I said, this is still theory. Identification and revealing character are the *effects* of a story. They're the results of a successful story. They're *what* stories do, but not *how* they do it. *How* they do it is the *cause*. Writers work with causes, not effects. Creating identification is the goal of every story. Showing you *how* to create identification is the continual goal of this course.

So, how do you reveal character? Well, the character can only be revealed if he acts. Action is character. The most wonderful character in the world will not get to us unless he does something. The character will not act unless he has to, unless he's challenged. Like the rest of us, he's not going to get up and push himself to the limit for no reason. He has to be urged, prodded, challenged. That challenge is CONFLICT, which brings us back to the story elements and the basic story form, which is:

CONFLICT, ACTION, RESOLUTION

CONFLICT is the first, the number-one critical ingredient, but it's important not for what it is, but for what it *does*. What conflict does is force the character to ACT—whether he likes it or not, and he will not like it, he cannot. Ahab, Scarlett, Hamlet, Lear, Gatsby did not like what was happening to them or what they *had* to do. They were *trying* to enjoy themselves, but they were frustrated at every turn. The character cannot enjoy himself. You, the author, cannot let him, because if he's enjoying himself, the reader is not. So, conflict is what we use to make the character act, to use himself, to *reveal* himself. *Revealing character* is what must happen before identification can occur.

THE NUMBER-ONE INGREDIENT AND
SOME THOUGHTS ABOUT IT

Conflict is the first, most important, and trickiest ingredient by far. There are a number of reasons for this. The first is a social reason. The first time I was told by a writing teacher that nothing happens without conflict, I went home and wrote a story, working conflict in at every turn, making everything difficult for the characters in every possible way. How do you think I felt after making all that trouble? I was worn-out. Working the conflict was stressful beyond the usual struggle of writing. That story was applauded in the workshop, but it had been a real strain to write.

Why was it such a strain and why will it be until you get used to it? Ask yourself how you get along in society, how you survive when you're out in the world. By making as much trouble as possible every chance you get? No, you survive by avoiding conflict, by playing it safe, by being careful, by doing **the exact opposite of what you need to do to write exciting stories.**

Writing compelling stories goes against the grain of all our socialized, civilized training. Creating fiction is an antisocial act. You, the author, are the one who must make all the trouble. And you must be merciless if you are going to incite your characters to the kind of action that is revealing and dramatic. This will be difficult when the time comes to pressure, to assault, to attack your character, a character that you have put your heart into creating and are attached to. But you must, because the more pressure you put on your character, the more he must use himself, reveal himself, so that we are able to experience him.

If you take the easy way out, which you will be prone to do, consciously or unconsciously, because of your civilized nature and your affection for your character, if you take that easy way, your character will not act in a compelling way, your story will sag, and the reader will leave. So you must be cruel to your characters. It's the only way.

Remember, the whale didn't kill Ahab. Melville did. The betrayed husband didn't kill Gatsby. Fitzgerald did. In *Gone with the Wind*, the tragic death of Rhett and Scarlett's little daughter falling from the horse wasn't ultimately from the fall. The author, Margaret Mitchell, had to kill her by making her fall from the horse. Why do that? Why cause such pain to Rhett and Scarlett? Pushing them to their limits was the best way to reach them on the deepest level and to reach us also—to *reveal character*, to create identification. So, you, the author, are the ultimate cause of all the trouble in the story and all the pain suffered by the characters.

This is what I call THE DRAMATIC PARADOX. What's bad in life is good on the page. The worse you make it for the characters the better it is for the reader. Why? Because it forces the characters to use themselves to the maximum and when they do that we experience them to the maximum.

Think about what makes a good game in sports. What makes a good game—one in which one team trounces the other one hundred to nothing? That might be a record-setting score, but does that kind of a game give us what we want? No, a good game is a close game. And why is that? You might say it's more exciting and suspenseful, but that's your reaction to what's happening on the field, not what's different about the game. The question is what happens down on the field that makes it more exciting and suspenseful? What does it make the players do? It makes them go all out, makes them give it all they've got. And when they give it all they've got, we experience all they've got. A good story has to have two forces, equally matched, struggling against each other, giving it everything they have, going all out. Ahab went all out. Romeo gave it everything he had, as did

Gatsby, Scarlett, and Rhett. So you must make your characters do the same.

We're capturing life on the page, but we do it in a way that could only be seen as perverse if we were doing it to real people. The more real your characters become to you, the more you must fight the urge to make life easy for them. To create compelling stories, you must develop and exercise SADISTIC LICENSE. As I said earlier, fiction is not polite society—even when you're writing about polite society. Happy lives make lousy novels. Because trouble is dramatic, fiction is the downside, the gory details, the worst-case scenario—always. The thing you must be ever wary of is your tendency to hold back, to go easy, to let up at the very moment when you should bear down. It's a great paradox that this antisocial process produces this most social and personal creation.

OK, shying away from using conflict is one problem. The other problem is not understanding what conflict is and what it isn't. We all know what conflict is, right? Your wife calls you an insensitive slob. You get cut off on the expressway on the way to work. Your boss tells you that your work is below par. Your mother disinherits you.

Well, guess what, not one of those is conflict, our kind of conflict—*dramatic* conflict. Oh, those examples are troubling, disturbing, upsetting, but not one of them is what's needed to set a story in motion. They're *false* conflict. Trying to create a story from false conflict is like dragging a dead horse around a racetrack: you might get to the finish line, but you'll never win the race.

What we think of as conflict in everyday experience—disagreements, arguments, insults, shouting matches, even fistfights—are not our kind of conflict—not dramatic conflict. They can be turned into dramatic conflict—anything and everything can, once you know how—but dramatic conflict is a different creature entirely. Dramatic conflict is made up of several elements. Get one wrong, and no matter how brilliantly you write, your story falls flat.

Conflict is the single most poorly defined and misunderstood of all the story forces and that is the cause of so many failed stories. In all my years, I have never had conflict defined fully enough in a class or seen it defined thoroughly enough in the many writing books (over 200) that I've read. One reason it's deceptive is: **All conflict is trouble, but not all trouble is conflict.** What we're looking for is a very special kind of trouble, the kind of trouble that I call *dramatic conflict*.

All right, so what exactly is dramatic conflict? In the last chapter, I defined it as **want + obstacle.** That's good, but not precise enough to keep you focused the way you need to be. We need to pin it down so there is no doubt you have a *dramatic want* and a *dramatic obstacle*, which are both needed to create *dramatic conflict*.

Want: How do you know if you have a dramatic want—enough of a want to incite the character to propel the story forward to a dramatic finish? For a want to be dramatic the character must *feel* that satisfying it is a matter of life and death. That doesn't mean that it *is* a matter of life and death, but the character must feel that strongly, must believe that deeply that things must change, that he or she can't stand to go on with life as it is. A wife who has been browbeaten for years and taken it quietly, for example, could feel that her husband's abuse this particular morning was so vicious and demeaning that she can't take it any longer, that she can't live with herself if she puts up with another moment of it. He must stop treating her with such contempt, he must change, or she will leave him. She must be *determined, driven, desperate* to make things change. She will settle for nothing less. (Now, that doesn't mean that she won't be forced to compromise, but only *after* waging an all-out battle, after using everything she has to prevail.) There's ur-

gency, a sense of crisis. If she can live with things the way they are, if
she has a choice, you have a *false* want, which will make for a *false* conflict. The want must be overpowering and pushing the character to
the limit. She has come to a point where she can't stand it any longer.
Her neighbor might feel differently. "Twenty minutes of abuse a day,
for all you've got. I'd trade places with you any day." But our wife can
stand it no longer. If she did nothing, she could not live with herself.
She would have no self-respect. This would eat her up from the inside.

Now, of course, there are gentle, subtle stories that may not go the
limit to this degree. But even the best of these follow this form. At a
minimum, they have a sense of urgency, an encounter/confrontation,
and a resolution. But don't get distracted by that now. Your job is to
learn to create drama. Once you can do that, you can do anything.

Obstacle: Following immediately on the heels of the want must come
the obstacle. But how can you tell if you have enough of an obstacle, a
dramatic obstacle? Well, first, the obstacle must be as determined,
driven, and desperate to block or deny the want as the want is driven
to overcome the obstacle. If they are not of equal determination, you
have an uneven match and a false conflict—one that will be resolved
quickly. The best way to measure the want-obstacle relationship is to
consider what would happen if the character ignored the obstacle. If
you have a dramatic obstacle and the character ignores it, if he does not
act, he will be seriously harmed or destroyed—emotionally, physically,
socially, financially ruined. If the character can do nothing and still suffer
no injury, you have a false conflict or no conflict—no drama, no story.

Obstacle First: Now, a person's want often doesn't get fired up until it's
thwarted. The obstacle often appears first, as in *Hamlet* (the ghost of
Hamlet's father appears out of nowhere) or in my Larry scene (my

wife kisses Larry). The want is there. It's understood, but it's dormant. We assume Hamlet wasn't longing to have the problem of avenging his father's death dumped in his lap. So, he doesn't give it a thought until it is. We assume that I don't want my wife cheating on me by kissing Larry, but it doesn't cross my mind until it happens. Often it's easier to dump a big problem on the character to get things moving than to try to work up a want first. Or you can create an obstacle, then start your story before the obstacle appears and build up the want that the obstacle will threaten or deny. Whether it's want-obstacle or obstacle-want, they need to appear as close together as possible.

Action: Activity is not action, not dramatic action. A character can be doing all kinds of things (ranting, raving, thrashing around) that are not to the point, not an attempt to make something happen. For action to be dramatic, it must be either a **direct attack upon** the problem or a **defense against** it. Trying to convince someone to loan you money so you can pay off a gambling debt is a direct attack upon the problem. Hiding behind the door with a baseball bat to club the juice man who's coming to break your legs at eight o'clock is a defense against the problem—a problem that's coming to you. In both cases the character must assert himself in a major way.

Thinking: Thinking can be action. Thinking that involves wrestling with the problem and planning an attack or a defense is action. The mind is a dramatic place. The written story is the only story form that can do the mind well, that can portray it to its fullest. All great stories involve the workings of the mind and the internal conflict, the character's struggle with himself. The mind is the deepest, most intimate connection that we can make. But all writers do not go into the mind to the same degree—mainly because it's the most difficult part of the craft next to using conflict. Portraying a character's thoughts is difficult and complicated enough that it needs a chapter of its own, which will come later.

WANT, OBSTACLE, ACTION
Your first line of defense. The never-fail tools.
The holy trinity of story.

Want, obstacle, action are the one, two, three of dramatic movement. If you get those three elements in place and working properly, your story will have the dramatic energy to propel it to a strong ending. The first questions to be asked when reworking a story or a scene are: 1. Who wants what? 2. What's the obstacle? 3. What's the character doing (action) to overcome it? If you don't check these elements first, if you fuss around with other concerns, you'll waste a lot of time and energy trying to fix things that can never make up for a weakness in these elements. If the want, obstacle, action aren't absolutely clear, if you can't find them on the page, that is what you must work on first—always. Nothing begins, nothing moves dramatically, until they are working. Never let yourself be distracted from working these elements first. They are what determine all else in your story.

Resolution: The ending. Many writers say they have trouble with endings, but the ending is rarely the problem. The major cause of difficult endings is: There is no real beginning. The fact that you have a lot of words and pages doesn't mean that your story has begun in the dramatic sense. Technically, until you have a dramatic conflict (want + obstacle) and a character acting to overcome the obstacle, your story has not begun. If those elements don't emerge until page 60, your story doesn't start until page 60. Some stories *never* begin.

The rule is: the end is in the beginning. This means that if you have two forces of equal strength struggling to conquer each other, you have a beginning. The story will end when one prevails after an all-out struggle. For example, it's easy to see what the end of my Larry scene and the eventual end of the story would be. The end, the resolution of the conflict, is merely a **victory** or a **defeat.** Romeo and Juliet are defeated. Hamlet is defeated. Ahab is defeated. Scarlett loses and wins. Now, reality is not so cut-and-dried, so the ending doesn't have to go all one way. There can be mixed victories, compromises, accepting less, just as it might happen in real life, but again, only after an all-out struggle. It can never be easy. But there can be moments when it can appear easy, which brings us to an important point.

THE USES OF HAPPINESS

Even though it can't *be* easy, it can *appear* to be easy. What would you feel if, in a 300-page novel, everything got good, the trouble seemed to be over, and the characters were home free on page 150. The characters are rejoicing, "This is great. Our worries are over. Life is wonderful." But you know damn well that trouble is going to strike soon; otherwise, it's over.

Early in *The Great Gatsby,* several pages are spent showing us Gatsby's grand mansion and describing how it glows through the night with his fabulous parties in and around his place and his pool. It's OK, but we don't need that much of it, if that's all there is to it. But, in fiction, happiness is a setup. We open with the wonderful, glowing Gatsby mansion. We close with the mansion darkened and Gatsby floating facedown in his swimming pool. If things are going to get better, they can't do so until the end. That brings us to another important point.

WORSE AND WORSE AND WORSE
The worse it gets, the better it is.

The course of good stories never runs smooth. Things get worse and worse and worse until they get better. **Things must be worse at the end of every scene and every chapter.** The drama *builds*. Building means getting worse. If you have two scenes that have a lot of activity, but nothing has gotten worse, your story hasn't moved. You have a scene that serves no purpose. *Romeo and Juliet* is a great example of how it gets worse and worse. Romeo and Juliet get married. Romeo kills Tybalt and is banished. That's a lot of conflict, a lot of pain. Shakespeare could let up, could give Juliet a break, let her rest a bit in her agony. But no, now that she's down, Shakespeare kicks her. Juliet's father, not knowing she's already married, suggests that she should marry Paris. When Juliet objects, he becomes enraged and orders her to marry Paris, and even begins making arrangements for the wedding. Each step leads into more trouble, more threat until the end.

So, we never have two characters sitting around having a conversation or a discussion or exchanging information. That will not move things forward. There must be confrontation—one character trying to get something from the other. Someone working on the problem, pushing for change.

If you have two characters getting along perfectly and acting in concert, you are not revealing anything about them except that they are alike. Your choice is to stir up trouble between them or get rid of one of them. Dramatically, you only need one character. No one is along for the ride in fiction. Each character must serve a purpose, which is to rub another in a way that will reveal something meaningful about both of them. Butch Cassidy and the Sundance Kid were partners and bosom buddies, but they didn't get along perfectly. There was plenty of friction between them. Characters (and people) are defined by their differences and how they handle them.

It's always confrontation, but confrontation isn't always challenging or ranting or threatening. It can be gentle. Someone trying to get something out of someone else, politely, carefully. But there must be a lot riding on the outcome of the interaction. If not, we don't need it. Nothing is neutral in fiction. Everything and everyone must move the story in one direction or the other and serve to reveal character.

Also, each scene and each chapter need to end in the mind of the character, with the character stewing and fretting and wrestling with what just happened and what he has to do next. The character might not know. He might be thinking, *This is bad. This is terrible. What am I going to do now?* The scene has moved forward and has moved the character to a new place, a more troubling, more worrisome place. We need to know where exactly that place is inside the character in order to relate. If the character isn't worried or scared at the end of the scene or chapter, your story is in trouble. Why? Because threat and fear go hand in hand. So, **if it's going well, it's going nowhere.**

Do I overstate my case? Perhaps. But you will never go wrong following these rules. Shakespeare didn't. Hemingway didn't. Fitzgerald didn't. Master these techniques first. Learn to be ruthless in this way. Nothing will serve you better.

Want, obstacle, action, resolution are the story elements that fit together to create the story *form*. There are two other critical issues that are not a part of the form. One is the critical *ingredient,* **emotion.** The other is the basic story *technique,* **showing.**

Emotion: This is where the ultimate connection is made, where the reader and the character become one. We feel what the character

feels. If we don't know what the character's feeling, we're not connected. Emotion is tricky. We'll spend a chapter on it later. For now,
you need to be aware that we must know what the character is feeling
at all times. In cases where the character is confused or trying to sort
out how he feels, we must know that. That's an emotional experience
we can relate to. An easy way to pin down what the character is feeling is to ask what are his **worries, fears,** and **hopes.**

If the character is not worried or scared, you don't have a conflict.
A conflict means that the character could lose something of great
value. He cannot be neutral if something dear to his heart is threatened. If the character doesn't care, the reader won't care. The reader
can't care more than the character. Stories are about crisis. In a crisis,
we **worry,** we **fear** the worst while **hoping** we can do something to
prevent it. So, for now, ask what are the character's worries, fears, and
hopes and express them on the page as best you can.

Showing: Showing is your basic weapon—the fundamental method
of capturing an experience on the page. Showing is almost always
scene/dialogue. It has the pace of reality, moment by moment, word
for word. The opposite of showing (experience) is telling (ideas).
Even though we call it story*telling, telling* is our *technical* term for being general, abstract, or conceptual. What we're really doing, in technical story terms, is showing a story. "He was a homicidal maniac," is
an example of telling. It's the idea, the words, but not the experience.
It's general, abstract, conceptual.

"Well, angel," he said, holding the knife to her throat.
"Where would you like me to cut first?" "Oh, please." "Oh,
please. Oh, please, yes, darling. Tell me where. Don't rush. You
have plenty of time—the rest of your life." "No. No." "Yes. Yes.

Pick the spot, lover. Anywhere you like. I don't want to start in the wrong place," he said and kissed her on the forehead.

Here the writing is *showing* us a sadistic maniac. Showing is making it happen right before our eyes, without the writer using the words *sadistic* or *maniac,* without his *telling* us about it in the abstract. We'll be working with showing throughout the course.

We started with an anecdote—Michael Jordan and the Bulls. And we end with an anecdote. This one concerns Jimmy Connors. When Jimmy Connors was at the height of his career, he was playing in a close match and missed a shot. As he was walking back along the baseline to get set, he was mumbling, scolding himself, about what he did wrong and what he had to concentrate on for the next volley. The greatest tennis player in the world, he'd been playing tennis for thirty years, and what do you suppose he was telling himself he had to do? Well, it was the thing they told him the day he went on the tennis court for his first lesson. That day the instructor put the racket in his hand and said, "This is the racket, Jimmy. You hold it like this," and wrapped his hand around the grip. "And this is the ball," he said, holding the ball in front of his face. "Remember, always . . ." What did the coach tell him? "Always keep your eye on the ball."

Thirty years later, why was Jimmy Connors still telling himself to keep his eye on the ball? And why am I telling you this anecdote? Well, I'm telling it to you because storytelling is all in the fundamentals, and no one can keep them in mind all the time. What does you in is not failure to apply some high-level, intricate, complicated technique. It's overlooking the basics. Not keeping your eye on the ball.

Your fundamentals, your ball, are *conflict, action, resolution, emotion, showing.* They're all you need to know to write successfully. They will get you there every time, because they draw out what's inside you that is exciting and dramatic. Remember, you know a lot more than you realize. There is much more of you than is in your mind at any one time. Exploring and discovering yourself is the thrill of creating stories. That doesn't mean you have to write about yourself. Even if you're writing science fiction or fantasy, it's you. It all comes out of your mind. You have all you need already, you just have to learn *how* to put it on the page.

And now it's time to put something on the page again. But first, let's go over what you wrote at the end of the last chapter. It's been a while since you've seen it. Time in between often gives you a fresh perspective. So, go over your writing and check it for **want, obstacle, action,** and **resolution.** The way you do that is deliberate and exact. If you don't, you'll slide over things and miss opportunities to get more out of your characters.

So, here's how you go about it. First ask, **"Who wants what?"** Then, find it on the page. Do not work in your head. Where does the want first appear on the page? Find the exact line. Is the want strong? Could it be stronger? Could it appear earlier? Next ask, **"What's the obstacle?"** Where does it first appear on the page? Could it appear earlier? Could it be stronger? Can the character ignore it and suffer no injury? (Remember, the obstacle can appear before the want.) Next ask, **"What's the action?"** What's the character *doing* to overcome the obstacle? Where does it appear on the page? Could it appear earlier? Could he be doing more or asserting himself more strongly or directly? Last ask, **"What's the resolution?"** Is it a victory or a defeat (or a partial victory)? If it's a scene resolution, there are more battles yet to fight. If it's a final resolution, the story's over.

The important thing in this is to go over your work in a **calculated, deliberate** way and identify these elements or the lack of them. This part feels intellectual, stiff, and even heartless at first. That's because these tools are new to you. In themselves, they do nothing. It's what they can do for you that counts. So, even though they are conceptual and heartless, once you master them, they'll show you where your story needs work. They are lifeless concepts that will lead you back into the life and energy of your story and yourself. A chisel and mallet have no life in themselves, but in the hands of a sculptor, they can release wonderful things from the stone. Without them, with only his bare hands, he couldn't make a dent.

After you've done that, you may have done a fair amount of writing, or you may want to work on the piece you started in the last chapter. If so, do that. If you're tired of it, here are some new exercises to work with. Follow the same guidelines that you used for the last writing you did. That's the plan from now on, always.

A Word of Caution: It's not necessary to know what the conflict is or where your writing is going when you start. You write to find out where things are going to go. Let your writing take you. So, don't get the notion that you must have these things in mind when you start. Some writers do work that way. If you find it helps to think things through first, do it. Neither way is better than the other. Just as many writers jump in with no idea where they're going as plan ahead first.

If you already have your own project, use that and try to work conflict and action into it. Or if you want to continue what you started in the last chapter and go forward with it, then ignore what I give you here. These will be here to use if you want to.

Also, this time I'm going to give you the first part of a **full-story exercise.** If you choose it, you'll do it in parts until it's finished. I'll give you another part with the other exercises at the end of the next chapters.

EXERCISES

First are the full-scene exercises. Pick one and write for a half hour—longer if you're able.

Here are some scenes:

- A child getting a sex talk from his parent(s).
- Someone breaking into your home at night when you're there.
- A romantic breakup: one character wants out, the other doesn't.

Here are some three-word combinations. Write a scene using one of these sets of three words.

- Hitchhiker, baby, sex.
- Penis, razor, witch.
- Guts, goblet, dwarf.

Here are some settings and characters. Pick one of the settings and put two or more of the characters in and have them interact.

- Settings: Bowling alley, pool hall, tennis court, ballpark, boxing match, roof, basement, factory, church, bus station, lunch counter, men's room, lady's room, desert.
- Characters: Homeless person, male chauvinist, conman, artist, pickpocket, waitress/waiter, busboy, judge, feminist, psychic.

FULL STORY, PART ONE:

This is a story of infidelity. It's from the point of view of the lover who is being betrayed. Part one is the character finding evidence of the other's cheating. It can be ambiguous evidence or solid, concrete, undeniable evidence. First there's the confusion and shock of discovery, with attempted denial, resistance to facing it. That will be followed by the horrible realization (if the evidence is undeniable). That's the end of part one.

That's plenty in one sitting, but if you get going, since the first part flows right into the second, you may want to go right into that. It's the aftermath of the discovery. That will be the character wrestling with implications: Is it true? Why, how could he or she? What to do next, etc. If you have time, you can have the character plan an initial action to try to figure out what's going on, without tipping his or her hand.

Use or Abuse

SELF-EDITING

Now that you've done your second writing exercise, the first thing to do is to go back, reread it, and see how you respond to it. More than anything, this is an emotional game, so relax, let it affect you, and pay attention to your reactions as you read. It's a passive game on your part. Working with your reactions on this level is the first step. If you haven't reworked your writing much, you should have some perspective on it. If you've reworked it a lot and feel stale, you might need to wait a day or two. But that doesn't mean if you have the time to write, you should wait a day or two to do so. If you have time, write. If you're not sure what to write, do another of the exercises from the last time.

Whenever you do go back to that first piece, what kind of reactions do you think you'll have?

SELF-EDITING

You may feel, *This is OK. I like this. This is damn good.* If that's your response, you're lucky. Often, you'll be feeling something like: *This isn't* moving. *This is kind of dull. What's wrong with this?* Still, that's pretty mild. The trouble comes with stronger reactions like: *God, this is stupid. This is so awful. This is such boring, pretentious, shallow crap. What am I going to do now?* Exactly! What are you going to do now?

First, you need to realize that your strong negative reaction is the **most valuable** thing you have. Also, what you do with it, how you use it, or how you let it use/abuse you are what will make you or break you. Too often, it goes like this: *God, this is dull, boring, empty garbage. I wrote it. That means I'm dull, boring, and empty. I'm wasting my time writing. I might as well quit.* And that's it for writing for a day, a week, a month, or more. Rarely will it be forever. The fact that you're this far into it means you probably have the disorder, the affliction, the desire, and the need to write. If you do, you're going to be writing for the rest of your life. But if you run away every time it's disturbing, you'll never get anywhere with it. If you're going to succeed, you must find a way of sticking to it when it's painful. This is one of many techniques you'll get in this course.

What do you do when you feel that your writing is dull, boring, and empty? First, every writer who ever was and ever will be has written dull, boring, empty garbage. And every writer has felt that he might as well give up. So, those reactions reflect nothing about your ability or what you're capable of. Remember that it's not whether you *can* do it, but whether you can *stand* to do it that makes the difference. Fine, but you're still sitting there feeling that your writing is lousy and so are you. As I said, it means nothing as far as your ability is concerned, but *it does mean something—something important.*

Fiction is a game of the heart, the emotions. Your writing isn't reaching your heart, or it's turning your heart away. You're sitting there with this negative reaction, feeling awful about yourself and your writing. That's the **effect** of your story. What can you do? Work on the effect? How would you do that? Sit there and try to convince yourself that what feels dull, boring, and empty is really fascinating? Will that work? Can you do it, and if you could, would it make your writing better? No.

Trying to brainwash yourself like this sounds ridiculous, but it's what we do, all of us, in one way or another. We sit there stewing over how bad our writing is, how bad it makes us feel, when what we need to do is to **get on with it.** But how do we do that? Get on with what exactly, and how? First, we need to stop lamenting the symptom **(effect)** and do something to treat the disease **(cause).** Your emotions are your best guide, but only if you handle them well, if you make them work for you rather than against you. You need to catch yourself before they attack you and you join forces and collude in the attack. The trick is to understand that your **negative emotions are merely a signal** that something *on the page* needs fixing and then to move on. Move on, OK, but move on to what?

You need to move on to what needs to be fixed. What needs to be fixed is something on the page—the **cause** of the problem. The cause can be fixed. And fixing the cause will change the effect. So, you must be aware of your reactions and then turn them into an issue of **craft.**

How does that work? How do you use the craft to fix the problem? Got any ideas? Think about it. How might you approach your writing in a focused, orderly way that will help you figure out what's needed? How about Michael Jordan and the plan? Jimmy Connors and keeping your eye on the ball? The one, two, three of dramatic movement? Enough hints. Maybe you don't need them, but often when you're feeling down about what you've written, you don't think to step back and get some perspective before you start changing things. You don't take the time to **use your tools.**

Another problem is that these tools are new. They take some getting used to. It takes time before they feel comfortable. But just because they're uncomfortable doesn't mean they won't work. Even if they feel clumsy or artificial, start using them anyway. The more you use them, the better they will work. It just takes practice.

Now I'm going to go over the story elements as I did earlier. And this isn't the last time I'm going to do it. You need to hear them many times. So, we'll go through them again. This is your practice, your training, your conditioning.

So, ask the first question, WANT: Who wants what? Now, the trick is not just to think about it, but to *find it on the page*. Where does the want first express itself and how? Locate it on the page and mark it. Could the want be stronger? Is the character absolutely determined/driven to satisfy his want or else? If the want could be stronger, make it as strong as it can be. Now, you may not have an answer right away. You may have to play around with it awhile. Plus, you'll have some ideas that aren't right or don't work. Just discard them and keep working and playing with it. For every idea we have that works, we have others that don't. Get what you can from yourself now. Don't strain. Then move on. Come back later.

The second question is OBSTACLE: What's the obstacle? Find where it first expresses itself *on the page*. Is the obstacle equally as de-termined and driven to prevent the character from satisfying his want? Is it as strong and as threatening as it could be? If it could be stronger, make it so. Can the character ignore the obstacle (not act) and suffer no injury? If so, you do not have a dramatic obstacle or a dramatic conflict. (Remember, the obstacle can appear before the want. Either way, these questions are the same. You just consider the obstacle first, then the want.) Again: relax, be loose, play around, ex-plore your writing, and don't worry about it being good.

The next question is ACTION: What's the character doing to overcome the obstacle? Where does the act first appear *on the page?* Is the character taking direct action to change things, to make some-thing happen, to prevail and get what he wants? Is he using himself to the limit? What else could he do? Consider everything. Is the obstacle counterattacking with equal or more force to thwart the character? If you go too far, that's fine. Just cut back.

Now, I have never seen a case where these three elements were working well on the page and the story or scene was not dramatic and compelling. Rarely will you have to go beyond these three. But let's complete the job.

What's next? We have conflict (want + obstacle) and action. The third element is

Resolution: Is it victory or defeat? The outcome of the struggle. Who wins? Who loses? Is it a compromise? How is the problem settled for now if not for all time?

That's our story form. We have two other issues, emotion and showing. It's early to get into them deeply, but in case you're that far into it, we will.

Emotion: What's the character feeling? We need to know at all times. Check your writing line by line and ask what the character's worries, fears, and hopes are, and how and where they are being expressed through the character. (We're going into this in detail in the next chapter.)

Showing: Are the characters acting and talking as much as possible? Are you creating a moment-by-moment, word-for-word experience that's happening right before our eyes with no general statements or summaries? Showing means we always have something we can picture in our mind. It's visual and almost always scene with dialogue. (We're doing more with this in chapter 7.)

The critical issue here is to use yourself, don't abuse yourself. When you become discouraged because you feel your writing is weak, let that be only a message to you that you need to shift gears and get into your craft and start working the story elements to make it work. When your writing feels boring, stupid, shallow, it's not the end of the world. It just means that not enough is happening dramatically. You need to get busy and fix what's wrong, practice your craft, use your tools, keep your eye on the ball.

This course is set up to allow you to do it yourself without having to run to others for answers every time you write a draft. The whole issue of using others—whom to use, how, and when—is tricky. There's plenty of misleading or bad advice around even among professionals—teachers, editors, agents. When you use a friend or family member, it's even trickier, because not only are they not trained, but each brings in his or her own taste, philosophy, personal bias, agenda, or even vendetta. Always, you want to **get the most out of yourself before you go to someone else.** This chapter is about self-editing, which you need to develop as your number-one skill. You need to do *all* the self-editing laid out in this chapter and in chapter 8 (rewriting) *before* you consider getting "help" from anyone else. The best lessons are those you teach yourself.

So, it's time to write again. As always, if you have your own project or want to continue what you started earlier, write on that for a half hour.

EXERCISES

Here are scene exercises:

- Going to confession. This can be any religious ritual about which the character has strong negative feelings about (fear, anxiety, guilt).
- This is called the "everyone hates Jim" scene. Use that line/idea, and write a scene based on it.

- A character being tempted to commit a crime and not doing it. The line between moral and immoral.

Here are some three-word sets to choose from:

- Fist, jealous, poodle.
- Breast, armor, tweezers.
- Parrot, crabgrass, sex.

Settings and characters are next. You can go back to the ones in the other chapters if you want. Here's a new set to choose from.

- Parking lot, Disney World, hotel lobby, bathroom, rooftop, sewer, mountain, classroom, restaurant, health food store, balcony.
- Banker, skinhead, stockbroker, doorman, TV star, musician, mugger, hit man, gypsy, boxer, paranoid, televangelist.

Next is the complete story exercise:

FULL STORY, PART TWO:

Infidelity story. You had part one in the last chapter and part two if you got rolling. If you have not done part two yet, do that. Part two is the aftermath of the discovery. In it, the character is wrestling with the questions: Is it true? Why? How could he or she do this? What to do next? etc. The next part involves the character planning an initial act to find out what's going on, without tipping his or her hand. Again, if you get going and want to go forward, do part three.

Part three can be the actual confrontation of the injured lover and the cheating lover. Or it can be the character preparing for confrontation by spying to get more proof or even to catch the cheater in the act. If it's the direct confrontation scene, the injured lover **wants** an explanation, revenge, love, consoling. The cheating lover is to resist giving it, perhaps deny the whole thing **(obstacle).** At the end of the scene, the situation needs to be worse, first, because what's revealed is more troubling, and second, because the injured character is more upset. The scene ends in the mind of the injured party. If the character is snooping for evidence, he or she **wants** to catch the cheater without getting caught spying **(obstacle).** This character can also seek help from others—friends, detective, family. Things must be worse at the end of each scene, and the scene needs to end in the mind of the character, with him or her in a state of heightened worry and fear.

6

The Active Ingredient

EMOTION

Suppose a committee went to Mother Teresa and said, "Mother, you've done so much for others. You've been so generous, so giving, so loving, so holy, and so self-sacrificing. No one can ever repay you. That's impossible, but there's an opening in Donald Trump's penthouse, and we've arranged for you to go and live there for the rest of your life. You'll have servants waiting on you hand and foot. You'll never have to lift a finger for another living soul as long as you live. It's high time you got some earthly reward for all your good deeds." Now, what do you think Mother Teresa would have said? "Praise God. It's about time"? No? What would she have said? Whatever it would've been, she wouldn't have gone for the idea.

Now suppose they went to Donald Trump and said, "Don, we've got a wonderful opportunity for you—a chance to do the most satisfying, most fulfilling, most gratifying thing anyone can do in this life. That is, devote yourself completely and totally and unselfishly to helping those less fortunate than you. There's an opening at Mother Teresa's place, and we've arranged for you to get the job." What would

Donald have said? "That's it! That's what's been missing. Why didn't I think of it?" No, Donald wouldn't have gone for it either.

OK, they're not going to switch. Why not? And what if they did? What would it have been like? Mother Teresa lounging around in silk pajamas in a penthouse. Donald holding a cup of broth to the lips of a leper in India. What would have been their experience? Satisfying, fulfilling? Would they have enjoyed it? No, they wouldn't. They couldn't. Why not? Because they would've been miserable—they wouldn't have *felt* right. The way they felt, who they were, would have prevented them from enjoying it.

The reason they wouldn't have switched isn't reason or logic. It's passion—emotion. Emotion is the trickiest part of life and the trickiest part of fiction. Emotion is the payoff, the ultimate connection, where identification occurs, where the reader becomes the character and *feels what the character feels.* Emotion is our subject. First, we'll look at *the nature of emotion,* then how we can capture emotion on the page so it moves the character and the reader as one. If the emotion's not there, the character's not there. If the character's not there, the reader's not there—and neither is the author in any satisfying way. It's not just about giving the reader an experience. It's about having it yourself, as you create. Character, reader, author—they're all having the experience, the emotion. Without emotion, nobody's having anything.

The first thing to realize is that the world is emotionally determined. Passion, not reason, makes things happen. We love, help, hate, and destroy each other not because of logic, but because of passion. How many times have you done something because it felt *wrong?* Even if you did something that didn't feel right, it was because it was the lesser of two evils. You'd feel worse, you couldn't live with yourself, if you did anything else. Our actions are determined by how things balance out emotionally.

A very successful pop psychology book came out some years ago. Its premise was: Your thoughts control your feelings and you control your thoughts; therefore, if you think the right thoughts, you'll have the right feelings. Sound good? An easy solution to emotional problems? Well, if it were true and you came home and found your house burned to the ground and you had no fire insurance, all you'd have to do is think the right thoughts, and it would be fun. Right? Wrong.

If anything, your emotions control your thoughts. They descend upon you without warning and overpower you. You wish to God you could control, reduce, or relieve them. For example, you have a problem to be faced the next day—to confront your boss about a promotion he promised you, then gave to someone else. You've thought it through. You're prepared. It's not going to be easy, but you know what has to be done. You go to bed early to get plenty of sleep, so you'll be fresh and focused. What happens? It won't leave you alone. You obsess over it. You know it does absolutely no good to keep going over and over and over it in your mind. You will gain nothing. You will lose sleep and be less able to handle things. The logical, sensible, sane thing to do is to forget it, go to sleep, be ready in the morning. But your worry will not let you. Your emotion has a mind of its own. It's controlling you.

Now, this is not an altogether comforting idea. The words *logical* and *reasonable* have a much more trustworthy, dependable, comforting connotation than the words *emotional* and *irrational*. "It was a highly emotional discussion" implies that it was impulsive and excessive rather than levelheaded and sensible. "It was a highly logical discussion" has no such implication. "He's so irrational" suggests that he's not in his right mind and can't be trusted. "He's so reasonable" is the opposite. Emotion is often considered unpredictable. Logic is not.

We like to believe that the world runs on something more dependable and solid and concrete than insubstantial emotion. We like to believe that the institutions that protect us are objective and rational and evenhanded—the U.S. Supreme Court, for example. When a case goes before the Supreme Court, every justice hears the same facts, the exact same presentation of the case, and reads the exact same constitution. They have the identical experience. The only difference is that they're seated at different seats during the proceedings.

We like to think that we can depend on the highest justices in the land to render an enlightened ruling and that wisdom, not passion, prevails. If that were true, then how do we explain a five-to-four split in their opinion? Well, we say, the law is a matter of *interpretation*. All right. And what determines how we interpret something? Interpretation depends on life experience (childhood, education, personal taste, philosophy, religion, prejudice), which shapes how we *feel* about everything. At the bottom of that Supreme Court ruling are the emotional leanings of each justice. Emotion rules.

Struggling with your feelings is a major part of any serious problem you have to face—the kind of problems characters must face in fiction, always. You may be able to talk yourself out of lesser feelings to some degree, but big emotions (serious pain), the kind stories are made of (the loss of a job, a lover, your life savings, an arm), have a life, a power, of their own. You don't control them. They control you. Emotions are the most powerful force in and around us, for good and for evil, but they're important for reasons other than power.

Betty says to Louise: "My husband is impossible. He cleans the house, cooks the meals, does laundry, goes shopping, takes care of the yard. He won't let me lift a finger. He drives me nuts." And what's Louise thinking? *Let me have him*, please. What does this tell us? They each have different feelings about the same thing, as do we all. And why is that important? Because **emotion defines us.** More than anything else, what we feel and what we have feelings about—who we love, how we love, who we hate, how we hate, and all the things in be-tween—define who we are. In the example, we have a woman who can't stand a helpful husband and one who would love to have one. That doesn't define who they are, by far (we need more of their emo-tions for that), but it's a beginning. The philosopher René Descartes, to prove he existed, said, "I think, therefore I am." He would have been just as well (or better) served to have said, "I *feel,* therefore I am."

There's an old movie, *Invasion of the Body Snatchers* (I'm thinking of the original black-and-white version, not the remake) in which crea-tures from another planet come to Earth and begin taking us over. When they inhabit you, you stay the same person except that you have no feelings, no emotions. "Don't worry. Don't fight it," the ones who've been changed say to those who haven't. "It's better this way. You'll see." It's creepy and frightening. Emotions—we wouldn't be who we are without them. How do we know? Our emotions tell us.

All right, emotions are the most powerful and defining force in our lives, but how do we portray them on the page in a way that reaches the reader with the full effect that they have in the character? In order to do that, we need to look at what form emotions take in us. First, we need to realize that we're born with a full set of emotions, but with no words to express them. Learning to express your feelings (to yourself as well as others) is one of the jobs of becoming a person. But at the be-ginning emotions are visceral, visual, global—nonverbal images in the mind. They're nonverbal, but writing is verbal—100 percent.

So, we have a language barrier. How do we overcome it? In science, in order to study something, it must be measurable directly, or it must have measurable consequences. What we're dealing with, to a large degree, are the measurable consequences rather than emotion in its purest form, since no one (psychologists, biologists, neurologists) has pinned that down. But we must pin it down, enough for our (verbal) purposes at least. Powerful emotion is all over the place in literature.

So it can be done. But how? Well, measurable consequences are where we have to look.

One of our best guides is reality. Even though a direct recording of reality won't make strong stories, it's our best guide, since our goal is to uncover, to reveal, the essence, the truth, of reality on the page. All fiction could be reality, but all reality can't be fiction. Fantasy and science fiction are exceptions, but even they must create their own world of believable reality.

OK, so what happens when you have an emotion? Had any lately? How did you know you were feeling one? What form did it take? How did it express itself inside you?

Let me give you a situation and see if you would experience an emotion. Here it is: You're going to your car, late at night, in a deserted parking lot. As you take out your keys, someone sticks a gun in your ribs and says, "Give me your money, or I'll blow your brains out." Would you have an emotion? How would you know you were having one? What form would it take? Now, we're talking about the emotional experience before you act (talk or move) outwardly.

The kinds of things you'd experience are a pounding heart, a knotted stomach, shaking hands, sweating, dizziness. These are all emotional responses. And they're all something else. Know what that something else is? They're all physical responses. Now, physical expressions of emotion are fine—up to a point. The problem is that all our hearts pound, all our stomachs knot, all our hands shake, we sweat, and we get dizzy pretty much in the same way. So, the physical expression will never individualize or define your character enough. If you try to portray your character's emotions by using physical expressions only, you will turn yourself inside out and never reach your character (or the reader) in the way you need to. You need something else to do that. Something else goes on that's much more expressive, more individual, and more personal. Know what it is? Think about it.

Your stomach doesn't knot, your heart doesn't pound, your hands don't shake in such a situation until something else happens first. Something happens between the time the robber says, "I'll blow your brains out," and your body reacts. I ended the previous paragraph by telling you to think about it. I'm going to ask you to *think* about it again. Your body doesn't react alone. Something else happens first. *Oh, my God. He's got a gun. I'm going to die.* You *think.* Not only do you think, but you *think first.* **The mind leads the body.** The only reason that your body is churning is the situation registered in your mind as dangerous and you had a thought about it—in fact, your mind takes off in the same way that your body does.

IT'S THE THOUGHT THAT COUNTS

What tells you more about a person—the way his body works, or the way his mind works? "How does this guy think?" is something you probably tried to figure out before. But "how does he sweat?" is something I'll bet you never wondered about. More than anything else, we are language. It's how we're different from all other animals. We put words on everything. And the mind never stops. We're always thinking, talking to ourselves—urging, coaxing, warning, pressing, punishing, praising. Heidegger said, "Language is where being dwells." Our thoughts are one of the most revealing expressions of who we are.

Now, I've given you an extreme situation (gun in the ribs) to make sure you'd have an emotion. In this kind of experience, the emotions, thoughts, and physical responses happen so fast that they feel simultaneous. Nevertheless, the thought is first. Something has to register in the mind. You have to recognize what's happening and evaluate it before you get frightened. In fiction, we slow it down and take it step-by-step to capture the feel (the truth) of the experience.

SOME THOUGHTS ON THOUGHT

Before we get into the nature of emotional thoughts, I want to examine the role that thought, the internal workings of the character's mind, plays in story. Thought occupies an especially important place in the written story because **the written story is the only story form that portrays the mind well.** The written story can portray the mind exactly as it happens, word for word, moment by moment, in the character. That can't be done on the screen or on the stage. Those forms have their virtues, but the characters have to speak their minds if we're going to experience them at all. Stage plays used to use asides and soliloquies (the character addressing his thoughts to the audience). Movies use voice-over once in a while, but a little bit of it goes a long way, and it usually seems artificial or comic (often unintentionally) or melodramatic.

In the movie *Alfie* it was done for comic effect. Alfie turned and addressed the audience directly. It was clever, charming, and funny and worked well. The old Bogart detective movies used it and got away with it in their day, but by today's standards it seems stilted. The classic movie *Sunset Boulevard* had a fair amount of voice-over narration, although a case might be made that it succeeded in spite of rather than because of it. More recently, the movie *American Beauty* used it well. Maybe moviemakers will find a way to use more of it and use it effectively. Whether they do or not, it won't change things for the written story.

Since we can move freely about the landscape of the mind and since the mind is a major part of the experience, it's an expected and necessary part of the written story. The doorway to the mind is always open in the written story. Since we *can* go inside, we *must* go inside. If we don't, it will always feel as if something is missing.

Without the mind, we don't get much from the following:

"Hey, Uncle Harry. How are you?" I said.

"Fine," Harry said.

"You look great," I said.

"Thanks. How are you?" Harry said, extending his hand.

"I'm good," I said, shaking his hand. "Good to see you, Harry. Listen, I've got to make a call. Be back in a bit."

Now let's try it with the mind:

Good Lord, Uncle Harry's here. Why didn't someone tell me? Damn, here he comes. "Hey, Uncle Harry. How are you?" *Look at that alcoholic flush and that booze nose.*

"Fine," Harry said.

"You look great," I said. *Wrinkled clothes. Matted hair. He doesn't look very clean either.*

"Thanks. How are you?" Harry said, extending his hand.

Christ, now I have to touch him. "I'm good." *His hand is mushy and slimy. Who knows where it's been?* "Good to see you, Harry. Listen, I've got to make a call. Be back in a bit." *Keep this hand away from everything until I can wash it. Where's the bathroom in this place?*

Could the reader possibly have any idea what was going on with the character without his thoughts? The character can be having wild, frantic thoughts while acting perfectly calm in the presence of someone else, and we have no problem portraying both happening together.

Another reason the mind can reach a level of intimacy beyond that on film or stage lies in the nature of the mind itself. In the written story, we can explore what E. M. Forster called "the secret life" of the character. The secret life is the private thoughts the character will tell no one. Such thoughts can be enormously revealing, since we seldom speak exactly what's on our mind or in our hearts. What the character thinks as it relates to what he says and does is a critical part of who he is.

He loved her, but at times she disgusted him—for no reason. And sometimes he disgusted himself. Was it him? Or was it just the way life was sometimes—disgusting? Familiarity bred contempt. But how much and how often? Maybe he should see a shrink. How did you pick a shrink? He wasn't asking his friends. They'd think he was nuts. Maybe he was, but he didn't want them knowing.

That's one level of the mind. There's another. That level is the part of the character that the character doesn't want to reveal even to himself, the part of himself he tries to avoid, tries to keep secret even from himself and wishes he could forget.

A character who trampled an old woman's prize rosebush to death might later in life feel the following:

Oh, God. Why did I do that? No reason. Cruelty. Plain cruelty. What a bastard. What a lousy bastard I am. What was wrong with me? But I've made up for it. But not to her. Too late for that. Christ, forget it. Quit punishing yourself. How long do you have to atone for something?

So, in the written story, we can go to this deepest level without any concerns about how to make it real. It exists as language, so we can portray it exactly as it occurs in reality.

Our ability to reach such a level of intimacy in this way with the written story is why a good novel will always be lacking on the screen. The exception is when a weak book is translated into a strong screenplay. *Midnight Cowboy* is an example.

All great stories involve the internal conflict of the character—the struggle in his mind with himself. This conflict is a way of expressing the relationship the character has with himself—how he feels about himself and how he manages himself. We're all of more than one mind. In a sense, we're more than one person, since different aspects of ourselves can be pulling against each other while we're trying to hold things together and function. That's part of what goes on whenever we're facing a crisis. And all stories are about crisis.

But all stories and all writers aren't great. Writers use the mind to different degrees. There are some excellent writers/storytellers, not great, but damn good, who don't go into the mind so much. They never reach the complexity of character that's possible by getting into the mind, but they give us enough. Since his thoughts are not revealed, the character has to speak, or express in some other way, what he's feeling. We need to know what's going on with the character emotionally, or we can't relate or identify. Literary novels tend to be more internal. Action-adventure novels tend to be less internal. The literary mystery is one that is much more internal than the run-of-the-mill whodunit.

Pay attention to this when you read. Almost always, you feel the strongest connection to the character when you're deeply into his thoughts. Creating the workings of the character's mind is the most difficult part of storytelling. It's the most demanding, but it's also the most rewarding. The more deeply you go into the character, the more deeply you must go into yourself. As in life, the most difficult part is often the most fulfilling.

THE EMOTION-THOUGHT CONNECTION

So, what's the nature of an emotional thought? What might be going on in your mind with that gun in your ribs? Anger? If you wrote, "He was angry," would that give you a real sense of the character and how he experienced anger? The word *anger* is a label, not an expression of an emotion. How about: *This bastard. This rotten bastard. Just one chance. Give me one chance, and I'll take that gun and pistol-whip him to death.* Those are angry thoughts, yet the word *angry* or *anger* isn't used once. Also, the character has no reason to tell himself he's angry. *I'm angry,* wouldn't help. That doesn't mean there might not be a case in which a character might think, *This guy is making me angry.* But that's a certain kind of self-consciousness that isn't there in most people. And even if the character has this thought, you still have to go on and give us his angry thoughts if we're going to experience the full extent of his anger.

How about fear? How might it express itself? Well, let's try it. See what kind of fearful thoughts you can come up with. Before you read the next paragraph, make a list of all the fearful thoughts that a person might have in such a situation. If the complete thoughts come to you, put them down. If not, make a list of all the things a person could have fears about, then translate each one into an actual thought that could run through someone's mind.

How did it go? It's tricky at first. It takes a while—a little time and practice, but remember: *It's already there.* It's *in you* already. It's just a matter of getting to it. The important thing at this point is that you know where to put your efforts so that you're progressing and not spinning your wheels or chasing your tail.

So, what kind of fears might someone have in this situation? Someone with a new family might fear for his loved ones. There are an endless number of ways for that fear to express itself in thought.

Here's one way: *Oh, no, I'm going to die. Lord no. I'm not ready. I can't go yet. I barely got started. What about my wife and baby? Who'll take care of them?* That's seven sentences, but it could pass through someone's mind in an instant. And it's a long way from saying, "He was scared," or "His heart started pounding." One of those statements is general, and one is physical and thus generic by nature. The thought is an actual expression of an individual person's specific fear.

After the fear, something like this might follow: *Calm down. Calm down. Get hold of yourself. You've got to get out of this. There has to be a way.* Now that's the internal struggle I talked about earlier, and it's expressing another emotion, hope—the hope that you might get out of this alive.

These thoughts are all pretty sensible and appropriate, but emotion, by definition, is not rational. In a desperate situation we're not usually sensible or logical. *If he kills me, I'll miss* ER *tonight* might pass through your mind. Your emotions have a mind of their own. In fact, we might say, your mind has a mind (or minds) of its own. So, *My cat will starve if he kills me* might pass through your mind even though it's not the most sensible thing to be concerned about at the moment.

Or how about: *Please, God, get me out of this alive, and I promise I'll never screw my secretary again. I'll be loyal to my wife till the day I die.* Now we're into something else—praying, crying out for help (still in the mind). I myself am not particularly religious, but when I'm in a serious jam, I'm not above thinking, *I don't know if there's anybody up there, but if there is, I'd really appreciate some help right now.* And if you have even less religious belief than that, you might think, *If I get out of this, I'm going to give a thousand dollars to help the homeless,* hoping to enlist the aid of any power greater than yourself that might happen to be lurking in the area—or you might just make a kind of magical deal with yourself (promise to be a more decent person) in the hope it will affect the outcome of things. When we're desperate, we try anything. And fiction is about people who are desperate, driven, in crisis.

I've put together a list of some kinds of emotional thoughts someone might have in this situation. It's by no means complete. You will become aware of more as you write. The character's thoughts and emotions are what you will spend the most time trying to figure out. I'll give you my list, then a simple technique to help you find the emotion in the character. Here's my list of the kinds of things we do in our heads when we're upset.

Disassociate: Thinking of something totally unrelated in order to protect yourself from pain. *If I die, I won't get to eat lobster ever again.* We're all capable of this. Disassociation is what severely abused children do when they develop multiple personalities. They become another person in their mind to avoid feeling the torture.

Deny: It's OK. *He only wants my money. He doesn't want to hurt me.*

Face It: This is the opposite of denial. More like rubbing your nose in it. *He only wants your money. Don't be stupid. You saw his face. You can identify him. Now he has to blow your brains out for sure.*

Negotiate: Beg, pray to, plead with God. There's a lot in this one since religion and God are something we all have to come to terms with in our own way. Someone might think: *Please, God, get me out of this alive. I promise I'll never screw my secretary again. I'll never cheat on my wife as long as I live.* Your life is at stake. You're going to give up something big.

How you pray, if you do, and what you pray for, is an expression of who you are. When I'm in trouble, even though I'm not a believer, I'm not beyond thinking, *If there's anybody up there, I'd certainly appreciate some help.* I'm not going to rule anything out. But that's as far as I can go. I'm not going to convert to a religion and start attending services. That's me. Another person with even less belief might think, *If I get out of this, I'll give $100 to the first homeless person I see.* Now, what's that all about? It's about making a deal with any power that might be lurking in the area—or just making a deal with yourself in hopes of influencing things—magic.

A character's religion or related beliefs (philosophy of life, morality, etc.) and how he/she came to them are ways of revealing who that person is. You don't want to be pushing a religious point, although you might if you do it the right way, but you're exploring character wherever and however you can.

Displace: *Look at what the world's come to since the Republicans (or Democrats) took over.*

How about something like this: *Ah, now you did it. You knew you shouldn't park here this morning. You knew it wasn't safe. But you were in such a hurry and had to have your designer coffee and were too damn lazy to walk an extra block. See what it got you? He should shoot you. You deserve it.* So, not only are you in a jam, but you PUNISH yourself for being there. This is the kind of thing that comes out of my Protestant background. Everything that happens to you is your fault, says the Puritan. Again, I'm drawing on myself or part of myself to create a character. John le Carré, author of many novels (*The Spy Who Came in from the Cold,* for one), said that every character he created was a dimension of himself. That has to be true in a sense for all of us, since all we have is ourselves, what's inside of us, and what's in our imagination.

Think Positively: *This will be good for me. This will make me stronger.* This was the philosopher Nietzsche's creed: "That which does not destroy me makes me stronger." A well-known, present-day disciple of

Nietzsche's is G. Gordon Liddy, who was one of Watergate's cast of characters. Gordon was terrified of rats when he was a kid. What did he do to overcome his fear of rats? He caught, cooked, and ate a rat to overcome his fear of rats. It worked for him. Now, what if I'd done that with my background? I'd be thinking: *Uh oh. When the rats hear about this, they'll be out to get me. I'm really in trouble now.* For Liddy it was strength. For me it would be guilt/fear.

Question: *Why is this happening? What does this mean? What am I going to do? How can I get out of this?*

What makes a thought emotional? It can be the words themselves, such as, *Help! Save me. I'm too young to die.* Or a thought can be emotional because of the *situation*. If I'm sitting in a theater at the end of a movie and I think, *It's over,* that's not an especially emotional statement. But if when the robber sticks the gun in my ribs, I think, *It's over,* that's an emotional thought. So, you're not necessarily looking for emotionally charged words; everyday objective words that express emotion in a particular situation can be enough. And often if you just concentrate on what the character would be thinking in such a situation, it will lead you where you need to go.

Planning: A lot of thinking in crisis is about what to do to protect yourself and to escape without injury (psychological injury, most often) and what to do if you fail: *What should I do if he raises the gun to my head?* or *What'll I do if my wife leaves me? Who'll get the house? Lord, I couldn't stand to date again.* or *What should I do to keep from getting fired? Who'll hire me at my age?* The mind is a dramatic place. A lot of action (planning an attack or a defense) takes place before we act outwardly. I've given you a short list of some of the kinds of thoughts we have in emotional situations. Now that you're aware of them, you can work on your own list.

Reaching the inner workings of your character, the secret life, is **a lifetime process.** It's important to realize that, just as in life, emotion is the hardest and trickiest part. So, if you're having trouble with it—and you will—don't panic. It's **the part of your story that tends to come last,** the part you will have the least of in early drafts. You will know that your character is having a big emotion at a particular moment, and you will have some sense of what it is, but you will not be able to pin it down. When that happens, when you can't reach it, don't fret. Just be aware of the kind of thing that's needed and move on. The next time around you'll get more of it. Each draft will give you more, and you'll piece it together bit by bit. It's the trickiest and most elusive ingredient of all, but it's the most rewarding. When you deepen the connection to your character, you deepen your connection to yourself.

WORRIES, FEARS, HOPES

I've devised a simple, direct method for helping you find out what's going on inside the character. With this technique, you go through your story and ask, every place it could possibly apply, "What are the character's *worries, fears, and hopes?*" There should be plenty of places where emotions are kicking up—on every page and in every scene. Stories are about conflict, about threat. If something of great value to you is truly threatened, you have to be *worried* and *fearful* that you will lose it while at the same time *hopeful* that you will be able to save it. These worries, fears, and hopes will be running through your mind until the problem is resolved.

If your boss calls you in and says that if you don't improve your work, he'll have to let you go, you're *worried* and *afraid* you'll get fired, but *hoping* that you can work overtime for a while and save your job. Romeo wants Juliet, but he is *worried* and *frightened* that their marriage will be discovered and he'll lose her before they can escape. He *hopes,* with all his heart, that they will succeed and be united. In the parking lot stickup, you would be *afraid* you'll be killed, but *hoping* that you'll come out of it alive. If the character isn't worried and afraid, you don't have a dramatic conflict, and your story will flop. If your character doesn't care, the reader won't care. The reader cannot care more than the character.

Fantasies are a kind of hope and can be especially revealing of the character. Some characters have elaborate fantasies, while others have few. "The Secret Life of Walter Mitty" by James Thurber is a classic story of someone who lives in fantasy. It's a famous story. If you haven't read it, you should. We all indulge in fantasies. Thinking about what we'd do if we won the lottery is probably one of the most common. In the case of someone whose job is threatened by an abusive, fault-finding boss, the character could dream of what he'd do if his rotten boss worked for *him.*

HOW MANY?

Who's a more complicated character, Dan Quayle or Lyndon Johnson? The answer is obviously Johnson. What was it that made Johnson complicated? Can you guess? It's related to emotion. Quayle is seen as rather shallow and bungling. He's pretty much a one-note personality. Johnson, on the other hand, was a symphony of contradiction. He was capable of enormous generosity and great viciousness at the same time. That's why we think of him as complicated. A complicated character is one who embodies many different, often opposing, qualities at one time. Which brings us to an important issue for creating character in story.

How many emotions/thoughts can be dancing in the mind of the character at one time? How many emotions can you feel at once? Well, you might feel guilt, anger, sadness, regret, and relief at the death of a loved one. And all of them will be pulling at you at once. Now, we can't do them simultaneously on the page, or we'd be typing one sentence on top of another. But we can have these emotions affecting the character one right after the other in a scene by having the character have a sad thought, a guilty thought, an angry thought, etc.

> *Oh, Lord. Mom's gone. I don't know if I can stand it. She didn't deserve this. What a rotten world. And I'm one of the rottenest. I really let her down. I could have done more—a lot more. But why me? I'm not her only kid. John never even called. Let it go. She's at peace. No more pain, thank God. It's over.*

What we're after in fiction is the full experience. We rarely feel only one thing at a time. Life is seldom so simple. Crisis usually involves being pulled in many directions at once, internally as well as externally. So, when you write, look for all the emotions that the character could possibly be feeling at one time. If he *could* be feeling it, he *should* be feeling it.

A LITTLE TENDERNESS

Here's a scene:

> "You're a rotten, lousy, self-centered, inconsiderate bastard," she said to her husband.
> "And you're a crude, ignorant, repulsive old hag," he said.

Are you sympathetic to these characters, moved by them, identi-fied? Chances are, you're not particularly touched by them. Why is that? There's plenty of emotion. Why isn't it reaching you? See if you can figure it out. It has to do with emotion—the emotion they're hav-ing and the source of it.

Let's try it again, only differently:

"I told you I was cooking your favorite dinner tonight and we'd eat at eight o'clock. You said you'd be home in time," she said. "At eight o'clock, I had everything ready—table set, can-dles lit, wine poured. All the food was ready. I waited. You weren't here at eight-thirty. I sat here like a fool, watching the food get cold. Nine o'clock, nine-thirty, you're still not here. You didn't call. Now you come through the door at ten o'clock act-ing as if nothing is wrong. You rotten, self-centered bastard. You make me feel worthless."

Is that version more involving? If so, why? What's in this version that isn't in the first? Can you identify it? The answer is not that there's more detail or more dialogue. It's a specific emotional ingredi-ent that isn't in the first version.

In the first version the characters are expressing *anger only*. Now, anger is a fine emotion. It's all over the place in literature and life. We need it. But anger is a response to something else. Something that happens first, something that makes us angry. What is anger a re-sponse to? Anger is a response to injury and pain. If something makes you angry, it's hurt you or caused you pain *first*. Without expressing the injury, the pain, you're not giving the reader (or the character) the full experience. Anger is only the surface.

We need to know what's causing the anger. This is true of other emotions also, like fear. If someone is frightened, we need to know what the cause is. But anger is the emotion where we go wrong most often because scenes are always confrontations with characters asserting themselves, so it's easy to get stuck in the anger and not go beneath the surface.

THE IRRESISTIBLE FORCE
Lessons from the gutter

The following scene was shown on the nightly news: A rat was trapped in the middle of a busy intersection in the heart of Manhattan, cars were whizzing by on both sides. The rat tried to run to the gutter. A car shot in front of it and the rat ran back to the center. The rat tried again and another whizzed by, just missing him. A crowd began to form on the sidewalk. The rat ran in the other direction, another car shot in front of him. He stood shaking and quivering in the middle of traffic. The camera panned the crowd. A big, tough-looking guy said, "Should we help him?" The camera turned back to the rat, running back and forth with cars cutting him off each time. Then a tire nicked the rat, it tumbled over, then stood twitching and cowering. The traffic stopped. A man raced out from the curb with a folded newspaper and scooped the rat toward the curb and into the gutter. The rat ran down the gutter, into the sewer and was gone.

The man jumped on his bike and started down the street. The camera crew ran after, calling, "Why did you do that?" The guy on the bike stopped. He looked a little sheepish and embarrassed. "I don't know," he said. "I've been scared like that myself."

OK, what's going on? Why did they care about a rat—a disease carrying vermin, the symbol of filth and deceit, an enemy we poison, trap, and try to obliterate?

They cared, because as the guy who rescued him said, "I've been scared like that myself," they had "been scared like that" too. "Like that myself" means "like myself," which means "myself." He, and they, became the rat. They *identified*. Why? Because they couldn't stop themselves. An irresistible force was at work—identification.

Identification, fine, but is that a complete answer? Or can we take it further? We can and we should. As always, we need to take it to the deepest level possible. So, exactly what is it about this rat that made it irresistible? What made this rat so different, so real, and so human?

It was in a different state from which we normally see or think of a rat. That state, that irresistible state, was vulnerability. And we identify with vulnerability. We cannot stop ourselves. That connection to vulnerability runs as deep as our evolution, natural selection, our very survival as a species. It's what holds the human race together. We can't help but identify with vulnerability.

Identification. Vulnerability. It works every time. And if your character is not vulnerable in your story, you have a problem because if someone is threatened and may suffer a serious injury, he must be worried and afraid. If he's not, he doesn't care. If he doesn't care, we won't either. The reader can't care more than the character. So, always be sure the rat is in your story.

WHAT YOU KNOW

You may have heard the old rule "Write what you know." It's what many writing teachers tell their students they must do. Here's a little anecdote that addresses that issue.

When E. L. Doctorow was being interviewed about his book *Billy Bathgate*—a novel about a young boy who ingratiates himself with Dutch Schultz the gangster, the interviewer asked him about a particular scene in which a veteran gangster takes the kid out in the woods, gives him a pistol, and shows him how to shoot it. The interviewer said that the scene stood out in her mind as unusually vivid and personal.

"You must've had a lot of experience with guns," she said.

What do you think Doctorow's answer was?

He said, "I've never touched a gun in my life."

"Then how could you write such a scene?" she said.

Doctorow went on to say (paraphrase), "I think about how it might feel to hold a gun, how it would probably feel, and how I imagine it would have to feel to me and how I would respond to it. Then, if I do my job well, you have the kind of response you did."

Write what you know? No. **Write what you can imagine.** After all, imagining is knowing—a special kind of knowing that can reveal as much or more truth than our real experience.

Then what about writing about characters who are totally different from you? Again, forget write what you know. Instead, **write what you can figure out.** And you can figure out most human experience. Why? Because you're human and all humans are made of the same stuff. We all start out with a full set of emotions and the same potential for good or evil, etc. We grow into adults with the same emotions and needs, *except* that they're in each of us to different degrees and in different amounts. Plus, we satisfy them in very different ways since our experience twists each of us into a different shape. Mother Teresa loved caring for others. Donald Trump loves making money. The hit man loves killing. It's the same emotion, but it's satisfied in different ways. In the first, it's an expression of good (Mother Teresa), and in the last it expresses evil (the hit man).

There's a little bit of everything in all of us. We all have a bit of sadism, masochism, homicide, suicide, etc., inside of us. Most, if not all, of us at some time in our lives have felt like killing someone. If you haven't, it might help to work on it. Having these urges doesn't mean that we follow through on any of them. That's what makes the difference between us and those who do awful things.

An excellent book that shows how the same psychological needs drive even the most vicious of us is *Mind Hunter*, by John Douglas. Douglas is the FBI agent who developed profiling to help identify and capture serial killers. There's an eerie and uncomfortable similarity between serial-killer psychology and our own. What the killers do is horrible, but it all makes complete sense once you understand their mentality. If it didn't make sense, Douglas wouldn't be able to look at a crime scene and say that the person who killed had poor communication skills and probably stuttered. He did, and he was right.

So, you shouldn't be intimidated when faced with the need to create characters you don't understand. The trick is to find a way to put yourself in their place in order to figure them out. Fine, but how do you put yourself or get yourself into their place, their frame of mind? Well, we can turn to the helping professions (social work, psychology, etc.) for some guidelines.

When working with someone who's emotionally disturbed and acting strange or crazy, there are two things to keep in mind. First, no matter how strangely someone is behaving, what they're doing makes perfect sense to them and would make sense to you if you understood how they experienced the world. There's nothing crazy about it to them. So, you need to look for the logic in the character and his actions. That's not so easy, so the second thing is to ask yourself, "What would make me act that way? What would be going on in me to make me, drive me, to do the same thing?" Answering these questions will take you close enough to create a believable character. All of our behavior (sensible, wacky, sane, crazy) obeys the same psychological principles. It's all in us. Everything is in every one of us. So look to yourself for the answers.

FINAL THOUGHTS ON THOUGHTS

As I said, the workings of a character's mind is the hardest part of all of this. It's the thing that you will have the least access to in the early drafts. Often, the physical reaction will be what emerges first. When it does, put it down, recognizing that there's more to it since *the mind leads the body*. Just keep moving, knowing more needs to be done next time around. On each successive draft, you'll get more and more of the character's mind, and eventually you'll have what you need. Once you do, consider getting rid of the physical response. Use it only if it's necessary. "Necessary" means it gives us something significant about the character we wouldn't get without it.

The mind is dramatic and wild and exciting, but it's also confusing and contradictory, so don't be surprised if it's where your writing is the most clumsy and obvious. Keep in mind that it is what will take you the longest to get right in any given story, and it is the skill that will take you the longest to master as a storyteller. That's fine. Like everything else in writing, it takes practice. The main thing is that you know what to work on.

EXERCISES

Remember the scene with Larry and my wife that I used in chapter 3 to demonstrate the story form? There were no thoughts included at all. We didn't know what I (the husband) was thinking. I'm going to give you that scene again so you can practice putting in the thoughts. Whatever you imagine the husband's reactions would be is fine.

Start with the husband watching his wife kiss his best friend in the kitchen. Put in what you imagine he would be thinking. Put in his **worries, fears, and hopes** at every possible opportunity. If you can't come up with exact thoughts, make a list of the kinds of thoughts that he could be having, and come back and make them more specific later.

Remember, this is the hardest part of all. You may only get little pieces of it each time through. That's fine. Also, if it's too difficult, let it go for now. You can come back and do it at a later date if you get the urge.

Start with the husband's reactions the moment he sees the kiss, then his thoughts as he goes to the door and enters the kitchen. Put in anything and everything he could be thinking throughout the scene. You can cut back later. Here's the scene:

"Hi, guys," I say happily as I come in. "Here're the smokes."

They thank me, and both light up. Larry pours himself some Scotch.

"How'd it go while I was gone?" I say, flopping into a kitchen chair.

"Fine," my wife says.

"How about you, Lar? Enjoy yourself in my absence?"

He glances at my wife quickly. "I did," he says.

"Good. I was worried you might get lonely. But, when I saw you through the window, I could see you didn't need me to entertain you."

"Well," Larry says. "We both missed you, and we're glad you're back."

"That's right, honey," my wife says. "It's not the same without you."

"Of course not," I say. "Say, hand me the butcher knife, darling."

"Butcher knife, what for?"

"No reason. I just feel like holding it."

"Don't be silly," she says.

"No, really. Indulge me."

"Will you stop?" she says.

"Stop what? You don't trust me with a knife? What is this: no sharp objects for the lunatic?"

"Very funny," she says.

Larry stares at me, smiling weakly.

"Afraid I'll hurt myself—slit my wrists—or my throat? What do you think, Lar? Can I be trusted with a knife in my own kitchen with my best friend and my loyal wife?"

"Of course you can," Larry says flatly, then downs his Scotch.

"Damn right. Hear that, angel? Larry trusts me. He trusts you. We all trust each other. So pass me the knife, sweets."

The above is a chapter-subject exercise (applying the craft presented in the chapter). But we still have our ongoing short exercises and the full-story exercise to work from. If you're into the ongoing story, work on that. If you want to do one of the short exercises (full-scene or three-word), do that. Also, you may be into something of your own. Work on whatever attracts you. The main thing is to write. However, I realize that you may have no time to write and are only doing the 5 minutes a day. If that's where you're at, do your 5 minutes. The 5-minute method is described in chapter 12. It can be used to work on any of these exercises.

First are the scene exercises:

- Hiring someone or trying to get hired.
- Firing someone or trying not to get fired.
- Death of a loved one.

Here are the three-word combinations:

- Bathtub, cat, marijuana.
- Dove, castle, midget.
- Gorilla, toupee, extraterrestrial.

If you want to work from the settings and characters, use those from the previous chapters.

FULL STORY, PART THREE:

A quick reminder. Go over what you wrote last time and check it for want, obstacle, action as laid out in the last chapter.

The next part of the infidelity story is the actual confrontation through action that the injured lover takes. She or he can confront the cheating party directly or can be trying to get the goods on him or her by spying, hiring a detective, getting friends involved—anything you can dream up that you want to use.

Remember that every scene is a little story *(want + obstacle + action)* in which the character is trying to make something happen, get information, etc. Each scene has a *scene resolution* but not a *final resolution*. In the scene resolution, things are still worse than they were at the beginning. They must be. If they're not, the story is standing still. The tension and drama rise from scene to scene and chapter to chapter. **Things are worse at the end of every scene and every chapter until the story ends** (final resolution), when they get better or end in disaster. In *Romeo and Juliet,* it's one continual downhill slide. If a character gets his hopes up early on, it's only to have them dashed in the next encounter. Each scene and chapter ends in the mind of the character, who is stewing over his plight and trying to figure out what it means and what to do next. We end in the character's mind, so we know where we're at, where the character (and we) have moved to.

Showing

If I say, "He was a dangerous person, a walking time bomb," are you gripped by the character? You may be interested or even a little hooked since a walking time bomb promises action and excitement, but you're not there yet.

See how the following excerpt from the short story *Aryam's Flight*, by Clayton Luz, affects you:

> He was going to kill somebody. Maybe kill himself before it was over. His six-shot Smith and Wesson lay in the glove compartment. She had a six-inch, ventilated, blue steel barrel, a tight coil hammer that bit into your thumb when you drew it back, and one of those polished crescent triggers, cool to the touch. She was fully loaded, so smooth and trim he got a hard-on thinking about her.

That gives you an experience rather than a general idea of the character. The first example *tells* you about the character in general terms. This one gives you the experience of him by means of personal specifics, *shows* you who he is, *shows* him acting in the immediate moment. The first statement is in the language of the author—from the outside. The second is in the language of the character—from the inside. The first we call **telling**. The second we call **showing**. An unfortunate choice of terms in some ways, since we talk about story*telling*. Then, when you get into the actual craft, we say that telling is bad and showing is good. "Show, don't tell" is the old writing rule. And rightly so, since showing is the most fundamental of all writing techniques. Showing is to story as heat is to cooking.

The author says, "He was an awful person." The reader says, "*Show* me." You have to prove it because **saying it doesn't make it so.** You must create the experience. You must make it happen because **the reader will take your word for nothing.** But if you *show* the actual experience, happening here and now, word for word, right before our eyes, the reader will be there, living it through the character.

If I went on to tell you our dangerous time bomb character was angry, narrow-minded, and cruel, it wouldn't do much to you. You wouldn't experience much more about him. But if I showed him acting angry, narrow-minded, and cruel, it would be another story. Here's another excerpt from the same story:

He could feel the heat coming through the floorboard as he pressed the pedal of the piece-of-shit Chevy he'd stole. He was on a two-lane, ass-backwards, redneck road somewhere in the Florida Panhandle. It didn't matter. It could be Texas, Virginia, or Arizona. It was all the same. Hauling his broken ass in this can of Sterno, getting to where he needed to go, which was any fleabag motel that would take him. The kind of run-down dump on the side of this dry lick road where some fat dumpling of a toothless daughter of her own brother/father snickers when you tell her you need a room and she thinks you want it to get laid or do something perverted to yourself.

Maybe he'd shoot her too.

The world's like that. You end up doing something you thought you never would. What the fuck!

The fuck was, it was hotter than an oven on Thanksgiving in this tin can with no air-conditioning. Just his goddamn luck, the first old fool he robbed outside of Jacksonville had a car that didn't have no air. Who the hell buys a car in Florida that don't have air? The stupid old fart actually tried to stop him from getting into the car. He'll see what a fool he was when he wakes up in the hospital and sees his foot looking like hamburger. He woulda shot him in the head if he knowed the son-of-a-bitch had no air.

That should have given you a feel for the character, given you the experience of him, *shown* you what he was about.

If I say fear, you don't experience fear. If I say, "Barbara was terrified," you don't experience Barbara's terror. But if Barbara is seven years old and is cornered in an alley by a seedy-looking man who says, "Come on little darling. We're going for a ride in my car," you might begin to feel something for her because of the situation. If she says, "Where's my mommy? I want my mommy," you start to feel her fear as she's feeling and expressing it even though the word *fear* isn't used. You have to give us the actions of the characters without labels or generalities. Specifics, specifics, specifics—the personal specifics of the characters and their actions *(showing)* are what do the job.

These are pretty clear-cut examples—all or none. The problem is, it's not always a matter of all or none. Sometimes you have a mix of telling and showing. Instead of a full scene, you give us a partial scene. A partial scene is one that gives us the setup in summary (generality) and mixes in enough dialogue and specifics to sketch it in and give us an experience. Think of it as the difference between highly realistic painting in which you can't see the brush marks, and impressionism, in which a few broad strokes give you the image. In partial scenes, you must give the reader enough (as the brushstrokes in impressionism) so that his imagination can fill in the rest. The thing to remember is that **showing a little is better than telling a lot.**

The showing example I gave you in chapter 3 is also a good example of partial showing. Let's look at it again. We started with the dictionary definition, the idea, of homely. "Homely, adj. Lacking in elegance or refinement. Not attractive or good-looking." That's the *idea* of homely. To create the *experience* of homely, to *show* it, it must be put in personal terms, a specific person's experience of homeliness. Here's the *showing* of it again.

"She's a homely girl. I don't know where she gets it," my six-year-old ears overhear my mother saying to my Aunt Beth. I don't know what "homely" means, but I know it's bad. I run to my room, bury my head in my pillow and cry. Eventually, I learn what homely really means. It means to be taken to the dentist for my buckteeth: "Can you make them straighter?" To the plastic surgeon for my nose: "Can you make it smaller?" It means I am dragged to walking classes, talking classes, and posture classes: "Chin up. Shoulders back. Enunciate. Smile." Homely means that everything I put in my mouth is carefully weighed, measured, and calculated beforehand so I don't take up more space than I already do. "Will she ever lose weight, Doctor?" my mother asks. "She's just a big girl," says Doctor Chen. Homely means that you see a look of disdain on the face of a mother who wishes her daughter could be a beauty queen. You see that look every day of your life.

—Elizabeth Brown

This paragraph skips a lot. It's an overview, a summary, of many years of the daughter's life with this mother. It doesn't give us everything, but it's personal and specific enough to give us an experience, to reach the heart, which is something the dictionary definition could never do. This paragraph was the lead into a scene of the daughter going home as an adult to visit this mother and still feeling intimidated and frightened by her. It was an excellent way to give us a feel for who's who and what's what as we are led into a painful and dramatic scene.

Here's another example:

> He lay in bed at night, his pillow over his head, trying not to hear his parents fighting—the banging and hitting. "You bitch, you lousy bitch," his father said. The sound of a slap, a thump, a kitchen chair skidding across the floor. "Oh, why? Why do you do this to me?" his father howled.

You get the picture pretty well, but you don't get the father coming through the door and the kid's thoughts, his running for cover in his room, the parent's conversation that led up to the violence, or how the fight finally ended. You don't get a lot, but if it's done well, you get enough—enough to stick with it. You can do it once in a while, but if you do it too much, you're leaving too much out to hold the reader.

The more you tell, generalize, the more you cut the reader out of the experience and yourself too, for that matter, since it's as much about you and your having the experience as it is about the reader having it later. **The best way to give the reader an experience is to make sure you have one first.**

Showing takes place in real time, the pace of reality. Telling generalizes, compresses, skips. No one wants part of a big experience left out—no one wants to have sex and skip the orgasm, or have soup and salad, skip the entrée, and go on to dessert. Now, if it's a lousy meal, you might want to skip the entrée, and if it's a weak part of your story, you might be tempted to skip over it.

If it was a lousy meal, then why tell us about the soup, salad, dessert, and coffee? Well, maybe they were great. Telling can be used to get through some sluggish material, which is fine, if you **do it rarely.** My personal advice is to go back and prepare an entrée worth eating. **Make all of your story worth showing.** Now, that may be unrealistic, especially if, after repeated attempts, you can't make it work. Quick vivid telling can be better than long sluggish showing if you don't do it often. Telling should be a last resort.

Another way to summarize *(tell)* is flashback, a memory of the experience that would naturally be fragmented. When you need to cover a lot of material in a short space. Also, you might do it if you don't feel you have the skill to do the whole job. Still, the issue is, Could you do better with showing? Try to show it with pieces of the experience that will suggest the whole.

Whatever the reason, just remember: telling is risky. Ideally, you want to create scenes worth doing in full, scenes that have the drama to justify giving us all the gory details. Even if you're going to do a partial scene, I would recommend, especially when you're new to writing, doing the full scene and trying to find enough drama to make it work, *then* cutting it down into summary/telling if you need to. That way, you're practicing your craft and improving your skill and not shying away from the task. All the big, dramatic episodes in a story should be done in full scene—should be dramatic enough to be worth doing in full scene.

So, what about the writers who get away with telling? I'm talking about authors like Thomas Wolfe, F. Scott Fitzgerald, John Fowles in *The French Lieutenant's Woman,* Joseph Conrad, Thomas Mann, etc. In order to get away with it, your ideas have to be striking, vivid, provocative, or brilliant in their own right. That's not to say the reader won't overlook some telling if the rest of what he gets is strong, which means the question you should always ask is: Does the story work **because of** or **in spite of** the telling? Readers will plow through a lot if they are rewarded for it, but don't count on it.

Tolstoy said, "All happy families are alike but an unhappy family is unhappy after its own fashion." A famous line. It's arresting and thought-provoking. It stands on its own. And it's telling. It doesn't give us the experience of a single family, happy, unhappy, or otherwise.

Fitzgerald entered into one of his stories when a young boy who had agonized about being an outsider had just been made to feel accepted.

> It isn't given for us to know those rare moments when people are wide open and the lightest touch can wither or heal. A moment too late and we can never reach them any more in this world. They will not be cured by our most efficacious drugs or slain with our sharpest swords.

These words are not the boy's experience, but a comment by the author on not only what was happening at that moment but on the nature of life itself, and it made the moment even more sensitive and touching.

That Fitzgerald passage is one of my personal favorites. But then you might hate it. And that's the problem with *telling*. It's ideas. Ideas are much harder to sell than experience. If they strike us the wrong way, we resist. Experience *(showing)* is what we live and feel. It touches our heart before we have time to judge. To deny it is to deny our own hearts.

Deeply held ideas come from a meaningful experience, usually painful. We learn not by being told about life, but through living it.

Life is showing. Ideas change us only if they relate to our life. The power is in the experience *(showing)*.

In terms of writing, the place where you will most often slip into telling (usually without realizing) is emotion. For example, "His anger turned to guilt," might come out of you. Can you see it? Can you feel it? Anger to guilt? How does that work? How it works is one of the most difficult problems in writing—getting feelings into words. It might go like this:

> Jesus Christ, he wrecked the truck, OK. It was his fault. He admitted it. Why were they still on his back? Rotten bastards couldn't let go. What the hell did they want, blood? Everybody screwed up. Nobody was perfect. He told them everything they wanted to know. Except about the drinking. He couldn't tell that. If they ever found out. Damn, that was stupid. Damn! Why the hell did he start having beers for lunch? He knew better. He'd promised himself never again. He was the rotten bastard, not them. Rotten worthless bastard. They were right.

You can lapse into telling with anything and everything, even description. "It was a frightening storm." "It was a dangerous-looking slope." "He had a disgusting face." There is no way to avoid it. And it's perfectly all right in early drafts when you're working to get the basic story down. In fact, if you have a sense of what you need to do, but you're not up to it, telling is your shorthand that lets you put something on the page so that you can move forward and not get bogged down. You do multiple drafts. One time you're good at one thing, another time at something else. Bit by bit, you get it all up to where it needs to be. That's the way of all writers.

You could practice showing with the three examples in the above paragraph. Here's a scene of telling that you could show also.

By the time Ed got to work, he was so freaked out about his wife asking him for a divorce that morning, he couldn't keep his mind on what he was doing. He kept thinking about going through a divorce and what it would be like, how he would get through it and if he could go on alone. He was so preoccupied he couldn't focus. Eventually, his boss called him in and asked what the problem was.

If you don't want to do that, here are some more exercises to choose from. Remember, if you have something that you want to go back to from previous writing, do that. If you're doing the full-story exercise, you'll be doing the next part.

EXERCISES

FULL STORY, PART FOUR:

This is the aftermath of the last scene, just as there was one after the first discovery. The character is wrestling with the newly revealed and more troubling facts, trying to make sense of them in the same way. If, by chance, you had the character be reassured in the last scene, then new, more incriminating discoveries need to be made in this scene. The character will be imagining the worst, planning for it, and hoping for the best. (He or she could consider spying on the husband, getting a private detective, help from a friend, murder, suicide, etc.)

Here are some full-scene exercises. They can be turned into full stories if they take off for you. Remember the point, always, is to reveal as much of the characters and their relationship as you can.

A family fight over a missing object.

Two people (friends, lovers, parent/child) fighting over the meaning of a word. Eventually they look it up in the dictionary and discover that they're both wrong. They then begin arguing over who was more right.

SECOND FULL STORY, PART ONE:

To bed or not to bed. A character is having dinner with someone she's been out with twice before and is trying to decide if she should go to bed with him or not. She *wants* to make the right decision but fears she might do the wrong thing and ruin the relationship *(obstacle)*. She's struggling with the question *(action)* by weighing things in her mind, by observing how he is acting toward her tonight and how he responds to her indirect, but probing, questions. This can be a little story in which the resolution is the decision to bed or not to bed. It's about making such a decision, and the goal, as always, is to reveal as much about the characters as possible.

Here's a second full story you can do if you want. It's in several parts. You'll get another part at the end of the next few chapters.

A character is waiting for his date. She's always late. Tonight she's especially late. He is agonizing over why she does it, why he puts up with it, what he can do, and what he's done to try to change her, etc. This story is also going to be about self-deception. In his thoughts, you need to show how he's possibly distorting things, how he's excessive, how he might be a problem also. He decides to pretend he's breaking up with her to teach her a lesson. He imagines the scene, how she'll beg and plead and how he'll let her stew before taking her back.

The Second Time Around

REWRITING

Here's a quote. See if you recognize it. "Yesterday, December 7th, 1941, a date that shall live in history . . ." Know who that quote is from? FDR (Franklin Delano Roosevelt, president). He was responding to the Japanese bombing of Pearl Harbor, which forced us into World War II. If you know your history, you might remember the quote differently. Even if you don't know your history, it's such a famous quote that you might have heard it anyway. And you might recall that FDR said, "a date that shall live in *infamy*," as opposed to "a date that shall live in *history*." So, which was it? "History" or "infamy"? And which is the stronger word? Even if you don't know the quote, I think you'll agree that *infamy* is the stronger word. *History* is general and neutral, while *infamy* is specific and sinister. "Infamy" is what he said.

So, if he said, "infamy," why am I saying, "history"? Any ideas? Well, he *said*, "infamy," but he *wrote*, "history." "History" was in his first draft—then he changed it to "infamy." The topic for this chapter is rewriting. **"Writing is rewriting,"** says the old writing rule. Make sense? Maybe. We'll see. It's a good idea to beware of writing rules. They're not always correct or helpful.

"Writing is rewriting" is one of the good rules, but it doesn't tell us what rewriting is or how to do it, only that it's important, with the implication that we should do it. Nor does it tell us how much rewriting we should do. So, what do you do—go back, over and over, plowing through what you've written, hoping something will pop into your head that will make it better? And how do you know when you've gotten it right? Or is rewriting a specific process with principles and rules and guidelines just like we have for shaping stories, techniques for uncovering the energy and drama in our stories and ourselves? Yes to the second choice. Even though you're often all over the place when you're creating, rewriting is an *orderly method* of approaching your work that keeps you on track and working in the right area.

Rewriting—what is it exactly, and what do we do when we rewrite? Well, first, rewriting is *not* polishing. Polishing is changing words and phrases and sentences so that your story reads smoothly. Just like it sounds, it's a surface issue. (If polishing is a face-lift, rewriting is a heart transplant.) Rewriting is reworking larger elements of the story to make it more immediate and dramatic. It's changing, adding, or cutting characters, scenes, and other story elements. Fine, but *how* do you do it, and *when* do you do it?

Fiction itself is a process of creating order from disorder. Working with and even creating disorder are a natural part of the process. So, we need an orderly way to approach this disorder that we've created. But before we get to the actual techniques, you need to get a feel for how much of a part rewriting plays.

How many drafts do you imagine it takes to get a story right? What would you suppose would be an average number of drafts—the number most successful writers *need* to get the most out of their stories? Remember, nobody gets it right the first time. From my experience and that of writers I know and have worked with and read about, it seems that 5 drafts would be an average—on average most writers do 5 drafts. Ten drafts are common. Tolstoy wrote *War and Peace* 10 times. Aristotle wrote some paragraphs 80 times, and Hemingway wrote as many as 60 drafts of a single paragraph. So, you don't write the entire story the same number of drafts. You might write a single scene many more times than the rest. Some lines or paragraphs and even a scene will stay untouched. Writing a full scene without needing to change anything is rare. The point is that you need to give yourself enough chances to get it right. You can rehearse as many times as you like, then take the best parts of each run-through and piece together your best performance.

All right, so you need about 5 drafts to get the best out of yourself and your story. But that doesn't answer the question of how you will know when you're done. I once wrote 12 drafts of a story. My normal number is around 5. On this 12th draft, a new dimension of the character and the story opened up that gave the story a lot more depth. That was nice, but it put me in a quandary. If I got this out of 12 drafts, what might I get with draft 24 or 36? Maybe greatness was just around the corner—1 draft away. How could I tell?

The old writing rule says: You've rewritten enough when the last draft is not as good as the previous draft—when you've made it weaker with rewriting. Sound like a good answer? Make sense? Think about it—and remember what I told you about writing rules—maybe they're good, maybe not. The trouble with this rule is, it really doesn't address the problem. The problem is: You have no idea which draft is better. You're lost and need a method to find your way back, to regain some perspective. If you could tell which draft is better, you could go on rewriting and improving it.

I've heard jokes that were so funny I couldn't tell them without cracking up and wrecking the punch line. After a while, I was able to tell them well. And eventually they weren't even funny anymore. That's what happens when you write. The more you work your story, the better you know it. There are no surprises. You lose perspective and become almost illiterate in relation to your writing.

Now, with time, if you don't look at it for a week or a month, you'll have a fresh response to it—for a draft or two, at best. Then you're back to being illiterate again. If you're writing a long piece, like a novel, and you go straight through and don't look at the beginning until you've gone all the way through, you'll have a fresh response when you get back to the beginning and be able to rewrite well. But even with a novel, you can get stale, especially since you'll need to re-work parts of it over and over. So, you can fall into the same rut with a novel.

For that reason, taking time off isn't a good idea—not to mention the risk of losing your edge, your nerve, or getting blocked during the break. No, time off is not the way to go. It's possible to refresh yourself, to regain your perspective, without having to forget what you've done.

So, it takes 5-plus drafts to get the most out of your story, but that still doesn't answer the question of how you know when you're finished. Now, we're talking about doing your best work at your present skill level—not writing the perfect story. The more stories you write, the better you get. You don't want to wear yourself out trying for perfection on a single story. You get it down the best you can at this time, within reason, and then move on. You can always come back and rewrite it later when you're a better writer.

John Fowles, author of *The Collector* (his first big novel/bestseller/movie) and later *The French Lieutenant's Woman* (also a bestseller and a movie—and a great example of a present omniscient narrator), also wrote a bestseller, *The Magus*, in between these two novels. Fowles, ten years after the success of *The Magus*, decided to rewrite the entire novel, which he did. This second version of *The Magus* was also a critical and commercial success and a bestseller for a second time. So, there are two versions of *The Magus*, each considered equally valid and different enough from the other to justify its own book. Your library should have both. If you want to see what happened to the author and how he changed as expressed through his craft, you could read both versions.

So, when are you done? *Never*. But when you've gone through all the story and rewriting techniques, touched all bases, you will have gotten on to the page most (nobody gets all, not even Fowles in his second time around) of what you have at this stage of your writing. You're done for now, as far as you can tell. But maybe not for all time. If one of your stories comes alive in you sometime down the line (usually more like years than months), if you find new excitement in it because of new ideas or (more often) new skills, you can always redo it. This reworking of old work is most often done on unsuccessful pieces you're attached to rather than on successful ones.

Another good comparison is a story written twice by Flannery O'Connor. The first version was called *The Geranium*, written in 1947 as part of her M.F.A. thesis. The second version, called *Judgement Day*, was done in 1964. There was a great difference in the way O'Connor approached this story the second time. Both versions are in *Flannery O'Connor: The Complete Stories*, published by the Noonday Press (Farrar, Straus and Giroux).

Another excellent example of the craft in progress (rewriting) is F. Scott Fitzgerald's unfinished novel, *The Last Tycoon*. There's a paperback version, published by Scribner's, titled: "The Last Tycoon (unfinished) with a foreword by Edmund Wilson and notes by the author." The important part is "notes by the author." The novel itself is 126 pages. Following the novel is a synopsis pieced together from Fitzgerald's notes and things he said to others while writing it. Then, most importantly, we get Fitzgerald's notes to himself—notes that appeared on the manuscript pages along with diagrams, outlines, and notes from his notebook. The most instructive part of it, for our purpose, is to see not only how he worked, but how much trouble he was having, how he struggled with getting the novel into shape.

Now, that doesn't mean his way will be your way. You may develop a simpler, more straightforward approach or one that's more complicated and roundabout. Every author works differently. Go with what feels right to you, but don't be afraid to try different approaches to see if they'll get you there more easily.

Story is about experience. So, one thing you do when you rewrite is relax and reread what you've written to see how it affects you and how much of an experience you get. Since it's all about emotion, you need to feel your story. But we know that you can lose your way in your feelings just as you can while writing. You may not be sure how your story feels or what's the better choice.

So, you're lost. What can you do? How do you find your way back into your story? Any ideas? Where do you go first, always? When you're in trouble, what do you do?

Michael Jordan: the plan. Jimmy Connors: keep your eye on the ball. CRAFT. Go to your craft. Yes, here they are again: WANT, OB-STACLE, ACTION. We just went over them in the last chapter, but you need to go over them again and again. We're going over them several times in the course. Even if you feel they're a pain or think you know them already, go over them anyway whenever you run into them. You need to. We all do.

WANT, OBSTACLE, ACTION: go to them first—always. Check for those elements before you do anything else. If you don't, and if the problem is a lack of those elements (which it almost always is), you will waste a lot of time and energy working elsewhere and never fix the problem. It's like waxing your car when it needs a new engine. No matter how much you get it to shine, you'll never make it run right.

So, once again, the first question always is, WHO WANTS WHAT? If no one wants anything, that's the problem. That's where you need to work. But don't gloss over it. Don't decide the character wants and wants enough without taking a careful look at what you have *on the page*. Do not work in your head. The only thing that counts, the only thing that exists, is what's on the page. So, find the want on the page and mark where it first appears. Then answer these questions: Does it appear as early as possible? How strong is it? Could it be stronger? Is the character as determined/driven as he can be to get what he wants? Does he feel that he absolutely cannot go on with things the way they are, that things must change or else? (Is he as in love as Romeo or Scarlett or Gatsby, as obsessed as Ahab or Hamlet?) Why does he care? What are his specific and personal reasons?

Note that the want does not always express itself first. It's always there, but not visible until it is denied or thwarted, as in *Hamlet* when his father's ghost appears or in my Larry scene when I see my wife kissing Larry. Hamlet was not wishing, *I hope Dad doesn't show up and order me to avenge his death.* Nor was I thinking, *I hope my wife's not cheating on me.* Nevertheless, the want must be there even though it's buried since it's satisfied.

The second question is always WHAT'S THE OBSTACLE? Where does it first appear on the page? Find it, and mark it. Does it appear as early as possible? Could it be stronger? Is it as determined/driven to block the character as the character is determined to overcome it? Could the character do nothing and suffer no injury? If the character can ignore the obstacle and get away with it, you have a false obstacle/false conflict, which means no conflict, no drama, no story.

Once you have the want and obstacle cranked up to the maximum (without violating the sense of your story—a character can be driven without being as whacked out as Ahab or Hamlet), then it's time for ACTION. WHAT'S THE CHARACTER DOING TO OVERCOME

THE PROBLEM? Is he making an all-out direct attack upon (or defense against) the obstacle? Where does this action first appear on the page? Find it. Mark it. Could it happen sooner? What else could the character do? Could he do more? Is he using himself to the maximum? If not, make it happen. Remember, thinking is action if it's struggling with and planning how to attack or defend against the obstacle. Remember, the obstacle must counterattack/fight back/resist with equal force.

Now, if you have WANT, OBSTACLE, ACTION working, it's very rare that you'll be in any real trouble. The RESOLUTION, which is simply a matter of a victory or a defeat, should not be a problem if you have a deep want, a threatening obstacle, and a character who is using all he has to overcome the problem. With those elements, the one, two, three of dramatic momentum, working, it's impossible to have a weak story.

Want, obstacle, action, and resolution are elements of form. The other crucial concern is not form, but a product of it. It's EMOTION, and it's more of an ingredient, a seasoning, that's all over the place, rather than part of form. But it doesn't matter what we call it, as long as we're aware of what the character is feeling *at all times*. A good way to get to the emotions in the character is to ask what the character's worries, fears, and hopes are at every important moment in the story. These should appear on every page and often several times on a page and should be expressed through both the character's inner thoughts and his actions, which are not always the same.

Anyone who is wrestling with a threatening problem that can harm him or something dear to him will be *worried* and *afraid* of what might happen while, at the same time, *hoping* that he can do something to win out. With such a threat, the emotion is intense and nearly constant and needs to be expressed in the character whenever you have the chance. Go through your story and ask of every line possible, "What are the character's worries, fears, and hopes?" Remember, emotion is the payoff. It's where the ultimate connection is made, where identification occurs, where the reader becomes the character. If the reader doesn't know where the character is emotionally, he doesn't know where he himself is, and he drifts away from the story.

The other concern is a matter of technique: SHOWING. Showing is creating the experience, making it happen right before our eyes, word for word, moment by moment, rather than describing it or generalizing about it. Showing is your constant method of presenting your story, your ongoing concern at all times. The purest and most effective form of showing is scene. You need to be showing as much as possible.

Those are your basic elements—CONFLICT (WANT + OBSTACLE), ACTION, RESOLUTION, EMOTION, SHOWING. They need to be working not only in the overall story, but in every single scene. For every scene and every chapter, you must deal with want, obstacle, action, resolution. Every scene is a struggle/confrontation between two forces, between the want and the obstacle. Every scene has a resolution—not a final resolution, but a scene resolution. In other words, every scene is a little story in itself. And at the end of each scene, **things are worse** than at the beginning. In stories, things get worse and worse, the plot thickens and complicates, until the final resolution—victory or defeat.

Romeo and Juliet, for example, is one complication after another. Shortly after Romeo and Juliet are secretly married, Romeo tries to stop his friend Mercutio from fighting with Tybalt, but instead causes Mercutio's death. In his anguish and fury, Romeo kills Tybalt and is later banished for it. Her lover gone, Juliet is despondent. That's bad, but to make matters worse, her father proposes that she marry Paris. When Juliet objects, her father flies into a rage and orders her to marry Paris and sets a date for the wedding. Shakespeare heaps one difficulty after another onto the "star-crossed" lovers. Stars are crossed—who crossed them? Shakespeare.

Things may get better in a story, or seem to, briefly. If they do, it's only a setup to knock them down and make things even worse—to reenergize the characters and the drama. Each scene needs to end in the mind of the character, who is more upset than he was at the opening and stewing over the new complication besetting him and what to do now. If things aren't worse at the end of every scene and every chapter, your story is marking time, standing still. If the story isn't moving, the reader will move—away.

It's these basic elements that make you or break you. They're all you need. If you get them right, any other mistakes you make won't matter. *Every* story that I've seen that failed was lacking in one of these basic elements. So, the first thing to do when rewriting, always, is to go over your story and check for these elements.

Once you're sure that you have these elements working, you're ready to try the other rewriting techniques in this chapter to get the maximum out of your story and yourself. You can take each of these techniques and go through and apply it to your story. There's a lot here, and it may seem like an exhausting list, but with practice, you'll master them and be able to apply several if not all of them simultaneously.

RULE NOTHING OUT

Go over your story, and let your mind run wild, imagining anything and everything that could possibly happen, what else the characters could think, feel, and do. Go for the far-out possibilities. Don't worry about going too far. At this point the problem is not going far enough. We shy away from pushing things to the limit—and beyond. We're organized personalities with boundaries and defenses. To create, we need to break through those boundaries, to be open to anything and everything that's in us. And because you can't really go beyond yourself, no matter how far-fetched an idea feels, it will have your personal stamp, your sense of order, on it.

If you do go too far out with your story, you can always cut back. An old writing rule says: The best way to find out what's enough is to do too much. So, if the man's wife shocks him by asking for a divorce and he's desperate to keep her, what might he do? Initially, you might have him argue, make promises, beg, or even threaten. But later you might consider having him attack, stalk, bribe, blackmail, murder, or slander his wife—or a combination of these—to uncover what's in him and you. He may not do any of these, but you need to explore every possibility. And even if he doesn't do them, he could well contemplate and dream of doing them. Thought is action. So, go as far as your imagination takes you, then see what you have and use what works.

LET NOTHING BE EASY

Let nothing be easy for anyone ever. Create and take advantage of every opportunity to cause trouble. Think about how difficult things were for Romeo and Juliet, Hamlet, Ahab, Gatsby, Scarlett O'Hara. Who made them difficult? Who drove Hamlet crazy? It wasn't his father's request for revenge. It was Shakespeare. The whale wasn't the real cause of Ahab's death. Melville was.

You, the author, do it all. Make all the trouble. Exercise sadistic license. One way to do that is to raise the stakes as much as possible. For example, if a young, successful lawyer, practicing in a prominent firm in a well-to-do county is asked to do something he feels is unethical, immoral, or illegal and he tells the senior members of the firm that he can't, in good conscience, go along, they might tell him:

> "Well, Martin, if you can't help us out on this, you don't have the kind of loyalty and team spirit you need to work here. In other words, you're out of a job."

OK, so it's play ball, or you're out. That's one level of conflict. But, for the same effort, without changing the meaning of the story, they could say:

> "You're out of a job, and we'll see to it you never practice law again in this county."

We've intensified the drama without changing the sense of the story. But have we gone all the way? Can we go farther? What if the young lawyer's bosses say:

> "We're sorry to hear you won't back us up on this, Martin. Frankly we had our doubts about you. So, just in case, we took some time to cook up a little file on you. Some of it's true. Some of it's not so true, but it'll stand up in court. If you don't go along, you're not only out of a job, but we'll have you disbarred. You'll never practice law again anywhere."

Now, we haven't changed the thrust of the story, but by raising the stakes we've made it more intense and dramatic.

Have we gone all the way? For this story, as I imagine it, we have. As *I* imagine it. That doesn't mean that someone else can't imagine it differently, push it farther, and make it work better. The senior partners could threaten to murder the young lawyer's wife and child. The story could get to that point, and it could be made to work, but it might border on becoming a different kind of story (a crime thriller) than I had in mind. That's my sense of it. You may go for something more extreme, and it would be just as valid.

Fiction reflects reality—the truth of reality. But fiction is not reality. It's concentrated, intensified reality. It's the essence of reality. In a sense it's more real than reality. It certainly reveals more truth than everyday reality. And it's never as mild as reality often is. So, you must put pressure on your characters to force them to use themselves. The more they use themselves, the more they reveal themselves. The more they reveal themselves, the more we experience and identify. You'll never go wrong by making everything as difficult as possible for everybody, bad guys as well as good guys, at all times.

TRY THE REVERSE

Consider having your character do the opposite of what he's now doing. This may seem like a violation of your character, but there's truth in it. The frustrated mother who says of her bratty kid, "I give him everything he wants, or I beat the crap out of him. Nothing works," is expressing this truth. When we're desperate, we go to extremes. So, the powerful man, after trying to intimidate his wife into not divorcing him, may fall to his knees and beg. The nerd who tries to avoid being harassed by blending into the woodwork or pleading to be left alone could get a gun and go berserk, blasting his enemies away. By considering the reverse, you're working to uncover possibilities in your characters, your story, and yourself—opportunities for your characters to express themselves and reveal themselves. Remember, **revealing character is the number-one purpose of fiction.** So, consider the reverse. If it works, do it. You'll be surprised at how often it uncovers new possibilities and gets you deeper into the heart of things.

DOUBLE DUTY—TRIPLE DUTY

Your story and you, the author, should never be doing only one thing at a time. Only *setting scene* (describing setting), for example. You never want the reader to be sitting around waiting for you to set things up so the story can begin. Set scene, OK, but at the same time you can be revealing character. We get character if the setting has meaning for the character, if the character is affected by it, if he has strong feelings about it. The setting should be a necessary element of the story, and the character should be reacting to it in a revealing way.

In good storytelling, everything has a purpose. Everything contributes. Nothing is just there. Nothing is neutral. Nothing is along for the ride. The old writing rule is: If it's not helping, it's hurting. Now, this is art, not science. So, you have some latitude—a lot in fact. If you can thrill us with brilliant, poetic description for no other purpose than the beauty and pleasure of it, you may pull it off.

Also, if something pops up on the page that you like, that feels right, that appeals to you, but you have no idea why it's there, leave it. If you put it in, it may have a connection that you don't see at the moment. The thing to do is to work on making it a necessary part of the story. When you do that, you challenge your inventiveness and often create a deeper and richer story. The last thing you do is pull something out that you like just because it doesn't fit. In the end, you may cut it, but only after trying your best to make it work. That's what fiction is about—relating things that aren't always related. In a good story, everything relates to everything else because that author has made them relate.

You should be doing *at least two things at all times*. If you have a character going to a cocktail party, he can't be neutral about it. He can't be going just because you're in the mood to create a cocktail party. The character has to have strong feelings about cocktail parties. He needs to hate cocktail parties because he feels so out of it or because he's an alcoholic and afraid he'll take a drink. You need to be giving us cocktails and *revealing character* at the same time—**double duty.**

But for the same effort you can be doing **triple duty.** The third thing you could, and should, be doing is *moving plot*. So, the character has to go to the cocktail party, which he hates, but he has to go to try to find his brother-in-law, who can't stand him, and beg him to loan him a thousand dollars so he can pay the bookie who's coming to collect his money or break the character's legs at eight o'clock. This way, he's on a mission. He has an objective. He's acting to overcome an obstacle. He has a *need* to be at the party. If he doesn't *need* to be there, he shouldn't be there.

So, **triple duty**—*setting scene, revealing character, moving plot*—is what we work for. And note how this example contains the story elements—**want** (one thousand dollars), **obstacle** (brother-in-law), **action** (trying to convince him to loan the money)—as every scene must. It will have a scene **resolution** (he gets the money or is refused) before it's over.

BLOCKS OF . . . ANYTHING

Check your work for long, thick paragraphs of EXPOSITION. Exposition is information the reader needs to know to understand the story. Often it's information you only *think* the reader needs to know. The reader needs to know who's who and what's what so he can have the same experience the character does. He needs to know what the character knows that's **relevant to the immediate situation.** But he needs **only what's necessary.** For example, if a husband is accusing his wife of cheating on him, we need to know, before the scene begins, why he believes she's cheating and that he himself is having an affair with his secretary if we're going to have the full experience. But we don't need to know that the husband has three brothers and once wanted to be a race car driver.

A common misconception is that giving the reader history and biography is a way of developing character. Your character is developed by the way he *acts* in the present, the way he deals with his problem. **Action is character.** We don't know where Ahab went to school, how many siblings he had, what his parents were like, etc. We know him by the way he behaves in the present.

If you have exposition (information you feel you need to deliver to the reader), first make sure it's absolutely necessary. If it is necessary, don't deliver it in one long stretch. Break it up and sprinkle it through the scene where it would naturally come up in the chain of events, thoughts, etc., and make it do double/triple duty.

FLASHBACKS

Avoid flashbacks if possible. If you need them, use them, but use them properly. Like exposition, a flashback should be broken up and sprinkled through a scene the way it might naturally come into a character's mind. Never launch into a long flashback midscene. For example, you wouldn't do this:

"Hey, punk, what you doin' 'round here?" the stocky, red-headed Chicano said as he strutted down the alley toward

Harry. Harry reached into his pocket and pulled out the switch-blade he carried ever since his Uncle Louie gave it to him after he'd been jumped by three bikers in the alley behind his house when he was fourteen. He'd always known the time might come when he'd have to use it. He was never much of a fighter, in fact rough stuff always made him queasy, especially since the time he saw his buddy blasted apart in a drive-by shooting.

This kind of long reverie should take place before this scene when the character has some leisure. In the heat of battle, no one drifts off into reverie. So, for the above, we would have Harry think about the switchblade earlier when he was under no pressure. Maybe as he gets dressed to go out that night and the switchblade is sitting on his dresser as he puts his wallet and keys in his pocket and thinks that maybe he should leave it home and how tired he is of carrying it around just to fulfill his promise to Uncle Louie. You will have time to go into it in the way Harry would think about it. Then, when the bad guy rushes him in the alley and Harry reaches into his pocket for the switchblade, "Thank God for Uncle Louie," is all we need to put us right there with Harry, having the full experience.

If it wouldn't happen in reality, it shouldn't happen in fiction. Reality is your guide, even though fiction is different from reality. Many things that happen in reality cannot happen in fiction (winning the lottery as a way of getting out of a gambling debt), but what's done in fiction should be possible in reality. All fiction could be real, but all reality can't be fiction. Even special cases such as fantasy and science fiction have to establish a believable reality and be internally consistent. So, don't launch into a long flashback in the middle of an intense scene.

If you need to do a long flashback, and you're sure it's needed, then go there and do it and do it all the way. That means your long flashback has to fulfill all the story demands—want, obstacle, action, etc. The reader will go anywhere you take him, gladly, and stay there as long as you want *if* you reward him with story.

You can often eliminate the need for flashback and make your story more immediate by simply starting your story earlier. Here's an example of an unnecessary flashback:

> "You're a rotten bastard, Dave, and you've exploited me for the last time," Larry said. His boss, Dave, had been taking credit for Larry's work for the last three years, promising to get him a raise and a promotion as soon as he could. Now he'd taken Larry's portfolio and used it to get a big job with another agency.

Can you see what happens? You start with high emotion, but the reader doesn't know who's who and what's what exactly, so to make it clear you stop the action and make the reader backtrack into a quickie flashback in order to catch up on what's going on. Even with that, we don't have a full sense of what's transpired, because a lot of dramatic material has been skipped. The natural beginning of this story would be the first time Larry discovered his boss was taking credit for his work, since that is the first dramatic event in the chain of events that makes up the story. Also, even though you hook the reader on the first line with high emotion, the reader will not fully connect until he knows who's who and what's what. It's like seeing an argument erupt on the street—it gets your attention, and you react to it, but you can't identify fully unless you know what's going on (who's who, and what's what).

In general, observing chronology is the best approach, because it's the natural order. The story flows forward, and the reader goes with it without being jerked around from one place to another. A story should start with the first dramatic event, but *far enough before* it so that we know what triggered the event. That way, we go into the scene knowing what the character knows, with full knowledge of who's who and what's what. Only with that awareness can we participate and feel the full impact of what's happening.

Another disadvantage of flashback is that the reader knows the character survived. If it was a life-threatening situation, you lose all the suspense of not knowing if the character will get through it or escape uninjured. If the situation is not life-threatening, the reader still knows that the character survived emotionally. Now, none of that may be important, and you may have a good reason for flashing back. If so, do it.

I've raised a lot of objections to flashbacks because beginning writers generally use them unnecessarily. But there are advantages. For example, if a dramatic or traumatic event takes place in a character's life and then nothing eventful happens for ten years, you don't want to ask the reader to skip ten years by saying, "Ten years later." You could do that, and I'm sure you've seen it done and seen it work. You might make it work also. But your story may be much better served if you start ten years later and get into some drama and then do the flashback at the appropriate time or times. What the right time is depends on your story and what *feels right* to you.

Again, it's art, not science. The rules are to make you aware of, to give you a *feel* for, how stories work. The rules are guides to keep you focused on the areas that will be the most productive. If you *feel* like going against them and it *feels* good, do it. The main thing is, if you take something away or leave something out, you have to give something back to make up for it. You can't just take something away and leave the reader with nothing. And I *feel* I must caution you again that it's not only a matter of doing what you feel, since sometimes you *don't know what you feel* or your *feelings turn against you*. That's why we have craft and technique.

DIALOGUE

Look out for blocks of dialogue. Some people are long-winded and go on a tirade and can't be stopped, and there are some wonderful long speeches in literature, but we're always looking for opportunities to reveal character. To do that, the characters must express themselves—not only to reveal themselves but also to pressure the other characters into doing the same. Also, in a heated exchange, people interrupt and talk over each other rather than taking turns. Even three lines of dialogue in a row can be a block. You need to consider the possibility of each character responding after *every* line of the other character. Considering it doesn't mean you'll do it, but you're always looking to create every possible opportunity for the characters to express and reveal themselves, realizing that you're never going to find them all. And, always, going too far is good. The more you have to work with, the better. You can always cut back. Here's a dialogue sample:

"You saw it. I can't believe she did that. Here's the deal, she just learned her husband has terminal cancer."

She shakes her head.

"I don't get it. You don't trust me? Look, she tells me her husband is going to die. She starts to cry. She's falling apart. I don't know what to do. I'm not good at that kind of stuff. You know that. Then she says, 'I'm scared. Please hold me.' What could I do? I patted her shoulder and gave her a peck on the cheek to comfort her. Before I knew it, she threw her arms around my neck and kissed me. She had me locked in an embrace. It happened so fast. Plus I was freaking out about the whole thing myself. How could you reject someone at a time like that? I feel awful that you have to humiliate yourself like this. I hope you don't believe I'm spending all my time fooling around with other women."

OK, there's something going on here, and we're getting some sense of the characters. I've seen dialogue in print that didn't give us as much as this. But how much more of the characters could we get if each responded after the other's line? A good exercise for you to do *right now,* before looking at the expanded version, would be to rewrite this little exchange and have each character respond after every line (sentence) of the other. This is a long chapter, and you haven't written for a while, so loosen up and give it a try.

Here's a rewritten version:

"You saw it. I can't believe she did that."

"She? What about you?"

"Here's the deal, she just learned her husband has terminal cancer."

She shakes her head.

"I don't get it. You don't trust me?"

"You get it. I don't trust you."

"Look, she tells me her husband is going to die. She starts to cry. She's falling apart. I don't know what to do. I'm not good at that kind of stuff. You know that."

"You seemed pretty good at it tonight."

"Then she says, 'I'm so scared. Please hold me.'"

"Good thing she didn't say, 'I'm so scared. Please screw me.'"

"I patted her shoulder and gave her a peck on the check to comfort her."

"That was no peck and it wasn't on the check. I haven't had a peck like that in months. Now I see why."

"Before I knew it, she threw her arms around my neck and kissed me. She had me locked in an embrace. It happened so fast. Plus I was freaked out about the whole thing myself."

"You needed comforting too."

"How could you reject someone at a time like that?"

"Rejecting or kissing? There was no in between?"

"I feel awful that you have to humiliate yourself like this."

"The humiliation is your doing."

"I hope you don't believe I'm spending all my time fooling around with other women."

"All your time? How about some or any?"

There's still a lot of direction in this version, but we're getting more of the characters, particularly the woman. We still aren't getting as much as we should, because we're not getting into the inner workings of her mind and heart. How to do that was covered in chapter 6 ("The Active Ingredient").

THE WHY TECHNIQUE

This could also be called the why-what-how technique. With this technique, you go through your story and ask *why?* of every single line. Now it won't make sense in some cases, so you just move on to the next line. Fiction is about finding answers, not raising questions. So, we're asking why in order to find answers. And we ask why of things that we would never question in normal society. So, if someone said, "Fred's depressed," we could ask, "What's wrong?" But if they then said, "His mother died," we wouldn't say, "Why does that depress him?" Not in reality, but in fiction we would ask—always.

In fiction, we're looking for the root cause, the deepest level of the experience, the most personal and specific reasons. We take nothing at face value. *Why* does his mother's death depress him? *How* is he experiencing it? *How* is it affecting him? *What* about her death, exactly, depresses him? If we're writing about grief, we want to get to the nature, the essence, of grief. What is it about grief that's painful, that's meaningful?

With Fred and his mother, he might be depressed because he loved her so much and will miss seeing her, miss talking to her, miss getting her advice and guidance. He might be frightened that he cannot survive without her guidance. Or he could be depressed because she disinherited him, leaving everything to the church two years ago when he was arrested for possession of cocaine and then she was just getting ready to leave everything to him again, but had not yet changed the will. He could be depressed because he'd failed to give her her medication and it killed her. Or maybe he was going to murder her and make it look like his rotten older brother did it, and now he has to find another way to destroy his brother.

And the depression might only be the visible reaction. He could be feeling guilt, anger, fear, sadness, and relief all at the same time. By running through your story and asking questions of every line and answering them, you will be creating a deeper, more dramatic story and a more complex set of characters.

OVERWRITE

When you go back and look at your work and you're not sure what to do with a section or a scene (or even if you are sure), run through it again, staying loose, writing anything and everything that come into your head as you do. In other words, **overwrite.** You're rarely going to be able to change or correct just one thing and nothing else. Trying to be that exact, to get it just right and no more, is a good way to get blocked. So, you need to give yourself enough to work with—to let enough out so you can see what you've got for this stretch. Remember, you make a mess first, then clean it up, make a mess again, and clean it up again, until you get where you want to go.

CUTTING

"Writing is rewriting" is the old writing rule. To that we need to add, **"Rewriting is cutting."** Cutting is one of your most important skills. Often, cutting alone will reveal what needs to be done. So, what is cutting? What do you do when you cut? And what exactly do you cut? What you do is go through your story and cut every word, every phrase, every sentence, every paragraph you can possibly do without. Now, I'm not talking about destroying it for all time. You're just marking it to see what you can do without if you have to, but saving it in case you need to put it back.

After you've cut paragraphs, then go on and cut every character and every scene you could do without. Then, cut time. Condense it. If your story takes two years, try to make it happen in two months, two weeks, or two days. Cutting is the best skill you can develop, because **cutting is not just cutting.** In order to cut, you have to (consciously or unconsciously) address every story issue there is. When you cut, you're deciding what belongs and what doesn't. Somewhere in you, you have a sense of what fits and what doesn't, what is relevant, what works. You don't have to know exactly what that is or why something doesn't fit, so long as you *feel it,* especially early on. The more craft you master, the more you'll *know why* something does or doesn't belong.

When you cut in this manner, what you end up with is *what works for you.* The material you relate to will stand out from the rest. And there will be gaps, gaps that will make it easier to see where you need to fill in. As when you focus a lens, sharpening the image, what's important to you pops out.

EXERCISE: TO CUT OR NOT TO CUT

OK, it's time to get active—to practice some cutting. Here's a quote from the first draft of one of the most famous writers of all time. See if you recognize it.

> To be painfully, torturously alive or not to be painfully, torturously, agonizingly alive—that my fretful friend, is the foul, wrenching, damnable question to be answered, here and now, for all God's good eternity.

Recognize it? Shakespeare. But doctored Shakespeare. It's Shakespeare that I've fixed up so you can practice cutting. The original Shakespeare is there, the right words in the right order. All you have to do is to cut until you pare it down and uncover the original. Just get rid of everything you can do without. Here's the full exercise:

> The quality of true mercy is not strained, nay not a drop, not a wit. Neither is it forced or pressured or driven. For it droppeth freely and softly as the gentle rain from Heaven above to settle tenderly upon the earth, this thirsty place beneath.

> How sharper and more piercing than a festered serpent's venomed tooth it is for a blameless, blemishless, doting parent to have a spiteful, spitful, thankless child next to thy own most tenderest of breasts.

> To be painfully, torturously alive or not to be painfully, torturously, agonizingly alive—that, my fretful friend, is the foul,

wrenching, damnable question to be answered, here and now, for all God's good eternity. Whether 'tis far far nobler for one, in the mind, to suffer unrelentingly the lashing slings and piercing arrows of this fickle, fiendish outrageous fortune, or take up strong, noble arms against a vicious sea of outrageous troubles. . . . To die, totally, completely, finally, to sleep the blessed snooze of the babe, to sleep—perchance to dream the wretched dream. Aye yie, frisky friend, there's the wrenching rub, the harshest, unkindest rub of all, the rub that soothes not, but beats and rends and tears asunder.

When you're done, check your version against the original Shakespeare on the next page.

> *The quality of mercy is not strained,*
> *It droppeth as the gentle rain from heaven*
> *Upon the place beneath.*
>
> *How sharper than a serpent's tooth it is*
> *To have a thankless child! . . . .*
>
> *To be, or not to be—that is the question.*
> *Whether 'tis nobler in the mind to suffer*
> *The slings and arrows of outrageous fortune,*
> *Or take arms against a sea of troubles. . . .*
> *. . . To die, to sleep. To sleep—per chance to dream.*
> *Aye, there's the rub.*

In chapter 5, on self-editing, I talked about doing the most yourself *before* seeking feedback from someone else. Again, it's important for your own development that you practice *all* the techniques in this chapter *before* you seek outside help. **Get the most out of yourself before you go to someone else.** That means you have to get through these techniques in a deliberate way and apply each one to your writing. If you do, you will solve your problems your way, the best way, and avoid the distraction and confusion that can result from seeking help too soon.

It's time to do some writing. I'm going to give you the same kind of exercises I did last time. If you want to continue what you did last time and go forward with it, then ignore these. They're always here for you to use.

EXERCISES

You now have two full stories to choose from. Here are the next parts of those:

FIRST FULL STORY, PART FIVE:

This is the infidelity story. Confrontation/scene. New things need to be hashed out. The betrayed character wants more answers and something more from the lover (realistic and unrealistic), wants to punish, etc. The scene follows the same form as all scenes: want, obstacle, action (worse at the end, finish in the mind of the character).

SECOND FULL STORY, PART TWO:

This is the late date story. The late partner appears. She makes a series of weak excuses about being late, which the other character deflects. After being nice in order to set her up, he launches his plan and tells her he's had enough and feels it would be best if they split up. To his shock, she agrees, saying that it's never going to work out, so they might as well cut their losses.

Here are two full-scene exercises:

Wedding day doubts. In the bedroom or waiting room with the bride or the groom, who is feeling uneasy and worried, full of doubts. Different people come in to help out (friends, father, mother, brother, sister, minister). The character asks each about their feelings on their wedding day, trying to get some help without coming right out and saying what the problem is. The advice given is off the mark, wrong, self-serving, shocking, maybe a bit helpful. This could be a complete story if the character struggles enough and makes up his or her mind to go ahead or back out at the end.

Dying and going to hell and meeting the devil.

Here are some three-word combinations:

- Dragon, fastidious, lawyer.
- Quarterback, dandelion, pirouette.
- Butler, truculent, buffoon.

Method

HOW TO. HOW NOT TO.

Method is the most wide-open part of this. No one can tell you how to approach your story. But they often do. Many writers think that their way is the only way. They find a way that solves their problems and think that it'll work for everyone. They espouse principles like:

- You must plan it out first. If you don't know the end, you won't know how to begin.
- Knowing the ending first takes all the fun and surprise out of writing.
- Don't go forward until you've gotten the beginning down.
- Write a first draft, straight through to the end, then come back and work on the beginning. (Even if you plan it, the ending is never what you expect. Changing the ending requires changing the beginning.)
- Never talk about your story, or you'll lose the energy and desire to write it.
- You must have a premise. Your story must fulfill that premise, or it will never be successful.

- Do all your research first.
- Write first, find out what you know and what you don't, then research.
- Know your characters before you start writing. Write full character biographies for your characters first.

Lots of advice and lots of contradiction. That's because what's right for one writer is wrong for another. So what's true? All of the above, depending on you and the story you're writing at the moment.

Planning: For some writers planning everything out first works great. It gives them a sense of direction and confidence that gets them writing. For others, who like the adventure, surprise, and discovery they get from *not* planning, planning is cramping, tiring, incapacitating. But it doesn't have to be all or none. Some stories lend themselves to planning, while others don't. Which is which is a matter of what feels right to you at the time. Even if you're not a planner, don't rule it out. There might be times when planning will work for you. And if you are a planner, don't rule out jumping in with no plan. You may plan parts of a story and not others. The only way to tell what's right for you or a particular story is to try it both ways. Respect your impulses and urges.

Some mystery writers say they need to know the end before they begin so that they can move the story to it. Elmore Leonard says that he doesn't know or want to know the ending. That's what he writes to find out—how it's going to end. If he knew the ending, he wouldn't bother. E. L. Doctorow says that, for him, writing a novel is like driving along a pitch-dark highway with only the center line visible a short distance ahead in his headlights. He only knows what he can see at the moment and has no idea where the road will take him. Ed McBain says he starts with a corpse or someone who is going to become a corpse. From then on he has to go on the same clues that the cops do. Probably, the nonplanners or plan-little writers are in a majority. No matter how much you plan, there's going to be plenty of surprises and discoveries. Neither method is better than the other. What's better is what works for you.

Often, if you believe something works, it will work, especially if it feels right. If it gives you a sense of confidence and keeps you writing, it's right.

Working the Beginning: Some writers (beginning writers especially) feel that getting the beginning right will make the rest easier. Maybe. It depends. It doesn't really solve any of the later problems *unless you feel it does*. If you feel strongly about it, if you believe in it, do it. But be careful that you don't hang yourself up on some preconceived idea about **how it's supposed to work.** There is no one right way. Often, you figure out the beginning by going forward and writing the middle or even the end. Again, what works for you is what's right. If you feel like doing it a certain way, try it. If it doesn't work, try something else, or try the opposite.

Get the First Draft Down to the End: This is good advice for writers who tend to get bogged down rewriting and rewriting. That's a danger for all of us, so it's probably a good idea to keep moving. If it works. The flip side is that while you're hot, you don't want to skim over things so fast that you don't get to the good stuff you've got in you for a particular part.

Never Talk About Your Story: Erskine Caldwell would never talk about what he was writing or was going to write. He said that if he did, once he told it, it was over—he would never write it. Many writers, however, get a lot out of discussing their ideas. It helps them formulate new ideas and sparks their interest even more.

You Must Write from a Premise: Some writers feel that knowing what their story is expressing in terms of its meaning, the point they're making, determines everything they do and makes everything more manageable. George Bernard Shaw was one of the great premise writers *(Pygmalion, Major Barbara)*. He always had a didactic point to make and even had his characters discuss the meaning of his story in the middle of the play.

Some writers say that you cannot write a successful or coherent story without knowing your premise. So what *is* a premise? It's a statement that tells you what the story is about. "Greed leads to destruction," is a premise. It's the point that your story (your characters' actions) proves.

One premise advocate says that even the writers who claim they write without a premise do fulfill a premise in their stories; therefore, they have an "unconscious" premise that's guiding their story. Well, if it's unconscious, then we don't need to concern ourselves with it.

However, this attitude that nothing works without a clear premise is based on a lack of understanding of what a full (want, obstacle, action, resolution) story does. *You cannot tell a full story without fulfilling a premise.* Once you set two strongly opposing forces against each other, your story will be making a statement about the nature of those forces and what happens when they collide. It will have meaning on that level whether you are aware of it or not. This kind of analysis belongs more to the realm of literature classes (meaning, theme, etc.) than to the realm of the writer. Premise is an irrelevant concern—unless it helps you write. It may be your thing, so it's worth a try. If it's not for you, forget it. Tell a full story (want, obstacle, action, resolution) and the rest takes care of itself.

Research First, Research Last: Lots of writers waste loads of time researching because they're reluctant to start writing. The longer they research, the longer they put off writing. They're looking for something in the research that will spark them to sit down and start writing. OK, if it works. But after a certain amount of time, you have to fish or cut bait. If your research is getting you revved up to start writing and as soon as you've done enough, you get rolling, OK. You may even be doing both (writing and researching) at the same time.

But often you think you need to know a lot more than you do. You may also be trying to make up for a lack of confidence by researching. What you know as a private citizen about the workings of the government, the police, big business, medicine, the stock market will be enough for you to start writing or even to finish your story. Remember, most of your readers aren't going to be experts. You know a lot about how the world works from the nightly news, books, movies, and your own life experience. One crime writer says he never researches first. He writes it the way it makes sense and how he imagines it would work, and then, once he's finished, he checks things out with the cops. He says he's always very close and has to change very little.

Character Histories and Biographies: Some writers feel you have to know all about your characters' backgrounds and lives *outside* the story (material that will never appear in the story) in order to create a convincing character and a believable story. They tell the rest of us that we need to write lengthy biographies about the character's education, siblings, parents, musical taste, what's in the character's clothes closet, medicine cabinet, refrigerator, etc.

If this helps you, OK. The problem is: 1. it's a lot of work, and 2. it *doesn't solve any of the story problems* you're going to face once you get down to it. The most revealing thing about a character is his actions, how he behaves when he's beset with a threatening problem. In a full story, your character emerges and develops automatically, because he must act in a meaningful, revealing way. He has no choice. *Develop-*

ing your character takes place automatically. Creating a story and developing character are not separate issues.

Tennessee Williams didn't think about where Stanley Kowalski went to school or how far he got or what kind of music he liked. Yet as soon as Stanley came on the scene and started behaving like Stanley, we knew. We knew he didn't listen to Mozart or love rare antique figurines. Character biographies are extra work, so do them only if they give you a feel for your characters that makes writing your story easier. If the idea appeals to you, that's enough reason to try it.

Two at a Time—or More: Some writers jump back and forth between two stories or even among three or more. If they're hot on one story, they stick with it until they cool off, then they jump to another one that attracts them.

It's always good to *follow your urges*. If you're struggling with chapter 2 and feeling, "I can't wait to get to the big confrontation scene in chapter five," go to chapter 5, and do it *now*. But be careful that you're not just trying to avoid facing a story problem. Even that's OK, since letting it alone for a while and coming back give you more perspective and also allow your subconscious to solve the problem for you. So, running away from trouble isn't necessarily bad if you go work elsewhere and then come back and deal with it later. "Gently but always," is the old writing rule.

Not Finishing: You can start many short pieces and not finish anything for quite a while before you have to worry. That happens a lot at the beginning. The important thing is to figure out as much as you can about the problem in story terms (want, obstacle, action, resolution, emotion, showing) before you leave one piece and go to another. Sooner or later, you will need to force your hand (gently) and start steering yourself toward writing a full story, taking each piece farther toward completion than the previous one, even if it's only by one paragraph.

This can be a problem especially for people who are in the habit of journaling (writing to themselves about whatever's in their minds or what's going on in their lives each day). Journaling can be an end in itself, a way of finding yourself each day. You will need to start shaping your journaling into story form, finding, emphasizing, or inventing the story elements (want, obstacle, action) in your journaling material. Again: little by little, until you get there.

We can say a lot about what a story is and how it works and what it has to fulfill in the end. But, how *you* do it, *your* personal creative process, is wide-open. It's up to you. If it works, if you're able to sit down and start writing when you want or need to, then that's right for you. Even if you have a way that works well, be open. Try different things, and always respect your emotions and urges.

EXERCISES

The infidelity ("Larry scene") thoughts. In chapter 6, you put the thoughts of the husband in. Now, play the part of the wife, and put her thoughts in. Give us her worries, fears, and hopes at every possible opportunity. Whenever she can possibly have a thought, put it in. Go overboard. You can cut back later.

FIRST FULL STORY, PART SIX:

The infidelity story. Depending on what the character wants and what needs to be hashed out, you will have one or more further confrontation scenes. A lot depends on how much trouble the character (and you, the author) dig up to deal with in the confrontation scenes. Eventually, you'll get to a final scene, in which a final resolution is reached. The character has to decide to stay or to split, to threaten, kill, commit suicide, fleece, blackmail—anything you want. Again, we end in the mind of the character at the end.

SECOND FULL STORY, PART THREE:

The late date story. In the last part, she agreed that breaking up was a good idea. Now, he's stunned and trying to recover, to take it back, to get her to reconsider, to salvage the relationship. But it's her turn to point out what's wrong with him, and she does a thorough and, to him, shocking job. (What she comes up with may well be new to you, the author. That means that you will need to work in some clues in the earlier parts when you rewrite so it's believable and so you're not springing something on the reader out of the blue.) He does what he can to get her to reconsider and stay, but she walks out.

Full scenes:

Getting mugged.

A criminal committing a crime—a bank robbery, a swindle, a murder. Do it from his or her point of view. Think of it as the portrait of a criminal.

Discovering your lover is a crook.

Here are some three-word combinations:

- Pizza, shark, waterbed.
- Dragon, rickshaw, bifocals.
- Anteater, income tax, cologne.

10

Under the Sun

UNIQUENESS. UNIVERSAL PLOTS.

"There's nothing new under the sun. Everything's been done before. All we do is tell the same story over and over." Ever heard this? If it's true, why bother? The reason to bother, even though it *has* all been done before, is that **it's never been done your way.** You won't be telling someone else's story, because you can only tell your own—your version of the way the world works. Your point of view is fresh and unique. It's your creative DNA. It comes from you and your experience. No one else has that to work from but you.

I don't mean you should write autobiographically. It's fine if you do, but no matter how or what you write, it's you. Your science fiction is you. Your fairy tale is you. Your superhero, private eye, four-headed monster are you. Uniqueness, difference, is your birthright. No two people are identical. But that doesn't mean you *feel* different. And you don't have to. Unless something about you or your behavior draws attention or rubs people the wrong way, you probably feel overall that you're a lot like everybody else.

If you don't feel different or unique, how do you make your writing original and fresh? You do that by being *specific,* getting it down exactly as you see it, by *showing*. Showing is the basic writing technique we went over a number of times. Here, as always, the answer to this *conceptual* problem (difference, originality, freshness) is a concrete technical/craft solution. If you get it down as you see it, as you imagine it, it will be different, fresh, one of a kind, unlike anyone else's.

Along the same lines, you may have heard that there are only so many plots in the world. If so, how many? Three, 6, 12, 20? Well, there's a book that's been around for a long time that's called *The Thirty-Six Dramatic Situations*. The author claims that he's covered all the basic plots with 36. Another book, called *Twenty Master Plots*, presents 20, but doesn't claim that's all there are. Aristotle, who's considered to be the grandfather of everything (if you say, "Aristotle says," no one's going to argue with you), claimed there were 6. Here are Aristotle's: 1. Man against man. 2. Man against society. 3. Man against the gods. 4. Man against himself. 5. Man against nature. 6. Man against machine.

So, we have 36, 20, or 6, depending on whom you believe. Having gotten this far in the course, what do you imagine I'm going to say? Here's a clue. When Einstein died, he was working on the *unified field theory*. He was searching for the one principle that explained how everything in the universe worked. Einstein didn't find it. But I'm happy to tell you that I 've found the unified field theory of fiction. The single, universal plot. It's the single plot they're all talking about, whether they give you 36 or 20 or 6.

The universal plot is a character's struggle to overcome a threatening problem—within himself, without, or both. Every one of Aristotle's plots follows this form. He changes the subject, the problem, what the character is struggling against, but not the plot itself. Whether the character is struggling against a man, society, the gods, himself, nature, or machine doesn't alter the plot in any way. It's still **someone against someone or something—always.** Life is a series of struggles. We're born. We have to learn to walk, talk, separate from our mother, get along with others, develop a sexual identity, get an education, find a mate and an occupation, rear a family, manage old age, die. It's **want, obstacle, action, resolution** over and over and over— one struggle after another. It's the human condition, the universal plot. The only one. That's all you need. That's plenty.

In using this plot (these elements), you need to be aware that your story and your characters do not live in the concepts of want, obstacle, action, etc. In putting together your story, you're working with your character, his actions, his words, his emotions. The word *want,* for example, may not be in your head at all. You'll be in a different region of your mind. You will have a character acting, talking, thinking, feeling, struggling on the page and in your imagination.

Sooner or later, depending on how you work, you need to go back and ask, "Who wants what?" Doing that requires a shift from the warm, real, living experience on the page to a colder, more analytical and objective frame of mind. That, in itself, can be irritating. Plus, this is new to you, so you may not be sure exactly what *want* is. You may remember there is *false* want as well as *dramatic* want. One works, and one doesn't, but you may not be sure of the difference. So, you may have to go back and review. All of this pulls you away from your story and may feel so irritating or intimidating that you won't bother.

Uncomfortable as it may be, **you must do it.** Step-by-step, check every scene and your overall story for want, obstacle, action, resolution, and emotion. At first, you won't be sure. It'll be hard to tell if you have dramatic want or not, but with practice it gets easier and easier, and eventually you will do it automatically without having to make a special effort. Whatever you do, don't blame yourself or start thinking that you don't have what it takes, just because it's tricky. Just remember this is the learning cycle. The learning cycle is: You start at *uncon-*

scious ineptitude. You don't know what you don't know. Then as you develop, you progress to *conscious ineptitude.* You know what you don't know—what you need to work on. Next is *conscious mastery.* You can do it, but you have to pay a lot of attention and it's not natural. Last is *unconscious mastery.* It happens in you as reflex and doesn't require conscious thought or control.

A good way to practice is to analyze someone else's story for these elements. A good novel to do this on is *Lonesome Dove* by Larry Mc-Murtry. *This Boy's Life* by Tobias Wolfe and *Gone With the Wind* are also excellent for this purpose. Some short stories that are excellent for this are "The Short Happy Life of Francis Macomber" by Ernest Hemingway, and "The Outstation" and "Macintosh," both by Somer-set Maugham. The stories of Flannery O'Connor are also excellent. Go over a few pages a day doing this if you have time. Eventually you'll close the gap between seeing these elements in other people's work and seeing them in your own.

The thing to remember is that, for a while and off and on even after you've mastered it, it's going to feel uncomfortable or irritating to switch from the creative flow of your mind into the analytical and conceptual frame of mind. That's fine. It's no reflection on you. Don't let it sidetrack you. Go there, and do it. If you master these few elements, if you can put a story together in this way, no matter what other mistakes you make, you will succeed.

Speaking of doing it, it's time to put something on the page again. If you have something you want to go back to from previous writing, do that. If you're doing the full-story exercise, you'll be doing the next part.

EXERCISES

Thought exercise (Larry scene): You still have to put the thoughts in for one more character in the infidelity scene. You did the wife in the last chapter. This time, go through and play the part of Larry, putting in his thoughts and emotions (worries, fears, hopes). Remember, he has no idea what's going on in the other character's mind.

SECOND FULL STORY, PART FOUR:

This is the resolution of the late date story. He's alone licking his wounds, trying to make sense of what happened and to come to some understanding of it. "Licking his wounds" means he's in pain. You need to ask yourself exactly what bothers him about losing her. What are his worries, doubts, regrets? He might find his way to some hope, eventually. He needs to see that he's the problem or consider that he might be. This is the moment of truth (longer than a moment), where either he has a painful realization that he's as screwy or screwier than she is, *or* he realizes it, but rationalizes his way out of it (distorting things even worse) by blaming it on her the way he has been doing all along. If he's back to blaming her at the end, it's a circular story in which he changes by becoming even more entrenched (even worse) at the end as a result of struggling with the dilemma. So, we know more about him than he does. We see his folly, but he can't stand to see it. Now, it's also possible to write it with a similar but different ending in which he has a true realization and feels, *Good Lord, what a fool I am*, as he sits alone staring into his drink.

Here are some scene exercises:

A husband and wife are doing dishes together and talking about winning the lottery. "If we won a million, we could retire," one says. "No, you have to pay taxes, and sometimes they give it to you over twenty years—fifty thousand a year." "Oh, then one of us could quit work." They go on to get into a serious and hurtful argument about which one could retire, which one deserves it more, etc. Remember, what you, the author, are up to, at all times, is revealing the characters and the nature of their relationship. That's what you need to do in this scene. If you do it well and bring it to a resolution (each discovers something awful or painful about how the other feels or about love/life; they both feel undervalued by the other; etc.), it could pass as a full story.

Taking a girlfriend or boyfriend to meet parents when he or she is the wrong class, religion, race, ethnic background, body type, looks. A boyfriend, for example, could be a pencil-necked geek and the father a macho jock.

Behind the scenes at a restaurant.

11

Point of View

The term *point of view* can mean several things. There are **person point of view, character point of view,** and **narrator point of view.**

Person point of view refers to which person (not which character) you use to tell the story. (First person = *I*. Second person = *you*. Third person = *he/she*.) You can tell a story from a *single character's* point of view (experience), but you can tell it in *different persons*. **First person** point of view uses **"I,"** and the **"I"** is a living character telling you the story. When you use first person, the character is automatically the narrator, a first person narrator. (More about narrators later.) "When **I** opened the package, **I** found a strange little statue." The **"I"** character is telling the story. He's the character/narrator.

Third person point of view uses **"he"** or **"she."** The characters are living out the story before your eyes, but they are not telling it, as with first person. "When **she (he)** opened the package, **she (he)** found a strange little statue." On the simplest level, person is merely a mechanical difference. First person can be changed to third, as in the above example.

Second person point of view uses **"you."** "When **you** opened the package, **you** found a strange little statue." One idea is that using **"you"** makes readers feel more a part of the experience since you're telling them that they're doing it by saying **"you."** It can also work in the opposite way by making readers feel that the author is presumptuous and intrusive in telling them what they're doing and feeling. So, it's risky for that reason, but if it feels right and it gets you going, it's worth a try. You can always change it to another person later.

First and third persons are used the most. So, what's the difference? For the writer, and for some readers, using **"I"** provides a feeling of closer contact with the character. For the writer, that's good, *if it's true*. If you feel a stronger sense of the character because you are actually more in touch with him or her, and *if it comes out on the page*, that's good. The downside is that the **"I"** may make you feel that you're more in touch when you're not. Since you naturally feel closer to this **"I,"** you may develop *a false sense of connection with the character*. Using first person makes no real difference in terms of what you must do to bring your characters to life and make your story move. However, an imagined difference or a felt difference should be respected if it works, if it makes writing easier. Just be sure that you are working your craft—*want, obstacle, action*—regardless of point of view or anything else.

Another issue is that first person allows you to write about the unreliability of the narrator in a way that you couldn't otherwise. First person *can* be objective, which means what the narrator is telling us is fact and not distorted by his perception or his telling of it. As long as the issue isn't raised by the way the character is presenting the story, the "facts," we consider him to be objective, and it's called **first person objective.**

Years ago, we were taught to never use first person unless we were also writing about the subjectivity and unreliability of the narrator. A famous story was used as the prime example of this strategy—Ring

Lardner's "Haircut." In it, the narrator is telling a story about a guy he (the narrator) thinks is a cut-up, a great prankster, and one hell of a lot of fun, and he's letting us know how much he liked the guy. In the story he tells, the prankster does a lot of sadistic, vicious things to people. He's so cruel that someone finally kills him "accidentally." The narrator is saddened by the loss of this "fun" guy in town. So, two stories are being told at once—one about the bastard and another about how the narrator interprets/distorts things. Here is some first person narration:

> My roommate is such a stingy bitch. She won't share anything. She went nuts, screaming and yelling, just because I wore her best dress on a date I had with this great guy. I didn't ask her because she wasn't home and this fantastic guy had just asked me out. So, I wore her dress, which I happen to look a lot better in than she ever could. Me and my date got really drunk and he wanted to go skinny-dipping. How could I refuse? So her stupid dress got a little wet and muddy and ripped, and now she's freaking out because she thinks it's ruined and can't be cleaned. Plus, she wants me to move out. All because of one lousy dress—and a couple of other things she's trying to blame on me. Doesn't she know people are more important than things? What a bitch!

In this paragraph, we know there's a lot more going on than the character is aware of. When the **"I"** character is being revealed by *the way* she's telling/distorting the story, it's called **first person subjective.**

Third person point of view uses **"he"** or **"she."** Because the character is not telling the story, and he can't be distorting the facts of the story as they are presented, it's called **third person objective.** That doesn't mean the character can't misinterpret or distort things, but because the story is laid out by the author and we have the same objective experience as the character, we know what the facts of the situation are. The character may misinterpret or distort events in his thoughts or when he relates things to someone else (dialogue), but since he is not presenting the experience in the first place, we don't have to read between the lines to figure out what really happened. It's easy to see if he's twisting things or not.

The facts aren't always so clear in first person, because with first person the **"I"** character has control over *what* is presented and *how* it's presented. The **"I"** is both participant *and* narrator—coach and player.

That's point of view as it concerns person *(I, you, he/she)*. The next consideration is **character point of view.** That means which character we inhabit. Whose eyes and mind are we experiencing the story through? In first person, we're in the mind of the narrator. In third person, we can be in the minds of a number of different characters. Almost always, the point of view is set in **the character with the biggest problem, the character with the most to lose,** because that's where **the biggest experience** is—the most intense, most exciting, most moving experience. We want to be there, on the spot, in his or her mind and flesh, experiencing it firsthand. If someone is setting out to climb Mount Everest, would you rather stay with the guy who observes from the ground and talks to the climber on the radio, or go with the guy who makes the climb? We automatically gravitate to *the person with the biggest problem,* because we know that will give us the *biggest experience.*

But what about telling a story from the **point of view of a minor character?** It can be done, but there are trade-offs—problems to be overcome, as always. *Moby-Dick* and *The Great Gatsby* are both told from the point of view of minor characters. When that method is used, the minor character must have an investment in the outcome of the story, and he must be struggling with problems of his own that he brings into the mix. Plus, he must be present, on the spot, for all the big scenes/struggles of the major character. Often his fate is closely linked to that of the main character. In *Moby-Dick*, Ishmael's (the narrator's) fate is linked directly to that of Ahab and the outcome of the whale hunt. In *The Great Gatsby*, the narrator, Nick, is having a meaningful, painful, and disillusioning experience.

Since we're in Nick's point of view, we don't get into Gatsby's mind. That means the author, Fitzgerald, had to find a way to get what's inside Gatsby's mind and heart out into the open. Fitzgerald does it in two ways: *First,* by making Gatsby a mysterious character who has a lot of notoriety and who is the subject of much gossip— gossip that Nick overhears and reports. *Second,* Gatsby feels compelled to tell Nick all about himself, his origins, his past with Daisy, his deep feelings for her, etc. Remember that neither of those two things (the rumors and Gatsby's confiding) just happened. They feel totally natural because the writing is so strong. But nothing happens in fiction unless *the author makes it happen.* Fitzgerald had to invent those devices to reveal Gatsby; otherwise, the reader would have no idea what was going on inside of him. In the case of *Moby-Dick*, Ahab is spouting off all over the place, so we know what's going on inside him.

Why choose a minor-character point of view? It's often chosen when the major character dies in the end and the author wants the story to go on after the death, as in both *Moby-Dick* and *The Great Gatsby.* Sometimes you may not feel up to tackling a wild character like Ahab and feel more comfortable portraying him from the outside as someone close to him would see him. Just remember, no matter what point of view you choose, you still must give us (reveal) enough of the main character to make him real.

You might be wondering about switching around from one character's point of view (mind) to another. That's called **multiple points of view.** A single point of view tends to be the strongest and most intense since we only have one point of view, one mind, in life. We settle into a single character and stay there without expecting to jump around into anyone else's head. If the writer does jump around, and the points of view are not handled skillfully, it's jarring and distracting.

But many great books have been written with multiple points of view. Flawless examples are *Streets of Laredo* and *Lonesome Dove,* both by Larry McMurtry. The point of view moves from character to character so naturally that you often don't notice. That's because of two things: *first,* you stay in a single character's point of view for a fair amount of time, and *second,* you switch from a *dramatic state of mind* in one character to an *equally dramatic* state of mind in another. Often the two different states of mind (characters) are wrestling with the same issue from a different angle. For example, you might have something like this:

> The wind lifted the little man's hat off his head, and he raced after it as it tumbled down the road. He wished to God he'd never come to this desolate place, leaving his wife home in New York City, doing heaven only knows what in his absence. He'd never trusted her, and now he had to come miles away or lose his job, to come to this hellhole to try and get this little bowlegged cowboy to help them catch the bandits.

Then in the next paragraph:

> The marshal stood on the porch, watching the man chase his hat, wondering what kind of a damn fool didn't have the good

sense to hang onto his hat and if this was the kind of person he wanted to do business with. He couldn't handle his own hat. What else was he going to lose track of and at what cost?

The one thing you don't want to do is to jump around for no reason. For example, if your main character gives his keys to a valet to park his car, you wouldn't go into the valet's mind while he thinks, "This guy sure looks like a hotshot. I wonder how much dough he pulls down a year," and then never use that character again. Also, you would never use another character to do your job; for example, you would never portray one character's nervousness by jumping into a bystander's mind and having him think, "That guy sure looks nervous. Wonder what's eating him."

The best approach is to learn to tell a strong story while staying in a *single point of view* in order to master the kind of skill you need in order to be able to switch points of view effectively. If you can't do a single point of view well, you can't do multiple points of view well either.

This switching of point of view is often called **omniscient point of view** or **omniscient narrator.** Here "omniscient" refers to knowing what's in everybody's mind. I like to distinguish between simple *multiple viewpoints* (switching point of view, but not expressing a knowledge beyond what's happening at the moment) and an **omniscient narrator** who comments, in a separate voice, on what's going on and anything else he or she wants to bring in (philosophy, interpretation, nudging the reader, etc.). The omniscient narrator knows everything about what's happening and what's going to happen and how it relates to the greater scheme of things, and he lets us know it by addressing us directly and telling us about it.

A modern example is *The French Lieutenant's Woman* by John Fowles. An early example is *Tom Jones* by Henry Fielding (one of the first great novels in the English language). Scott Fitzgerald's works provide other good examples. He often makes comments to the reader in otherwise third-person objective stories and novels. When done badly, this approach is called *author intrusion*. When done well, it's called *omniscient narrator*. If it appeals to you, do it. It takes a lot of practice to do well. Your comments have to be so clever, astute, penetrating that they do not distract the reader from the illusion you must create to make your story believable. Fitzgerald often made sparkling little comments that were nuggets of insight and well worth taking time out for.

An example of a more broadly omniscient narrator could be the following statement (paraphrased from *The French Lieutenant's Woman*), inserted after a man has just shown a great attachment to his mother. "Now, remember, this was fifty years before Sigmund Freud. It was a time when a man could show deep devoted and obsessive love for his mother and no one would question it." Here the narrator is not only addressing the reader but also referring to events that won't take place for fifty years and that will never even be a part of this story. That takes guts. But he pulls it off with great charm that adds another dimension to the novel. It's a tricky game. As always, the question you must ask is, Are you gaining more than you're losing when you do it?

A **nonparticipating narrator** is one who rarely carries his weight and is often in the way. He's part of the story but is used as nothing more than the teller of the story. He's an observer, and that's all—a bystander with nothing to gain or lose. This approach used to be fashionable, and some great stories have been told this way, but these narrators often seem heavy-handed and artificial—characters whose shoulders you have to peek over to see the story.

Another issue is **tense.** Present tense is being used more and more. "When she opens the package, she finds a strange little statue." Some people feel present tense makes the experience more immediate, more present. The only thing that makes your story and your character present and immediate is story craft—your skill. Tense cannot make up for weak storytelling, nor can it hurt strong storytelling. If the story and characters are alive, the reader quickly becomes oblivious to tense. The tense fades to the background as the characters come forward and take over. Present tense is being used a lot today, so it's your choice.

So, we have person point of view, character point of view, narrator point of view, and tense. It's not so important how we label any of these. What's important is that you have an idea how these devices work and realize that you do not have to use any of them exclusively. You might find ways of mixing and blending. If it feels right, do it. If it wants to happen, let it.

EXERCISES

A child wanting her rejecting, abusive mother to love her. "If you loved me," the mother tells the little girl/boy, "I would be happy. I'm not happy, so you don't love me." The child does everything that she or he can think of to please the mother—gets good grades, cleans the house, takes care of the mother—but it never works. The child feels that if she loved the mother enough, her mother would treat her better. The child and the father have a good relationship, and the mother is envious and tries to wreck it.

A man (or woman) goes to the doctor for a physical and gets a clean bill of health. He begins wondering what would've happened if he had terminal cancer. The character goes home and tells his family that he's going to die soon. He wants to see how upset his family will be and how important he is. He may not be totally conscious of his reasons when he does it. He will find out painful things about his family and himself.

A character discovering one of his or her parents is gay.

12

The Ticking Clock

FITTING IT IN

Someday you're going to write. Someday? Which day? When you're suddenly faced with a few free hours on a weekend, when the work levels off on your job, when you get promoted and have less pressure, when you go on vacation, when you retire? How much free time do you need before you start? How long should you wait? Will you know when the time is right, and will you know what to do when it comes? Well, I can tell you, do not wait until your life opens up and you're faced with starting cold with no discipline or writing skills. The longer you wait, the harder it's going to be to start, and the less chance you'll have of succeeding if you do start.

So, you should (and *can*) start now. The promise of this course is that I can show you how to write a novel, screenplay, or stage play without disrupting your lifestyle or sacrificing your sanity—and that it will be possible and *relatively* painless.

In this chapter the techniques are tailored to helping you overcome the particular difficulties you face in making writing a part of your daily life. If you're serious about writing, you can (and *should*) start now. If you do, when your life opens up (if it ever does), you'll be ready and able. But what if it never opens up? Well, you don't need to wait around for such an opportunity. This system makes it possible for you to do it now.

You have a full-time job, a wife, kids, extended-family obligations, and maybe lots more. Where are you going to find the time? Even if your life isn't that loaded down, even if you do have the time, but you're not getting anything done, how do you manage your time (and yourself) and make something happen? Where do you start?

Well, first, I don't believe you have *no (zero)* time. With this method, you have to find a tiny bit of time. How tiny? How about 5 minutes—5 minutes a day? Think you can find that much? You can always sneak away to the washroom and lock yourself in a stall to steal 5 minutes. OK, let's say that you're willing to try it—**the 5-minute method.** It's not much time. Most of us, no matter how busy we are, can take time out for 5 minutes once a day.

What can happen in 5 minutes? Well, has anything of great importance ever happened to you in that amount of time? Ever make a discovery or have an inspiration? How long did it take? Einstein said that all of his great ideas *just came to him*. He was a genius, so your ideas may not be as great as his, but the process that gets you there is the same. Great ideas often occur in a flash. A 5-minute inspiration would be very, very long—and rare. What can happen in 5 minutes? Plenty—*if* you know how to use them. And you will, because that's what this technique is all about.

It's not just the 5 minutes themselves that are important. The effects of these sessions **reach beyond the actual time you put in.** So, in a sense, the 5 minutes add up to more than 5 minutes, especially when you consider the results. Also, it's the first step in preparing yourself to write a novel when the time comes, which is sooner than you think, as you'll see when we get to the rest of the technique.

But remember you can't afford to be casual about these 5 little minutes a day. Just because the time is only 5 minutes doesn't mean it's not crucial. It's the key to making everything work—your first important step forward.

Of all the methods I've devised to get people started and keep them going, this 5-minute method has been the most successful. It's a daily fix that keeps you connected to your writing. OK, but what are you going to do in those 5 minutes? Not much, at first. The first thing is to simply get the *feel* of taking these 5 minutes out, get used to the routine, get comfortable in this little piece of time away from everything else you do each day. So, you don't do anything more than tell yourself, "OK, this is the time I'm going to use to work on my writing once I get used to being here on a regular basis."

It's a relaxed, meditative state of mind that you're getting into. For our purposes, this meditative state is just awareness of yourself and where you're at, awareness of being here in this place for this time. That's all. So, at first, you go there and do *nothing*—you put in your time, and that's it. No matter how foolish or ineffective it seems or makes you feel, **do it.**

This meditative state is the place where everything begins. And later, once you're into using this time to get something done, whenever you feel too pressured or strained or under the gun to *do,* to accomplish, anything, you return to this state, you fall back to doing nothing, to regain your balance.

Now, some people have trouble relaxing, doing nothing, wasting time, not going anywhere. I know because I'm one of those people. As soon as my foot hits the floor in the morning, the pressure is on to move, to do, to accomplish, to get something done, to make something important happen, etc. I've learned to let up, but it's something I have to look out for. And that kind of pressure is a major obstacle to doing anything creative, since there are so much mess and waste that are a natural and *good* part of the creative process.

If you're the type that pressures yourself in this way, it helps to first realize that maybe this old puritanical ethic (an idle mind is the devil's workshop, etc.) is excessive or even nutty. It certainly is in my case. I once sat down to try meditating for 5 minutes and nearly jumped out of my skin because, in my world, you were never supposed to be doing nothing, and if you caught yourself doing nothing, you damned well better not be enjoying it. (This is all very Western. The Eastern cultures have a tradition of meditation, of letting go of the mind, of letting it settle down, to achieve an inner state of emptiness and relaxation that brings on insight and enlightenment. Now, I'm not talking about religion or spirituality, but simply a way to reach a deeper level of your mind.) So, if the Puritan is in you, it usually helps to be aware of it and consciously tell yourself it's OK to just sit.

Also, relaxing your body in a conscious way is a good way of relaxing your mind. (The mind, if left alone, will relax and clear itself. That's not only meditation, but part of what's called the *relaxation response*, which is well documented in Western science.) I want to leave no stone unturned in all of this, so I'm even going to give you a method for relaxing your body.

Start by taking a deep breath. As you let it out, let your body go. Keep your breathing relaxed. As you go on, concentrate on what you're relaxing, get a sensation of it, and then let go of it. Now, relax your face. Your scalp. (Sounds wacky, I know. Do it anyway.) Your ears. Relax your eyes and all the muscles around and behind your eyes. Then one at a time, relax your mouth, tongue, neck, shoulders, arms, hands, fingers, chest, stomach, back, pelvis, legs, feet, toes. Take another deep breath and exhale, letting everything go all at once. This helps a lot to get me started, and I'm a pretty tense guy. Once you've done it a few times, you can do the whole thing in thirty seconds.

This whole relaxing, letting go, *do nothing* approach should assure that you will do your five minutes, that you will put in your time, because you can never use the excuse that you're not up to doing it, that you don't feel you can accomplish anything, that you're not in the mood, or that you can't handle it today, etc., since **the only thing you have to accomplish when you don't feel up to it is to do nothing,** and you can't claim that you're incapable of doing nothing, can you? Well, even if you can, don't let yourself get away with it. The important thing is that you go there, **put in your time,** do your five minutes, each and every day—no matter what. No excuses, no time off.

Now, there are exceptions to all of this. Some people find that trying to relax in this way only makes them more tense. If you're that kind of person, don't do it. Also, some people *like* to work from tension. There's good stress as well as bad stress. And you don't have to do it the same way every time. One time, you might feel the need to settle yourself down and relax first. Another time, you might be charged up and ready to go as soon as you sit down.

FIVE FOR THIRTY

The other critical part of this method is that you must commit to following it for **30 days straight** before you evaluate or reconsider it or debate with yourself about the value of it. Since it takes a while to get used to and since the goal is to accumulate momentum, the only time you'll be able to see the results and possibilities is after you've done 30 days. So you must make a *nonnegotiable* contract with yourself to do them. Just do them. Thirty days. Keep your mouth shut. Don't evaluate. Don't discuss it. Keep a record. Then, after 30 days, look back and see what you've accomplished. You'll be surprised at how much you've done and how much you're in the swing of the whole thing.

The 5 minutes a day will in themselves help you to make progress, but they will also keep your imagination stirred up, start things moving in the deeper levels of your mind and keep them moving, so when you do get more time, you'll be ready to go.

Deeper levels of your mind? What does that mean? The subconscious—the place where most of your mind and your imagination lives (or hides out) when you're not using them. No one has the final answers to how the mind works, but it's easy to see how it works for our purposes. I'm sure that you've had trouble trying to remember something, racked your brain, then finally given up, only to have it jump into your head hours later when you're doing some totally unrelated activity. That's the subconscious. Ask, and you will receive. Believe it or not, you can learn to use the subconscious and depend on it to help you write—**even when you're doing something else.**

Now, that's pretty far-out, and I don't want to give you the impression that you're going to write an entire novel subconsciously. But your subconscious is your best friend in all of this. It keeps things warm, primed, and ready to go when the time comes. But you must make daily contact with it in order to keep it focused and working.

How much can your mind do, on its own, without your conscious direction? Well, we know it can retrieve a forgotten name. How much actual work it does varies with the person, but it can do a significant amount for everyone. After you get into this 5-minute routine, you'll often find ideas and solutions waiting for you when you go there. That's because **your subconscious doesn't stop just because you do.** It goes on for some time after you leave. How long? Who knows? No one knows the mind that well, but you'll often find chunks of your story (character, scene, plot) popping up the moment you turn your attention to it.

The most extreme example of this is the famous poet John Milton *(Paradise Lost),* who had a photographic memory. He'd so internalized the process of creating poetry that he dreamt poetry written on a page, remembered it when he woke up, and then copied it down. His subconscious was serving up completed poetry. Consciously, he was totally absent.

Milton is the extreme. If you had that kind of brilliance, you'd know it by now. But, in principle, that's how the mind works in all of us. And it's the steady, regular, *daily* practice that makes it happen. When you internalize the craft, more and more ideas pop out of you fully formed, without your having to bang away at yourself all the time. That's when it gets a lot easier and a lot more fulfilling.

Unfortunately, many writers quit long before they master the craft and experience this kind of excitement. And they quit not because they lack ability, but because they *believe* they lack ability and blame themselves for the inevitable troubles *every writer* has to overcome. So, sticking with it until you master the process, until it becomes part of you, is the key. And the first step is to write or make contact with your writing for 5 minutes every day, 7 days a week, 365 days a year. No days off. No 5-minute vacations.

One caution: easy as these 5-minute periods seem, you must plan ahead for them. If you have a busy schedule, you can't count on remembering, in the midst of the flurry, to do your 5 minutes. If you have the kind of life that allows for 5 minutes and little more, your chances of thinking of it during the day are slim. If you just leave it to chance, you may find yourself in bed at night ready to drop off, realizing that you didn't do your 5 minutes. By then it's too late and too difficult to try to do it. **You must take steps ahead of time to get it done.**

Even though it's just 5 minutes, you have to plan ahead for how you're going to work it in. These basic 5 minutes a day are so important that, at the risk of going overboard, I'm even going to give you some tricks to ensure you remember to do them. Here they are: Put a note on your dashboard, and do 5 minutes before you take off in the morning. If you take the bus or train, wrap a note around your pass or ket or your money so that as you get on the train, you're reminded to do 5 minutes on the train. Put a note on your desk if you want to do them first thing at work. A trick I use when I need to remember something important is to write it on a three-by-five card. OK, but where do I put the card so it'll remind me? I crumple it up into a wad and put it in my pants pocket with my keys and change. (A flat card is too smooth and easy to miss. I know. I've tried it.) That way, I run into this crumpled, out-of-place lump several times during the day. A whole sheet of paper crumpled in your pocket is even bigger and might be the size wad you need. Wacky as it seems, this is the kind of trivia you have to attend to, and this is the kind of determination you have to have. One writer I know puts his watch on backwards to remind himself to do his 5 minutes. (If you're worried about remembering why your watch is on backwards, put a note in your pocket that tells you why your watch is backwards.) Putting messages on your own voice-mail is another method.

So, once you remember and take the time out, the first step is to settle in and get comfortable with your daily 5-minute sessions. Once you've done that, you take the next step, which is to approach the issue of a story. If you're up to it or in the mood, you can get into this right away, in your very first 5 minutes. But don't rush it.

Now I don't know what stage you'll be at when you begin the 5 minutes. Whether you've written a lot or never written doesn't matter. If you're starting cold and have no story or no idea what to do, that's where you start. If you have something in mind, you work with that. Wherever you are is fine.

You begin by simply thinking about what you might like to write about. Mull it over—no pressure, no straining to accomplish anything. Explore whatever comes into your head. You may not even be able to stay on the topic. Your mind may wander. You may not be able to keep from thinking about what you need to get back to as soon as you've done your 5 minutes. That's fine—all of it. Even if you only have a thought or two about writing and then drift away for the rest of the time, you've done a good job as long as you've spent 5 minutes away from your other activities. For a while, a few days to a week, go with this low-pressure, explore-whatever-comes-up approach. If it goes well and you're making progress, making something take shape, stick with that.

Sooner or later, you're going to lose your way or get stuck, or you may not be able to get started in the first place without more direction. That's when you take the next step, which is to use the **story work list.** That list is at the end of this chapter. It's there and not here, because I want to give you the rest of the time plan before you get into the story part.

The next part of this system is making bedtime contact. What that means is that, each night before you drop off to sleep, you visit your writing in your mind. Just take a moment to check in and go over where you're at and where you want to go. That's all. Often, you'll find ideas coming out. When you're closer to your subconscious, as you are when you're near sleep, you have more access to your imagination.

The problem with the bedtime contact is that, if you get a good idea, you'll be torn between getting up to write it down and just dropping off, hoping you'll remember in the morning. You may remember, or you may not, but don't count on remembering. If you have an idea that you really like and fail to record it and then can't remember it the next day, you may start agonizing over it. Whether it really was a great idea or not doesn't matter. Forgetting it can drive you nuts either way. Pretty silly maybe, but that's part of the game. The whole idea of this system is to minimize trouble—all trouble, whether real, imagined, serious, trivial.

One solution is to have pen and paper at your bedside. It's possible to write in the dark if you have to. I've done it many times. Another method is to have a pocket tape recorder at your bedside so you can record your ideas. You can do it in a whisper if you have to. Again, as with the 5-minute sessions, you're making contact and keeping things moving and churning in the deeper levels of your mind and imagination.

With this bedtime contact you have to take steps to remember, just as you do with the 5 minutes. So put a note on the alarm clock, your pillow, your pajamas, etc., so you'll be reminded when you get into bed.

All right, so your daily routine is a 5-minute session plus a visit before going to sleep. Now, there are all kinds of times when your mind is free or unoccupied. I said that all of Einstein's great ideas just came to him, but where do you think they came to him? When he was working hard in his study on the very thing the great ideas were related to? No. He said *all* of his great ideas came to him **in the shower** when he was *not* thinking of his work. The lesson is that big ideas come to you when least expected. Also, believe it or not, many great ideas have occurred **in the bathroom.** You spend a good deal of time in the bathroom each day. It's also a place where you can get into the habit of checking in with your writing. A lot of reading is done in the bathroom—why not writing?

Ideas, insights, breakthroughs, inspirations often pop up after you've worked on something and then gone on to some repetitive, monotonous, mindless activity—such as taking a shower or doing laundry or raking leaves. Walking, cleaning house, washing the car, weeding the garden are also repetitive, monotonous, mindless activities—times when ideas jump out of you, times when the pressure to produce is off, when your conscious mind lets up and makes room for your imagination and creativity to come to the surface. It's no accident. It's the way your mind works.

So, if it's possible, if your life permits, plan to do some drudgery right after your 5 minutes and after your writing once you get into it.

Or you can do it the other way around. That is, do your 5 minutes right before you have to do some drudgery. And even if you don't plan for it, whenever you find yourself involved in humdrum activity, check in with your writing to see what's there. First, let your mind go without any pressure to do anything, then gently steer it into whatever you're working on in your 5-minute sessions. And carry something to write with or a pocket recorder at all times.

So, now you're doing 5 minutes a day, checking in at bedtime, and opening the door from time to time to see what's there when you're doing drudgery.

This 5-minute plan adds up to 35 minutes a week. Once you get going, you'll be able to do 2 or 3 pages a week, or 100 to 150 pages a year. Pretty good for someone who has *no time to write*. Plus, it's not just a matter of pages, but the progress you'll be making in developing your skills and improving your writing by keeping your hand and your mind/imagination in on a daily basis. Two old writing rules are relevant here. The first is "Gently but always." The other is "Not a day without a line."

Now, these 5 minutes plus bedtime are the first level. If you find you have more time and the desire to do more during the 30 days, you can move on to the next level.

The next level is **5 minutes plus one half hour a week.** But what if even a half hour a week is too much? Sounds impossible, but let's assume it's too much to fit in your schedule. What are you going to do? You can't do two things at once. Right? Wrong!

You can ride the train or bus and write. That assumes you don't have to use that time for something else. Even if you do, you might be able to take 10 minutes out to write as much as you can. We're shooting for dashing off a full page *of anything* in that 10 minutes, but a paragraph or a few lines are fine. So, this level is **5 minutes a day and 10 minutes three times a week,** however you can fit them in. When you write 10 minutes, it replaces the 5 minutes. So, if you did 10 minutes a day for 3 days, you would do 5 minutes for the other 4 days. If you got rolling and did 10 minutes three times in 1 day, you'd do 5 minutes for the other 6 days. At that rate, you'd be doing 50 to 60 minutes a week (2 to 6 pages—100 to 300 pages a year).

The next level to shoot for would be **10 minutes every day.** That would be 70 minutes a week (2 to 7 pages—100 to 350 pages a year).

The main thing in all of this is to pick a plan you can manage, make a commitment, and **stick to it for 30 days,** before you reconsider or evaluate in any way. You will not be able to make an accurate judgment before that.

With this next level, I'm recommending finding as many 10-minute stretches of time as you can and shooting for a total of **20 minutes a day.** It can be 2 10-minute stretches or 1 20-minute stretch. If you can't do 2 10-minute stretches on a particular day, just do 1. If you *can't* do 1 10-minute session, **you must do your 5 minutes.** That's your lifeline, your fallback position, always. You must do one or the other *every* day. With 20 minutes a day, you'll be doing two hours and 20 minutes a week (5 to 14 pages—250 to 700 pages a year).

Whether it's 1 10-minute stint or 2 or more 10-minute stints if possible, how do you manage to do them? Well, how about doing 10 minutes before you leave for work? If it's hectic in your home, get up 10 minutes early, and do your 10 minutes in the car before you pull away. If your family won't leave you alone sitting in the car, drive away and pull off the road. If you're taking the train or bus, get up 10 minutes early, and do the 10 minutes at the station or on the train. Writing on the train or bus is another possibility. Then, at the end of the line, in the train station or the parking lot, do 10 minutes before going into the office. Sneak away and take a 10-minute break during the morning (in the bathroom stall if you have to). Try for 10 minutes at lunch. Then do 10 minutes before going home (in the car, at the station, etc). Or if your workplace clears out near the end of the day and you have time, do 10 minutes at your desk. Do 10 minutes as soon as you get home, or, if you must, before getting out of the car. Ten minutes after dinner (in the bathroom again, if need be). Ten minutes in the bathroom again right before a bath. Ten minutes before bed. If you walk, jog, or do Stairmaster or treadmill, that's a great time to connect. Take a pocket tape recorder in a waist pouch. If you're shy about telling people that you're writing, tell them that you're dictating business.

Now, chances are, you're not going to do all those 10-minute stints. But from those possibilities and others you can find on your own (start looking around to see where you have useable time), try to put together 20 minutes a day. Again, if your life is that busy, you're going to have to plan ahead and take steps to remind yourself to do them, or you won't do them. In that little time, once you've gotten into the swing of it, you can write one to three drafts of a novel in one year. (One page a day is 365 pages, one novel. Two pages a day is over 700 pages.) You're not doing the 5 minutes anymore, but if they have time, many people do them as a meditative connection to their writing that helps them keep their balance.

If you can't do anything more than 5 minutes a day, try to make a deal with your wife (family, whomever) for **20 minutes on Saturday** and **20 minutes on Sunday.** Sounds simple, but it may not be possible. It might be easy enough to get everyone to agree to it, but when the time comes for taking the 20 minutes, they may not be there. Even if it is possible, it's a new thing for you and for your family, so it'll take some getting used to. The best thing is to give them plenty of notice and keep them aware that you need to do it. So, with the weekend plan, you'd be doing 5 minutes 5 days (25 minutes) and 2 20-minute stints over the weekend, 65 minutes total (2 to 6 pages a week—100 to 300 pages a year).

Sounds easy? Maybe, but at first **it's going to hurt.** The stop-start routine might drive you nuts. You'll probably feel jangled or fragmented or disconnected. But don't despair, and don't let that stop you. You'll get past that. (Remember: 30 days before you reconsider.) If you keep at it, these little stints will become not only a natural part of your day, but one of the more satisfying things you do.

And it's not as if you've never done this before. Did you ever have a hot idea about a project you were working on or a problem you were trying to solve, an idea that you couldn't wait to get down on paper and that you took time out to put down, and it took 10 minutes or more, and it was great? So, getting something significant done in 10 minutes isn't unusual. This is the same thing—once you get the hang of it. Well, almost the same thing.

In the above example, the idea descended upon you. In your regular daily routine, you will be setting out without the surge of inspiration to carry you forward. Instead, you will often feel as if you're descending upon ideas, as if you're on an idea hunt, looking for something to pounce upon. But that's not the best way to think of it. What you're doing in all of this is simply setting the stage so that it can happen, opening the door, *letting* it happen as opposed to *making* it happen or *forcing* it to happen. Again, the relaxed approach is best. Accept whatever you get from yourself, and don't despair if it's not inspired. That's the attitude to cultivate, but I want to give you more to go on than attitude, since all of the story craft and technique applies to these short sessions.

These next issues are what you work on if you can't get started. They're also what you need to make your story move. You'll need to address them sooner or later—sooner if you're stuck or lost, later if your writing takes off. These elements may come to you in this order (you may think of a situation before you have a character), or they may come in some other order (you may have a character you like, but no situation). It doesn't matter where (or how) you start. Go over the list to get a feel for it, then find the element or elements (character, want, obstacle, action, etc.) that you need to start.

Again: If at any point you feel like writing, do it. You don't have to have everything (or anything) figured out to start. If the urge moves you, forget the list and go. When the momentum stops or when you get lost or blocked, come back to the list. Jumping around is fine. It's never an orderly process. Go where your urges take you. Come back to the list when you're stuck. Don't forget, **writers get stuck a lot.** So, in your 5-minute sessions, when nothing is happening or when you want to focus in on things, work from the following list. I'm going to give you a list with full explanations first, then some short versions that you can carry with you for when you do your 5 or 10 or 20 minutes.

First: Do you have an **idea?** If you don't and you can't think of one, go through the course and pick one that appeals to you. If you can't find any you like, take the one you dislike the least. If you still can't make up your mind, pick the third one you look at. Don't make it an ordeal. Whatever you pick will evolve into something that will work for you once you get into it. You may have a **situation** that interests you—a blind date, for example, or a cheating lover.

Second: Once you have an idea or a situation, you need to decide which **character** you want to write about in the situation. If you're not sure, pick one who **wants** something. If you want to write about a blind date, your **character wants** a lover. If you want to write about infidelity, your **character** is either the betrayed party and **wants** a loyal lover, revenge, etc., or your **character** is the cheating party and **wants** to have an affair without getting caught. So, **character + want** is what you need to find.

If you can't figure out what the character wants, ask: what *could* he want, what *might* he want, what *should* he want? until you figure something out. (**Remember:** You don't have to have quick answers. Mull it over, relax, explore what's in your head. Don't rush. Put in your 5 minutes, and don't worry about what you're getting done or not getting done.)

You may have a character in mind and know what that character wants. Or you may have a character who interests you, but you're not sure how to build a story around him. If that's the case, take the character trait you're interested in and frustrate/threaten it. That's **want + obstacle,** and they equal **conflict,** which is where a story starts. If your character is stingy, put him in a situation where he must be generous, where he must give up some wealth **(want)** or suffer a serious loss (his job, his family, his reputation, his lover, etc.). So his **want** is to protect his wealth. The **obstacle** is donate or suffer. **Want + Obstacle = Conflict.**

You can do this with any character trait. If you want to write about a compulsive neat freak, throw him in with a wild slob, and you have *The Odd Couple.* If you want to see an example of a serious, disastrous odd couple, read Somerset Maugham's short story "The Outstation." This setup was here long before Neil Simon used it with Felix and Oscar. People getting under each other's skin, rubbing each other the wrong way, for personal/temperamental reasons, and going to war over it is nothing new. It's also a story that can be told over and over. There's always room for one more. For you to tell it *your* way.

Third: Once you have the conflict established, the next step is **action.** What's the character going to do? If you have a true (dramatic) conflict, the obstacle is breathing down the neck of the character, and he must **act** to save himself. It's time for him to try to impress his blind date, regain his lover's loyalty (infidelity), or protect his wealth and reputation. He must be taking **action** in order to do that, in order to *make something happen*. He must be trying to change things, trying to get something from someone who is determined not to give it up. This taking action is confrontation and is done in scene.

Fourth: Your first confrontation scene has your character trying **(action)** to get something he **wants** from someone who doesn't want to give it up **(obstacle).** There are a few critical elements that must be part of a dramatic scene. At the end of that scene, things must be **worse** than they were at the beginning. The scene ends **in the mind of the character,** with him stewing and trying to figure out what to do about this even bigger dilemma that now threatens him.

Your scene will have the same shape as a story, with want, obstacle, action, and **resolution.** The difference is the resolution is a **scene resolution.** In a **scene resolution,** things have settled down for the moment, but the worst is yet to come. Your character is licking his wounds, wondering and worrying about what to do to save himself. Besides trying to figure out what to do, the character will be trying to make sense of things (the new complication or set of troubling facts uncovered during the confrontation). And he will be trying to figure out why this is happening, what it might mean for him, what will happen if he loses the struggle, etc. His worries, fears, and hopes will be churning in him. You, the author need to ask what he's afraid will happen and what he hopes will be the outcome. His fantasies may be working overtime also.

Fifth: If you've gotten this far, your story should be up and running. You should be on your way to more confrontations (two or three, usually) and a dramatic final showdown that will result in the **final reso-**

lution to the story—a win, a loss, or a mixed victory. If you're having trouble deciding what to do, remember your ongoing purpose is to **reveal character.** You do that by challenging and rechallenging your character—by raising the stakes, by making everything as difficult for everyone as you can, by letting nothing be easy for anyone—ever.

Push things to the limit, to the extreme. Stories are about extremes. And don't worry about going too far. At this stage your biggest problem is not going far enough. If you go too far, you can always cut back. Going too far and then cutting back is what writers do continually. Creating more trouble forces your characters to use more of themselves. In using more, they reveal more. When they reveal more, you, the author, and the reader have a deeper experience of the character—identification.

If what I'm telling you now still isn't helping, go to the chapter on rewriting and follow the steps for getting into your story and characters. Go through the motions, step-by-step, even if it feels stupid. If you're in that state (nothing is any good), the main thing is to keep moving along, following the plan, until it gets good again—which it will, always, *if* you keep at it.

OK, that's a pretty meaty list. It's a lot to be going over in a five-minute session, so I want to give you some abbreviated versions you can carry with you and refer to easily in your five-minute sessions, especially if nothing seems to be working. Here's one shorter list:

One: Do you have a **situation** (blind date, unfaithful lover, an enemy out to get the character, etc.)? If not, explore possibilities in yourself. If that doesn't work, pick an idea from the course.

Two: Who is the main character? (The main character is the one with the biggest problem—the most to lose.) What does he **want?** If you're not sure, make a list of *possible* wants **(want list).** Once you have a want or a want list, figure out what the **obstacle** is. If you can't decide, make a list of *possible* obstacles **(obstacle list).** If you're not sure, don't lock yourself into anything. You're just exploring possibilities—for five minutes a day and in free moments.

Three: Want + Obstacle = Conflict is what you've explored in the second step. Now it's time for the character to **act,** to assert himself to try to overcome the obstacle and satisfy his want. So, what can he do to win out? His **action** should be a direct attack upon the problem. Again, if you're not sure, make a list of *possible* actions **(action list).** This list should include the result, the **resolution** to the struggle between the character and the obstacle. The resolution is the outcome. You may not (and do not have to) know what it is until you write your way to it.

Four: Each scene ends in a **scene resolution** in which things are **worse** than they were at the beginning, and it ends in the mind of the character as he is stewing over the problem, trying to figure out what's going on and what he should do next to win out.

Five: Your story should have some momentum by now if you have **want, obstacle, action** working. If you don't or you're not sure, go to the chapter on rewriting and follow the steps for getting the most out of your story and characters.

Here's an even shorter pocket list:

1. *Situation.* Check course story ideas if you have none.
2. *Character* want + obstacle (conflict).
3. *Action* (confrontation/struggle).

4. *Resolution*. Scene resolution. Things are worse at the end. End in character's mind.

5. If it's not working, go to the rewrite chapter and follow the steps.

Remember to analyze any scene or story to see what you've got. Always remember: **Want:** Who wants what? Where does the want first appear? *Find it on the page. Do not work in your head.* What does the character want? Could it appear sooner? How much does the character want it? Could he want it more? How? **Obstacle:** What's the obstacle? Where does it first appear? Find it on the page. Could it appear sooner? How threatening is it? Could it be more threatening? How? **Action:** Is the character taking direct action against the obstacle to defeat it and get what he wants? Where does the action first appear? Find it on the page. Could he act sooner? Is he doing his utmost? Could he do more? How?

Yes, it's WANT, OBSTACLE, ACTION, over and over and over, until it's coming out of your ears. It may seem like I'm overdoing it, but these are your keys to creating compelling stories. It cannot be done without them.

FROM 30 TO 365

I've stressed the thirty-day trial period to get a feel for what this method can do for you. Once you've done the thirty days and are able to see what you can accomplish in five minutes a day, your next commitment needs to be for one year.

To find yourself as a writer and experience some substantial progress, you should not be fussing around evaluating what you've done or how well you've done it on a daily, weekly, or even monthly basis. There are too many slumps and surges and losses of perspective in all of this to permit any accurate judgments in the short term. Plus, we tend to evaluate our work when things are going badly—the worst possible time to judge anything. So, don't do it. It's been many a writer's downfall. And if and when you do evaluate, do it when things are going well and never when you're down.

So you must follow the system for a year straight, and keep going no matter what, if you're going to give yourself a fair chance. You should shoot for at least one hundred pages in that year. If you do that, at the end of the year, when you can look back over what you've done and compare your year-end writing with what you did at the beginning, I guarantee that you will be pleased.

The next few sections offer some cautions, tips, and reminders.

THE WORST

The worst thing you can do in all of this is to *not write and not make meaningful contact with your writing* for an extended or not so extended period. With this plan, there is no need to ever be away from your writing for any significant amount of time, because 5 minutes a day keep you in touch. The CARDINAL SIN in all of this is skipping the 5 minutes a day. Always, always, always make that daily contact. If you don't, when you get a chance to do some writing, you will be lost or, at the very least, creatively tense and stiff, and you'll flounder around trying to get into the swing of it, to loosen up, all the while losing time and running the risk of giving up. Do your 5 minutes—always.

BUT if due to forces beyond your control, you do miss your 5 minutes, never, never, never do extra to catch up. Don't say, "I missed yesterday, so I'll do ten minutes to catch up." Or worse, if you're into writing say a half hour a day and miss, don't ever tell yourself, "I didn't write for the half hour I had scheduled yesterday, so I'll do an hour to-day to keep my string going." Thou shalt not double up, ever. If you miss, forget it and go back to it tomorrow. If you're doing a lot (e.g., a half hour a day) and miss, you're better off dropping back a level for a day.

NOTHING = SOMETHING

With this method there is always something for you to do—even if it's nothing. With this technique, **nothing is something.** Your job, first and foremost, is to put in your time, always, no matter what. When you do, you actively, deliberately do nothing for 5 minutes, or you do something. Either way, you get full credit.

OUTPUT

Once you get into it, it's a good idea to limit the amount of time you spend sitting and mulling things over. The best way is to do a certain number of pages in the time you have. The minimum you should shoot for is one page every half hour. A sensible upper level would be three pages a half hour if you're writing by hand. You might do more if you're typing. I know people who can write five pages in a half hour by hand. A half hour a page leaves room for a lot of thought, too much maybe. Remember, it's better to **do your thinking on the page.** And faster writing is better writing. Dash it off. Come back and work it later.

FEELING IT

Writing is something you want to do—at least part of you does. But rarely when you sit down to do it, will you feel like it. And rarely will you feel like even sitting down to do it. So, never wait to feel it. Once you sit down to it, you will usually encounter more resistance. Especially at the beginning. Don't be surprised if you feel something like: *This is crazy. What can you do in five minutes? I don't even get warmed up in fifteen minutes. A writer in five minutes a day, B.S. This is stupid. I'm wasting my time. Cleaver is a wacko, and I'm just as nuts for trying this,* etc., etc., etc. To all of this you respond: *OK, it's stupid. I'm stupid. It's a waste of time. Fine! But, I signed on for thirty days. I'll do it for thirty days and be done with it.*

Another excellent way to defeat this kind of resistance is judo. Judo is using the power of the enemy to defeat him. With creative judo, you don't resist, ever. You go with whatever is in you. So, you say, or write: "I'm not writing today because . . ." "I can't stand doing this because . . ." "What I hate about this stuff is . . ." or "Why is there always resistance? Is it worth it? Will I ever get there?" etc. Whatever is in your mind, go with it, explore it. If you do, eventually it will lead you into something you feel is worth pursuing.

SLOP

No one's mind is 100 percent accurate. It's not supposed to be. The mind did not evolve for accuracy alone. It was never "intended" to be 100 percent accurate. This inaccuracy causes us to mix things that don't go together so that we can invent new ways of solving problems. There is no such thing as a photographic memory. Eighty percent is the maximum anyone has ever demonstrated. So, the very best we can do is 20 percent error, 20 percent slop. That, and the fact that we are looking for new combinations when we write, account for why the process is messy, disorganized, sloppy. In this game, mistakes and errors are good. They help us uncover new relationships. Fiction is about finding order in disorder—how everything relates to everything else. So you're supposed to make mistakes, get lost, drift off on a tangent. The slop can be maddening, but it's also your friend.

LEAPING AND LOOKING

One way of thinking of what you're doing in all of this is you are **training your imagination.** Which isn't exactly true, since it's not particularly trainable. But it's always there, and it's always willing to work for you. It's going all the time whether you're in touch with it or not. What you *can* do is **get in the way.** When you're in the way, you may feel that you have no imagination, but your imagination is a lot stronger and more durable and inventive than the rest of your mind. But it obeys its own rules. (The more you push it, the less you get, etc.) So, you don't train it. If anything, it trains you.

You have to learn how to follow your imagination's rules. Now, that's something you knew from the beginning. Little kids know it, since they haven't learned to approach things in a way that stifles the imagination. They haven't learned to plan ahead, to prepare, to think it through, to organize their thoughts before starting, to outline, to be careful, etc. All of this is what the educational system and the work world train us to do. And all of it is death to creativity. In creating, you **leap first** and **look later.**

If you want your imagination to work for you, you must learn to open the door and step aside. It leads. You follow. And if you do it long enough, if you don't allow your doubts and worries and fears to do you in, you will be rewarded. You will do less, and your imagination (subconscious) will do more. It will carry the load if you learn how to let it. Then, when you get into bed at night, when you turn onto the expressway or take your seat on the train, **your mind will go there on its own.** Your imagination will take you where you need to go.

There's nothing new about any of this. This is *daydreaming*. The technique I've laid out follows the natural currents of your mind. It takes some doing, but if you stick with it long enough to make the connection, to internalize it, to make it a part of you, you will discover what a great game this can be.

EXERCISES

Dealing with a nasty waiter/waitress or salesperson.

Dealing with a difficult child.

A character trying to figure out if he or she loves someone or not—if it's "the real thing."

13

Dead Weight

WHAT YOU CAN IGNORE

Earlier, I said that this story model is important for what it is, for what it includes, but just as important for what it isn't, for what it **excludes**—for what it saves you having to grapple with. Now I want to be more specific about what's excluded so that if you run into any of it, you'll recognize it and won't be confused or waste time wrestling with it. The few story elements and techniques (conflict, action, resolution, emotion, showing) I've given you take care of everything you need to do to create successful stories.

THE RAZOR

There's a principle in science called Occam's razor. It says that the simplest, most direct explanation is the best. So, although the theory that the Sun revolves around the Earth can actually be made to work with some mathematical contortions, we go with the simpler explanation that the Earth revolves around the Sun. It's simpler. It's more direct. It works better.

This issue comes up a lot when we have an unexplained phenomenon, especially the kind that people start attributing to extraterrestrials. One of the more recent ones was the crop circles in England. Perfectly formed circles imprinted in the crops started appearing on farms. Visiting spaceships, right? Look far away for an explanation. That's more exciting and romantic. They set up all-night cameras in some crop fields in the area, and guess what they found? Two guys sneaking into the fields dragging weighted platforms around to make the circles. The more immediate, direct explanation turned out to be true.

Writing is tricky enough. You don't need any vague concepts, any excess baggage, to drag along while you're doing it. I'm going to go over a couple of things specifically to show you what I'm talking about, then give you a list of unnecessary terms and considerations that you need not bother with.

The concept of **beginning, middle, and end** is a good example. In the introduction I told you about my first experience with this idea. I'll repeat it here and then tell you what it really means. "Be sure your story has a beginning, a middle, and an end," one of my writing professors once said.

Ah ha! That was it. It made perfect sense. That's what I needed to do. I went straight home and sat down to write a story with a beginning, a middle, and an end. I stared at the paper. A beginning? What did that mean, exactly? And what was the middle of a story, and how was it different from the beginning and the end? And the end, that's what I was having all the trouble with. Damn, I was back where I started.

At the next class, I asked, "Last time you said to write a story with a beginning, a middle, and an end, but I'm not sure what they are exactly."

"Well," he said with a little smile, "the beginning comes first. The middle comes next. And the end comes last."

Everyone laughed. I didn't ask again.

But now I know what they are, and so do you. The beginning of a story is the emergence of the *conflict* (*want* meets *obstacle*). The middle is the struggle *(action)*. The end is the *resolution*. They're already covered by conflict, action, and resolution, so there's no need to get into terms like *beginning, middle,* and *end* that are once removed and unnecessary.

Then there's this thing they call **character development.** I often have people come to me and say, "My plots are good, but my characters aren't developed enough." That tells me that the plot isn't working well either. What does character development mean? How does a character develop? How do we get a sense of who he is? A character is expressed (developed) by the way he handles his problems—how he acts when he's faced with an obstacle or a threat. *Action is character.* If you write a story using the model I've given you, your character will develop whether he or you want him to or not. He must develop. He must get off his ass and act in a meaningful way no matter what. This story model *makes* him act, makes him develop.

Voice and style are two other issues that come up. Some workshops' single goal is to "help you find your voice." Well, you don't need any help in finding your voice. Your voice and your style will emerge on their own if you write enough. They're a product of who you are, of your personality and your preferences. I don't differentiate between voice and style, although I'm sure there are people who do. Also, there's nothing wrong with trying to write exactly like Hemingway or Faulkner (two very different styles/voices). In the end, you will find your own way of doing it. It will emerge automatically, because of who you are.

Two other unnecessary issues, **character biographies** and **premise,** are covered in chapter 9, on method.

Another issue is **outlining.** At least one prominent author says that to be successful you must outline your story before you start. (Remember, anyone who tells you what you *must* do is talking about himself and what *he* must do.) Again, there is no real need for outlining—unless it helps, unless it's your thing. Most writers feel it's just another burden. Most writers don't want to be tied down to a whole story plan at the beginning. They prefer the adventure of exploring things on the page as they go along—feeling their way, being open to whatever pops up. One writer said, "Outline? Sure, I'll give you an outline—as soon as I finish the book."

Again, outlining (planning your story out) is worth a try if it makes sense to you. It might be your thing. Also, it's never one or the other, never all or none. You may plan one story and just jump in with no plan on the next one. You might lay out a scene or a chapter in great detail and jump in blind for the next chapter or the rest of the book. Outlining might be your thing for a long time, but then you might outgrow it. Nothing is static in this game.

Likeable character. Few things are more intimidating than having someone tell you that your character isn't likeable. And a good way to get stuck is to try to make him likeable. How would you do that? Have him help an old lady across the street or donate money to the poor? Likeability isn't a technical term. But *identification* is. Identification we can make happen. A character who is struggling with a threatening problem and is worried and frightened that it will defeat him will cause us to identify. Identifying is liking.

What about the need to pick a story that's **interesting?** One writing book says, "If you're going to bother to write a story, for God's sakes, be sure to make it interesting." The book fails to tell you what creates interest in a story or how to make it happen. The book did not even define "interesting" in a useable way. Be interesting! How intimidating is that? And why be just interesting? Why not be fascinating, captivating, mesmerizing? The answer to "interesting" is the same as the answer to likeability. Identification. If you've identified, you're interested—at the very least. Creating identification (revealing character through conflict and struggle) is what it's all about. Don't let yourself get distracted.

Here's a list of other concepts we don't get into and don't need to get into because the story model we use covers them all: Inciting incident. Plot points. Back story. Through line. Sequels. Verisimilitude. Believability. Beats. Context. Text. Story spine. Story event. Story value. Sequence. Story arc. Character arc. Arch plot. Mini plot. Antiplot.

How would you like to be loaded down with all that when you set out to create a story? These concepts are the result of examining story from the outside rather than from the inner dynamics of the characters and the conflict.

That said, if any of these issues that I'm calling unnecessary or burdensome strike your fancy or if you run into anything that sounds like it would make your task easier, try it. If it works for you, it's good. Just don't load yourself down with a lot of unnecessary things to do because you feel you're *supposed* to.

14

The Long and the Short of It

FROM SHORT STORY TO NOVEL

The short story versus the novel, the difference between the two, and how you can turn any short story into a novel, are the subject of this chapter. The first question is, What's the difference between a short story and a novel? The outstanding difference, of course, is length. The question then becomes, How long (or short) is a short story, and how short (or long) is a novel? And then there's that novella thing that comes in there somewhere. A novella is too big to be a short story but too small to be a novel—too big to be little and too little to be big—a kind of literary adolescent. So, how big or small is the novella? Is it at 90 pages, 110, or 120 that a short story turns into a novella? And when does that novella turn into a novel? If we say that a short story becomes a novella at 110 pages, how much different would that novella be if we cut 1 page so that it was 109 pages and fit the definition of a short story? Or what if it were only one word shy of 110 pages?

OK, so there's no clear cutoff, no point where a short story transforms itself into a novella and a novella into a novel. But that doesn't mean it's not a meaningful distinction or that we shouldn't draw a line somewhere. After all, there's no such thing as a 1-page novel or a 1,000-page short story. So, number of pages is the most visible difference. But is that all there is to it—more words, more pages? What accounts for those words and pages that turn a short story into a novel? Is it just a matter of taking more words to say the same thing? Is it that concise writers write short stories and long-winded writers write novels? Or is there a story ingredient that makes the novel longer—some element that demands more words and pages to do the job?

Many people who write short pieces think that they'll never be able to stretch a short story into a novel (300 pages or more). It seems impossible to them, because it *is* impossible—in the sense that they're thinking, in the sense of padding and stretching out a short story until it's long enough to be a novel. That'll never work. That's not how it's done at all. When you write a novel, you need to have so much story that you don't know how you'll ever fit it all in. If you're used to writing only small pieces, you may be wondering where you're going to get all that material. Before we're done, you'll know exactly where to get it and how to use it.

You often hear people talking about the difference between short stories and novels from the aspect of such things as *theme* and *scope*. Those terms, first of all, are not writing terms. They're most often used by literature professors or critics. They're fine for what they're doing, but they're at the other end of the process. *Theme* and *scope* are not the terms writers think in or create in. They are the effect of the story, someone's idea of what the story means translated into abstract, intellectual terms, but they are not the story itself.

This is so important that I want to digress a moment and say something about English literature classes and their relationship to writing. The reason I know this is important is that over the years I've had so many writers come to me, usually when they're frustrated and discouraged, and say, "I've decided to go back to school and get a master's degreee in English literature so I'll be able to write better." Will it help? It will not. What you learn in literature classes is how to analyze and interpret literature. You do not learn how to create stories. I know from personal experience and because I've had so many Ph.D.s in English literature take my workshops. They know a lot about literature, but they are no better at writing stories than anybody else. The thing to keep in mind is literature classes are to writing as art appreciation is to painting. Literature classes are fine for what they are but they won't make you a writer any more than art appreciation classes will make you a painter. The only way to learn to write stories is to dig in and write stories.

I've gone to great length to rid us of all the abstract, analytical, literature-class terminology, because they only confuse the issue. Writers work with the meat of experience, what we can sink our teeth into. From that come theme, scope, meaning, etc. So, while most novels have a larger theme and greater scope than a short story, we need to be thinking not about that, but rather why, *in story terms, in craft terms,* that is true. What is it about the novel that gives it that broader scope and theme? It has nothing to do with covering more time. Some short stories cover years, and some novels take place in one day. And it's not territory. Some short stories circle the globe, while some novels never leave the house. So, what's the difference?

I want to get to the answer by having you experience the difference. First, I'm going to give you a plot that could be a short story, then retell it and turn it into a novel. Your job is to see if you can tell what I'm doing to turn it into a novel, what I'm adding so that it *has* to be a novel, so that it's too big to possibly fit into a short story. Here's the short story version.

This is the old boy-meets-girl plot. It goes something like: Boy meets girl, falls for her, and tries to get her interest. She rejects him. He tries again to woo her. She shuns him again. He tries harder and harder and finally charms and wins her. Now, that could be a short story of 20 or 30 pages. He could win her and lose her and win her again without adding more than 10 pages. Either way, we're not approaching anything even near a novella. It's a short story.

Now, I want to change it into a novel. To do that, I need to be more specific, but that's not what will account for the length. I wasn't specific in the short story plot, because we didn't need specifics and they would have just slowed things down. So, for our novel: These are college-age people. The boy already has a girlfriend. They've been living together for a year and getting pretty serious, especially the girl. They're going to graduate soon, and it's time to make some serious decisions about commitment. Now, the boy isn't sure how he feels about the whole thing. Does he really love the girl? How can he tell? He'd always imagined it would be more consuming and thrilling than this. Is this the person he wants to spend the rest of his life with? Should he split and look for someone else? But what if this is as good as it gets? What if he splits and loses her and regrets it for the rest of his life? How can he tell?

This is his dilemma, and he's stewing about it at the opening of the story as he and his girlfriend are getting ready to go out on a double date with a friend of his girlfriend's he's never met and her boyfriend. They're going to meet the other couple at the pub for beers before going to a movie together. OK, they get to the pub, meet the couple, sit down in the booth, and order a pitcher. And what happens? Can you guess?

Zap! His dream girl. Love at first sight. The boy knows instantly that the other girl is what he's been waiting for—if not this particular girl, then one who makes him feel this way. He's sure. It's this or nothing. He can't settle for less.

OK, what's next? What's his next move? He has to break up with his girlfriend. Now, he could keep her until he finds someone else, but we're going to have him do the decent thing and end it now, since he's sure about it.

So, now we have a breakup story. He wants out. Is she going to let him out easily? Is she going to go quietly? No, it's going to be messy, messy as you can or care to make it—big trouble, big pain (always). She could become suicidal or homicidal. She could stalk him and be lurking around throughout the entire story. But I'm not even going to use her that much. Just remember that we could.

OK, it's messy, but eventually he's rid of her, and things settle down. What's his next move? To make contact with the other woman. Now, is she going to be interested in him? Is he going to be just the kind of guy she's always dreamed of? No way. Her present boyfriend is a big, handsome football type. Our hero is nothing special—decent, but no knockout, no giant, no tough guy. She wants no part of him. "Are you nuts?" is her attitude.

So, he's got to work harder. He's got to make contact with her when her boyfriend isn't around and convince her to spend a little time with him. Let's say he dares or begs her to just spend a half hour with him so he can show her what kind of a guy he is. If he can't stir her heart in that half hour, he'll accept any decision she makes. Reluctantly she agrees, saying he's wasting his time, but she'll do it just to get rid of him. But, she tells him, they'd better be careful, because if her boyfriend finds out, he'll tear him apart. So, they meet. He makes his grand play, doing everything and anything he can think of to charm her.

It's possible that he could win her over in this scene. Or she might say she'll think about seeing him again. Or she might say that she's not impressed and leave, and he'd try again, breaking his promise. Or she might later call him, and say that she wanted to see him again. This could go on for quite awhile, but to keep it simple and not wring too much out of it, we'll say that she thinks he's pretty cute and wants to see more of him. So, now we have our character wooing and charming her and overcoming her resistance. Eventually she falls for him.

OK, what's the next step? She's got to break up with her boyfriend. Is he going to go quietly? Never! He's big and dangerous, and he's going to raise hell. He's got to run into the two of them together and to get the hero alone and have a scene or scenes with him. But I don't want to milk that for too much. The ex-boyfriend could be an ongoing character throughout the novel, but I'm not going to use him much.

So, things settle down and are relatively peaceful. I'm not going to get into the kinds of issues and troubles people have to face and work out in any relationship, but just note that we could. But where are we now? Short story, novella, or novel territory? We're at least into a sizable short story if not bordering on a novella. But, it may not feel that it *has* to be a novel. So, let's go on.

What's the next natural thing people do in normal, conventional society when they fall for each other? They get engaged, have sex, live together, but I'm not talking about any of that. That's all there to go into if you choose. I'm not. The next natural step is to meet the parents. So, she takes the boy home to meet her parents. And is he going to be the kind of person they always wanted for their daughter? Or is he going to be the wrong religion, wrong class, wrong ethnic group, wrong race, wrong profession (damn fool wants to be a writer!). Yes, he's all wrong, 100 percent, total. He has to be.

OK, so it's dinner at her house. I'm making the parents wealthy, and giving the new boyfriend a working-class, blue-collar background. He's the first offspring to go to college. So, we have four characters at dinner. What can happen there? One thing is that **every character could have a meaningful scene with every other character.** We can have a scene with all four characters together (1), a scene with the boy alone with the mother and father (2), a scene with the boy alone with the mother (3), a scene with the boy alone with the father (4), a scene with the boy, the girl, and the mother (5), a scene with the boy, the girl, and the father (6), a scene with the girl and the mother and father (7), a scene with the girl alone with the father (8), a scene with the girl alone with the mother (9), a scene with the boy and girl alone together (10), a scene with the parents alone (11).

Now, that's too much to hold in your head at one time. But if you think of each possibility, you'll see it makes sense. In each of these possible scenes, the characters would act, and have reason to act, differently. For example, the father could be perfectly friendly and encouraging to the boy while others are present. Then, when he's alone with the boy, he'll say, "Look, you punk. I'll buy you off, or you'll find yourself floating face down in the river. Take your pick, because there's no way in hell you're getting my little girl. Repeat one word of this, and you won't make it to graduation alive."

Now, you don't always do all the possible scenes, but you should consider each of them—consider every character having a scene with every other character. In this case the dynamics and the possibilities are there to do them all if you choose to. If you do, you'll have eleven scenes at, say, 3 to 5 pages each. That's 33 to 55 pages for the dinner. However you do it, it'll make a hefty chapter.

So where are we? We're not done, but are we approaching novel length? Does it feel like it's beyond the short story, that it can no longer be a short story and *must* be a novel? And can you see what I'm doing to make it a novel?

Let's work on story possibilities a little more before getting into the specifics of craft. So, the boy has survived dinner with his new girlfriend's parents—for the moment. What's next in the natural sequence of events in conventional society? Meeting *his* parents. And how is bringing the girl to dinner in his parents' home going to go?

Not well. It cannot. It would be nice if there were alcoholism, spousal abuse, gambling problems, inappropriate flirting from the father, a possessive mother. And here we have four characters again, which gives us another possible eleven scenes, another meaty chapter.

All right, they've met each other's parents. What's the next step? Parents meet parents. Where will that take place? I'm thinking that the working-class parents go to the girl's mansion. And what could go on? Now, we have six characters. How many scene possibilities do you imagine we have with six characters? Fifty-seven. Now, this is not mathematics or science. It's art. I'm making my point by showing you the magnitude of possibilities. Many things enter into which scenes you choose to do. But with dinner at the girl's parents, you should be able to feel the kind of discomfort, unpleasantness, sparks, fireworks that might take place—all opportunities for revealing who these people really are (girl and boy included).

The lower-class father might ask all kinds of inappropriate questions. He could even try to bum some money from the girl's father when they're alone in the study. Or perhaps he's a union shop steward—uneducated, but crafty and clever and a master of insinuating and provoking. He could pocket a valuable knickknack. The movie *Guess Who's Coming to Dinner* had only 6 characters having dinner, and that was a feature-length movie. We're way beyond that. Don't forget that we could use the ex-boyfriend and ex-girlfriend. And we haven't brought in siblings or other relatives, who could also be involved. And then there's a wedding or plans for it, possibly. *Father of the Bride* was an entire movie about a wedding. So, we're not into any of that, but it should feel that our short story has turned into a novel.

OK, it's a novel, but what have I been doing? What have I been adding to the story to turn it into a novel? What's the difference between the short story version and the novel I've been turning it into? There are more conflict and more scenes, but what accounts for them? One thing and one thing only: MORE CHARACTERS. More characters, who are more trouble, more scenes, more pages. Believe it or not, that's all there is to it. That doesn't mean it's easy. It takes work, but it is that simple.

As long as each character you add brings into the mix a problem, a complication, an obstacle that has to be overcome, your story will grow and grow until it becomes a novel. Each character must have a natural connection to the story and add to the problem. No one is just there in fiction. No one is along for the ride. Everyone must serve a purpose, our ongoing purpose, which is to **reveal character.** Additional characters cause more trouble, forcing the other characters to act and reveal more of themselves. The novel is longer because the problem is bigger, the conflict more complicated and longer running. That larger, longer conflict is created by the presence of more characters. In terms of story elements, more characters are *the* difference between the short story and the novel.

In the short story version, the boy and girl both had parents and might each have had lovers when they met, but we didn't get into any of that. We didn't get into whether they were students or employed. It was about him and her and that's all. To turn the short story into a novel, I added characters who were naturally connected, closely and intimately, to the boy and girl, characters who had or felt they had something to gain or lose by the boy and girl uniting. We've by no means exhausted the logical supply of characters. To turn a short story into a novel, add more characters, characters who are invested in the outcome of the story, who feel, for reasons good or bad, real or imaginary, that they stand to win or lose by that outcome.

Now, that doesn't mean you have to know what a character's connection or investment is when he emerges in your mind or on the page. He doesn't have to qualify to get in. You may just have an urge to put someone in the story. If you have such an urge, follow it. Respect your urges. Then, as you write, you can work him in, make him necessary, find the character's connection or create one. Remember, in the end, and at the beginning, this is a game of the heart, the emotions. If it feels good, do it. In between, you use craft and technique to get the most out of the story and yourself, to make it all fit together, and to relocate your heart when it gets lost in the shuffle. Craft and technique are the tools that you use to keep yourself on track.

So, it's more characters that turns a short story into a novel. This more character stuff I like to call *the mathematics of fiction*. Now, this is art, not science, so putting numbers on things goes against the spirit of it all. I'm not trying to turn it into math or mechanics. But I put numbers on things whenever it will help give us a feel for the magnitude or the degree of some story issue. This is an elusive game. Whenever putting a number on things will make them clearer, it's worth doing, as long as you keep in mind that it's only an estimate.

So, exactly how much does adding characters increase the length of a story? Well, let's say that a 2-character story has one fundamental scene or character combination—the 2 characters together. Now, for this example, I'm not counting repeat scenes or scenes that the character has alone with him or herself (and there are many of both). To keep it simple, we're talking about possible scenes as determined by number of single scenes between characters.

So, 2 characters give us 1 scene. How many scenes would adding a third character give us? Three characters give us 4 possible scenes (all 3 characters together and each alone with 1 of the other 3). When we add a fourth character, the number of possible scenes jumps to 11 (more than doubles). Five characters give us 26 scenes. Six characters give us 57 scenes. Seven characters give us 120 scenes. Eight characters are 250 scenes. Nine are 520. Ten are over 1,000 possible scenes. Ten characters are not a lot of characters for a novel. I was reading a Larry McMurtry novel, *Comanche Moon*. It had 16 characters in the first fifty pages, and it didn't feel crowded, nor was it hard to keep track of who was who.

Note that I'm talking about *possible* scenes. At some point it isn't practical or true to the story to have every single character having a scene with the other characters in every possible combination. But this mathematical example should give you a sense of the magnitude of *possibilities* for scenes and story. Whatever your story, it's critical to always consider every character having a scene with every other character. If you have a dangerous, threatening, impulsive character and a frail, defenseless character in the same story, they must meet in a setting where the weak character is at the mercy of the dangerous one. Otherwise, what's the point? Fiction is about exploring the forces at work in us and what happens when those forces collide.

Many opportunities for drama, excitement, and expression of character are missed simply because the author didn't have characters come in contact with each other. Considering a possible scene doesn't mean you'll do it. But not doing it because you thought about it and decided against it is a lot different from not even thinking of it in the first place. By not considering each character having a scene with every other character, you often miss an opportunity to discover something about your characters, your story, human nature, and yourself.

Now, there are exceptions to everything I say. It's conceivable that there could be a story in which the dangerous character and the weak character wouldn't meet. But there must be a good reason for it not happening, a story reason. What would such a reason be, and how do you make such a decision? That reason has to do with the very purpose of story itself, and you get to it and make your decision by asking, always, which way is *more dramatic*, which way *reveals more* of the characters?

So, in this case, you would have to work it so that it would be *more dramatic* and *more exciting* and *more revealing* if the dangerous character didn't meet the weak character. That would be difficult to accomplish. Doing (meeting and confronting) is almost always more dramatic than not doing (avoiding). But then, it doesn't have to be one or the other. In this game you try to consider everything. It's possible that it could be both—not meeting and meeting. If you create excitement by having them not meet but come close, you can still go on and have them meet. It's often possible to have it both ways and get a lot more out of the characters than by just doing one or the other.

I find the idea of not meeting being more dramatic than meeting hard to imagine, but this is not science, so we need to allow for it (and anything else that might pop into our heads). Just remember that the way you make such decisions is to ask, **"What's more dramatic?"** and **"What reveals more character?"** Those are your main considerations—*always*.

So, the number of possible scenes skyrockets as you add characters. It more than doubles with each additional character. When you add repeat scenes between characters and scenes with characters alone with themselves, you generate enormous amounts of material. That's exactly where you want to be when you write a novel. You want to have so much material that you feel you're going to have trouble fitting it all in and not feel that you have to stretch and push and pad everything to have enough. If you don't feel you have enough to begin, that doesn't mean you can't start without it. You simply need to keep in mind that you can generate as much as you need by adding more characters where you can as you get into it.

Some writers start with little or nothing and expand the story as they go. Those writers (who are in the majority) like the adventure and surprise of not knowing where they're going. They solve problems when they come up. Other writers (a substantial number) plan the story ahead. If planning ahead works for you, do it. Just watch out that you don't get paralyzed worrying about problems ahead of time. That's another reason why the majority of writers tend to plan less. If you do plan, do it on the page. Working in the head is a bad choice for almost all writers.

Also, it's not that you're either a planner or not a planner. You don't work in the same way on every story. Sometimes you might plan because a particular story comes to you that way. The next time you start with no plan. You may plan some parts of the story and not others. The main thing is not to lock yourself into a single approach. Do what feels right, and don't get tangled up in how you *should* do it. The only *should* when it comes to creating is, **you should do what works.** No matter how strange or weird or illogical it seems, if it works, do it—and don't waste time trying to figure out why. Just go!

That's the novel, but there are a lot of different kinds of novels, different genres—science fiction, mystery, adventure, crime, spy, fantasy, romance, historical, etc. Which kind should you write? That depends on a lot of things. It depends on your taste, what's in your heart, your skill, what you want to achieve (publication, money, prestige), the marketplace.

First, the book market is great. Agents are being very creative in approaching publishers and getting huge sums for their authors. Publishers often seem willing to bid on a book they have seen little or none of if they are attracted by the concept. All of this drives the price up. Money for some of these not so well or even poorly written novels is in the millions.

David Baldacci's *Absolute Power* got five million. It was his first novel and not well written by any stretch. It's worth checking to see how little you can actually get away with. OK, but what *did* it have? It had a hot idea and perfect timing and a sharp agent going for it. It was about the president of the United States who gets into a fight with his mistress and kills her. The Secret Service is there and they have to cover up the murder. Now what better idea could you have for a novel with Clinton in the White House and Sexgate in full swing?

OK, you're deciding what kind of novel to write. You certainly can't count on the kind of thing Baldacci's novel had going for it. But knowing what gives you the best chance (the easiest kind of novel to write and sell) is important. We'll get to that but it's also important to know what is the most difficult kind of novel to write and to sell. That's what we're going to look at first.

The hardest kind of novel to write is the one more beginning writers pick to write than any other. It's a very personal story that relies heavily on the internal world (the mind) of the character and on the character's internal growth as a person. For that reason, I call it the internal novel. There are some great ones and all writers are capable of doing it successfully since every one of us has a dramatic and complex mind, but it requires the most skill. Even so, if you're dying to write a personal internal novel, if you have your heart set on it, then do it.

"Personal" doesn't necessarily mean it's autobiographical. It often is, but it doesn't have to be. How much the story depends on the character's relationship and struggle *with himself,* how much it hinges on or is about *internal growth* and insight, are what make it personal and internal. It's a type of story. It tends to be autobiographical, often about the author's big lessons in life, but it doesn't have to be. It's what would often be called a "sensitive" novel. *Silence of the Lambs* has plenty of sensitive writing, but it's not what comes to mind when you think of sensitive novels. Sensitivity is part of *Silence of the Lambs* but not its outstanding quality.

All novels have to be sensitive enough, or we won't give a damn about the characters or the story. Also, it is not that a novel is one or the other. The different elements blend, and how they do so depends on the story. All *literary novels* have a major personal, internal, sensitive dimension. It's where the strongest connections (see chapter 6) is made to the character. So, you've got to have that dimension, always, but the whole novel doesn't have to hinge on having a lot of it and doing it really well unless it's what I'm calling an internal novel. *The Catcher in the Rye* by J. D. Salinger and *Of Human Bondage* by Somerset Maugham are both internal novels.

It's this sensitivity to the character's internal world that makes the internal novel so difficult. It's a lot more about how the character feels (self-esteem, adequacy, irrational fears, etc.) than what's going on outside. The internal struggle in the character is much more difficult to figure out and express dramatically than what would be going on in the character if a maniac were stalking him. In the slasher story, all of the character's internal energies would be mobilized and focused on survival. Personal and internal issues are being played out, but they're more a response to the external threat and don't have to get deeply into the character's personal struggles. The mind is a dramatic place, but it's complicated, many leveled, and it's the trickiest of all to get right on the page. See chapter 6 on emotion for a fuller examination of this.

When you write an internal novel, the biggest problem, beyond creating the character's internal world, is keeping the drama going *outside* the character. Fiction is never a head game only. It's about how the world affects our head and how those internal effects influence how we relate to and affect the world. To write an internal novel you have to do both the external and internal well to succeed. The beginning writer's biggest failing is (1) focusing too much on the internal world while not having the skill to do it well and (2) not creating enough external drama to move the story.

My concern with what novel you choose to tackle first is based on my thirty years of working with writers, and with the high risk of discouragement and quitting that comes with trying an internal novel first. My advice is to realize that you're a beginner and pick the kind of novel you're going to learn the most from and have the most pleasure writing and the most chance of success, which is what we'll be getting to soon. If you're set on doing an internal novel, the story craft is identical. It does not change from genre to genre or form to form (novel to movie to stage). But be sure to pay attention to keeping the external drama and excitement going. It has to be about big trouble outside as well as inside.

So, that's the most difficult to write. What's the easiest kind of novel to write? It so happens that the easiest to write is also the most salable. Any idea what it is? Often half to two-thirds of all novels on the bestseller list are this type of novel. It's the mystery.

The mystery has its own *built-in* drama and energy. Any time there's a dead body, everyone's interested in who did it, why, and how. It's human nature. But why is that so? It's worth looking at—especially for our purposes.

Often in the news, there's a killing and, from what's reported, you can tell the victim was a rotten son-of-a-bitch who had been causing people all kinds of trouble and pain. But do we say, "Well, what the hell. It was a good thing. Let the killer go."? No, we don't. And why not? Well, we can't very well let people get away with murder, now can we? Of course not, because, who knows, they might get around to *us*. Ah ha. Now this worthless dead guy has become *us*. Here it is again. Good old identification. And not only do we identify with this dead creep, but also we identify pretty much with anyone who is dead, especially if he's been murdered. After all, someone who's dead is vulnerable to the max and vulnerability is what we're designed to relate to. Death, it's something we're all concerned about, worried about, afraid of. Murder, dead body—instant identification. If there were a dead body on the sidewalk in front of your workplace, there's no way you wouldn't want to know what happened. No way you wouldn't go into work and talk about it, or check the news to find out.

So the audience is there. Also, for the mystery, you don't have to write so well to pull it off. Check the writing in the mysteries at the bookstore next time you're browsing. It's often pretty mediocre. One reason is there's such a huge market. It's just harder to find enough decent mysteries to fill the market so the standards are lower.

Now, there are some classy writers writing mysteries. Mysteries in that class are called literary mysteries. So, even though there are a lot of shabby mysteries around, we shouldn't be looking down our noses at the genre. I'm including crime novels with mysteries. In a crime novel, you usually know who did it from the beginning—how to catch them is the issue.

So, you don't have to lower yourself or write beneath yourself to write a mystery. Dostoyevsky's *Brothers Karamazov* was a mystery. The Nobel Prize–winning author William Faulkner's book *Intruder in the Dust* was a mystery. In a mystery, your story and characters can have as much depth as any other kind of writing. One way to write a mystery is to create a murder that seems impossible to solve. Then you and your characters work like hell to figure it out and catch the killer. You don't have to have any idea who did it to begin writing. The famous mystery writer, Ed McBain, says he starts with a corpse or someone who is going to become a corpse, and from that point on he has to go on the same clues as the cops do. Other writers like to start by knowing who did it and work from there. Both methods are valid.

It's possible to turn any story into a mystery. Know how? Kill someone. A dead body gives us instant drama, suspense, mystery. We identify with anyone who's been murdered as long as he's not a villain. Let's try it. Take our boy/girl romance we just went through. Who's our victim? Whom shall we kill off? Well, it can be anybody except the boy, because it's his story. He's the main character. So, who's a prime candidate to murder? Whom we kill will cast suspicion on different characters and push the story in a different direction.

Without dragging it out, I'll give you my version. Yours will be just as valid if you see it differently and murder someone else. Personally, I would kill the girl's father. If we murder the father, who would be the prime suspect? For drama, suspense, and tension I would have the boy be the main suspect. The father doesn't like him; he's threatened him, and the father's in the way of the boy winning his daughter. And, if he's the prime suspect, that almost always means he's innocent. Who might be the killer?

It could be the ex-girlfriend trying to get revenge, knowing the boy would be blamed, expecially after she leaves some incriminating evidence at the crime scene. She could have something of his with his fingerprints on it and use it as the murder weapon. She might or might not be in cahoots with the ex-boyfriend who would have a similar motive and who would have easier access to the father since he knows him. Also, since the ex-boyfriend is stronger than the ex-girlfriend is, he would be better able to do the father in. A plot complication could be that the ex-girlfriend has also set the ex-boyfriend up as a fall guy if the police came after her. Or the ex-boyfriend could have masterminded it on his own, recruited the ex-girlfriend to help, setting her up to take the fall if he got cornered. Or they both could have set the other up to take the fall. Or he could be in it alone, but have set it up to look like the boy and ex-girlfriend did it. He could testify they were still lovers and were in cahoots from the beginning to win the girl, marry her, then kill her for her money, but the girl's father discovered their plot and they had to kill him. That's a complicated one, tricky to follow, but the kind of stuff that makes for dramatic unraveling.

Or it could be the girl's mother who'd discovered her husband had been cheating on her and planned on leaving her. She saw the opportunity with the new boy on the scene whom the father disliked, and she made it look like the boy did it. Then it could also be either one of the boy's parents who did it. That would bring in a whole other set of motives that would have to be worked out. All of these choices are equally good, depending on how you work the characters and the story.

Anything is possible. No matter how far fetched or strange it seems at first glance, you can make it work if you get deeply enough into the characters' logic and motives. Human behavior is so wide ranging, if you can imagine it, no matter how strange it is, somewhere in the world some screwball is probably doing it right now.

The mystery is the easiest and most salable. It's ready made with excitement and drama built in. It can be lightweight and succeed like Agatha Christie's, which were excellent but in no way approaching the literary mystery. Like any other novel, there are no limits on how deeply you can develop your characters or on how strongly it can be written.

So, the main difference between the short story and the novel is the number of characters, but I don't want to give the impression that there are no novels with just a few characters. There are and some are excellent. But it's a lot trickier to keep the drama going for a full novel with only a couple of characters. Stephen King's novel, *Misery,* is an excellent example. It's a tighty written, well-crafted story that holds you all the way through. I recommend reading it.

EXERCISES

A search for a lost or stolen priceless object. It could also be something intangible like a lost reputation. Setting out alone to seek one's fortune. The search can take place on home turf (small town, big city, school yard, health club), in a strange foreign land, or across the globe.

A character sets out to find someone, seek revenge, get information. To catch a bad guy or rescue someone from himself (drugs) or from another person. Again, the story can take place within a single family, within one room, or across the globe.

A character's romantic adventures and misadventures.

You can find a lot of material by outlining your own life—the high points and trouble you had at each phase. How you accomplished your developmental tasks, starting with childhood, at home with family, in elementary school, high school, college, and with friends and enemies. Make a list of all the schools you attended and the places where you lived and what happened there. List your friends and enemies—those you loved and those you hated in your family and outside of it. Most families are a mess. There are loads of material there. However, that doesn't mean you should use it if you're not drawn to it. Some writers do well by writing about themselves (auto-biographical novels), such as Hemingway, Maugham, Roth. Others need more distance and stay away from their own lives. Neither way is more valid, creative, or valuable.

15

Hitting the Wall

BLOCKING AND UNBLOCKING

When Rex Harrison was on the stage, he timed it so he barely had enough time to rush into his dressing room, throw on his costume, put on his makeup, and race out onto the stage just moments before the curtain went up.

When Laurence Olivier was on the stage, he got there early like most actors and got into costume with some time to spare. Then, when the house was full, but the curtain was still down, he would go out onto the stage and stand behind the curtain facing the audience on the other side and say to them, but so only he could hear, "Not one of you lousy bastards can do what I'm going to do here on this stage tonight."

Harrison and Olivier, two great actors—what were they up to? Why all the antics? What were they struggling with? Performance anxiety. Fear. Stage fright. Harrison was trying to distract himself by making himself frantic about something else—something he could manage easily (costume and makeup). Olivier was trying to psyche himself up, trying to overcome his fear by turning it into something else.

Do writers have stage fright? Yes, they have a kind of performance anxiety that can be just as terrifying. They have *page fright*. Unlike stage fright, where you must go on when the curtain goes up, ready or not, writers can sneak out, put off the performance again and again. Because of that, page fright often lasts longer and grows more disabling the longer the writer puts off writing. Some writers have been **blocked for years.**

Blocking is the writer's affliction, so we're going to treat it like one. We're going to look at the nature of the disease, determine the causes, and then put together a treatment plan. Diagnosing the disease and its causes helps, but diagnosis is not a cure. Understanding alone will not solve the problem. Understanding is not mastery. You have to know how to treat the ailment (what to *do*) if you're going to cure it. That's where we'll wind up—with an aggressive plan of action to get you onto the page and back up to full strength.

AUDIENCE AS ENEMY

Fear of the audience. How would Olivier and Harrison have felt if they had no audience, if it were just a rehearsal? They wouldn't be panicky if there were no audience. Do you have an audience when you write? Readers are your audience, but do you have an audience while you're actually performing the act of writing? Yes, you do. The audience is yourself, and that's **the toughest audience in the world.** No one can terrorize you like you can terrorize yourself. Actors often perform without an audience, but can you write without an audience? Can there be *no you* there?

Have you ever heard someone say, "He was lost in his work," or, "She was so absorbed she didn't know what was going on around her." That's what we're talking about when we say writing with no audience. The difficult, frightening audience is gone. You're aware of what's happening, but you feel as if *you are the process, you are the story*. Now, that's the ideal state, what keeps us going, what we hope for, but certainly not the state you must be in *before* you can begin writing and definitely not what you wait around for in order to start. Waiting would only compound the problem.

THE AFFLICTION

You're blocked. OK, where does it hurt? How does it hurt? What's the experience of it? Exactly what happens when you're blocked—what goes on inside you?

You sit there in a knot staring at the wall or your computer or a blank page or something you've written, thinking, *Writer? Who do I think I am trying to be a writer. I'm wasting my time. I'll never publish. I have no ideas. I have no talent. I used to think I had it. I wrote a couple of decent pieces once. But that was long ago. They weren't that good anyway. Now I can't think of one thing worth writing about. I can't even bring myself to put a single word down on the page. If I had what it takes, I wouldn't be having all this trouble. I might as well forget it. Who needs this misery? Who cares? Why put myself though this?* And on and on and on, totally out of control, attacking your talent, your character, your moral courage, your worth as a human being. It often turns into all-out character assassination.

The strange thing is that it has nothing to do with what you need to be focusing on at the moment. **Blocking has nothing to do with the act of writing anything.** You're totally off the track, worrying about your talent, your future success, the ideas you *don't* have, all the things that *aren't* happening and that you *can't* make happen, instead of all the things you *can* do something about at the moment. Of course, you aren't aware of what you can do, because you're so consumed with mourning the loss of your talent and your demise as a writer.

The first thing to realize is: **You're wrong—about all of it.** These kinds of negative emotions should never be trusted, because they're *always* distorted, excessive, irrelevant—completely off the track, totally beside the point. The problem is, this is an emotional game. Your emotions are your best guide. They're 99.99 percent accurate. Most of the time, there's a good reason for feeling what you're feeling. But never when they turn against you. When they do that, **they're always wrong.** So, it's like having a trusted friend who helps you with everything, whom you *must* depend on to get anything done, but who every so often without warning and for no reason decides to clobber you.

None of these worries have anything to do with actually writing something. But they come over us when we write—or when we're trying to write, so we call it writer's block. What's really in your way, what's really blocking you, are all kinds of concerns you drag into the process (is it any good? am I any good? will I ever make it?)—concerns that are irrelevant to actually putting words on the page. It begins to seem impossible. It seems impossible because it is. You've made it impossible by loading yourself down with so many concerns that you can't move. Nobody can deal with all these issues and write at the same time. It can't be done. But you can unload them so that you can start writing again. Writing doesn't have to be so hard, and it isn't. Once you learn how it works, you'll find that **easier writing is better writing.**

Putting words on the page is the simplest of acts. If I were to give you a thousand dollars for every page you filled with complete sentences (anything you wanted as long as you didn't write the same sentence over and over), you'd get going fast, you'd fill a lot of pages, and, without even trying, you'd come up with lots of good ideas. So it's not objective reality, but your state of mind (subjective reality) that's in your way. Writing is not in your way. Your **worries about writing** are paralyzing you. **Worrying and writing are two completely different acts.** These are the kinds of problems we create for ourselves when we write, and because they're so closely connected with the act of writing, we don't realize that they're not part of the writing process at all.

OK, I don't want to be splitting hairs or quibbling about definitions, but it's important to realize that **writing is a simple act,** but because of what we drag into it, we make it complicated, miserable, impossible. So, when you're blocked, you're completely distracted, you've lost all sense of proportion, and you're waging an *all-out, unrealistic,* and *unfair* attack on your work, your talent, your imagination, your chances for success, and anything else within striking distance. It's self-abuse of the highest order. I said in an earlier chapter that you have to be a sadist in order to tell a good story, to create conflict that hurts your characters and incites them to act, and you must be a masochist in order to write. This kind of pain/lunacy is why most people give up. They think they don't have what it takes (ability/talent), but that's **never the case.** What it takes, what makes you or breaks you, is whether or not you can withstand this kind of misery while you find some way around it. Identifying the source of the pain is the first step. Then, you must have an orderly, step-by-step way of treating it.

THE CULPRIT

When you get blocked, whom do you blame? Well, who's there? You. Nobody but you. So you blame yourself. And since you're to blame, whom do you punish? Same deal. You're the only one there, so it has to be your fault. You're the one who deserves punishment. Makes perfect sense, right? Maybe. Let's take a look at who gets blocked.

WHY ME?

Who suffers such misery? What kinds of writers get blocked, and how long do you have to write before it stops happening, before you outgrow it? In chapter 1 I gave you some examples of the kind of trouble some great writers had. That was a while ago, so it's worth repeating. Gustave Flaubert *(Madame Bovary)* struggled for three days, threw a monumental tantrum, rolled on the floor, banged his head against the wall—all to produce a grand total of eight sentences. Oscar Wilde *(The Picture of Dorian Gray, The Importance of Being Earnest)* said, "I spent the morning putting in a comma and the afternoon taking it out." Joseph Heller took ten years to write the novel *Catch-22*. Tom Wolfe also worked for ten years to write *A Man in Full*. So, **who gets blocked? Everybody.** Some less than others, but it's unavoidable.

What does that tell us? First, you're in good company. Second, if it happens to everybody, it's part of the process, and you shouldn't be blaming and punishing yourself for it. True, but realizing that isn't going to stop you. You *will* get blocked. You *will* blame yourself. You *will* punish yourself. You can't stop that, *but* it's possible to minimize it, to learn to catch yourself quickly, so it doesn't take you ten years to write a novel. The goal is to get the most out of yourself with the least pain and the most pleasure.

When a new writer tells me, "I never get blocked," I usually say, "You have something to look forward to." What I would like to say, but don't, is: "You don't know enough yet." The more you know, the more possibilities there are for blocking yourself. The better you write—the more inventive and skillful and ingenious you become at ambushing yourself. You're never beyond it. You never outgrow it, because it grows with you.

So, if it happens to all writers, does it make sense to blame yourself when it happens to you? Could it be that something in **the process makes blocking inevitable,** something that has nothing to do with you personally and is in no way a reflection on you, your character, or your talent? It could be and it is. It's the process, not you. It's all part of the game of writing, and you can learn to master it just as you can learn to tell a compelling story.

HOW LONG IS TOO LONG?

Heller and Wolfe took 10 years to get their novels done, but, as I pointed out in chapter 1, Nabokov wrote *Lolita* in 3 months. A famous novel of some years ago, *Goodbye, Mr. Chips,* was written in 4 days. It was a slim little novel, but if they had been written at the same rate, Heller and Wolfe's novels would have been finished in months instead of years. A number of full-length novels have been written in a couple of months. So, the question is: how long should it take? Well, that's going to vary. Four-day, 2-month, or 6-month novels are rare. A novel a year is very prolific. One to 2 years is respectable. Serious novelists often take 3 to 5 years. Philip Roth says he writes for 6 months to produce one hundred pages, from which he then pieces together one decent page. If he's lucky, he says, that page is the start of his next novel. Six months for one page—does it have to be?

The 10-year novel, the four-day novel—what's the difference? I'm sure that Heller and Wolfe didn't bang away, writing every day, full-time for 10 years to write their novels. Their novels took 10 years, but a lot of time had to be spent stricken, disabled, spinning their wheels. But, as I keep saying, it doesn't have to be that way. What makes the difference is not **how much time you spend writing,** but **how much**

time you waste trying to write. Most writers *waste* enormous amounts of time and energy *trying* to make it happen.

And then there's another issue that squeezes in here somewhere.

YOU'VE GOT IT, OR YOU DON'T

There are those who say, "You've got it, or you don't. There's no substitute for talent." Talent—what part does it play in all of this? How do you know if you've got any? What if you don't? Can you get some? How much do you need? Is it necessary? Is it worth worrying about? Well, I can tell you: There's no special talent needed to write publishable stories—all you need is your own emotions and your own life experience. In the other arts—music or painting, for example—you may need a special, inborn talent. But writing is different. It's different because life skills are writing skills. Everyone has a full set of emotions and plenty of dramatic, painful, and exciting experiences to draw on. You have more than enough inside you already than you'll ever be able to use. That doesn't mean you have to write about yourself or your personal experience. But what you have in you now is enough to imagine any kind of story you choose. Plus, the standards for publication aren't high. Plenty of talentless writers are making fortunes. Look around. They're not hard to find.

Have you ever heard the saying "It's ten percent inspiration and ninety percent perspiration." Well, it is never truer than when referring to writing. And 90 percent is a damn good average—plenty good enough to get published. Now, that's not to say there isn't such a thing as talent or genius and that it doesn't come into play at some point. But that point is for something like the Pulitzer Prize or the National Book Award or the Nobel Prize, but not for making a living or writing a bestseller. Most successful writers don't get those big awards. The only talent you need to be successful is a talent for work. **Storytelling is an acquired skill, not an inborn talent.** There is a substitute for talent. It's **work + craft.** Work hard, learn your craft, and the rest will take care of itself. Craft is the issue. You have everything else already. **No special talent needed.**

OK, let's get back to our examination of blocking.

THE LITTLE MAN UPON THE STAIR

One way to get some insight into the state you're in when you're blocked is to compare the symptoms to those of psychological depression. One of the symptoms in clinical depression is a sense of doom—eternal gloom and doom. Things are awful. They're going to stay that way. They'll never be good again. The depressed person doesn't think, *I feel horrible, but I'll get through this, recover, and feel good again.* And when you're blocked, you're never thinking, *This is awful. I feel worthless and talentless, but I know that's just a state all writers get into. I'll get through this and write really well again.* No, if you have that much perspective, you're not in the throes of a serious block. When you're truly blocked, even though you may know that all writers get blocked, you're certain your block is like no block in writing history. For you, it's truly the end. You'll never write a decent sentence again as long as you live.

The other symptom of this kind of depression is hostility turned against yourself—an all-out attack. Olivier, in belittling the audience ("Not one of you bastards . . ."), was instinctively doing the right thing—trying to turn the hostility away from himself. Of course, no one in the audience was hostile toward him. They loved him. He could have fallen on his face, and they would have applauded. They weren't the enemy, but it was better to attack them than himself. The enemy without is less threatening than the enemy within.

My Psychology 101 textbook defined what they called *free-floating anxiety* as "a vague objectless dread." That's especially apt for blocking. Vague, yes, because often you don't even let yourself think about writing; you keep it out of your consciousness as much as possible. You have a vague dread that if you go sit down, it's going to be awful. You keep it out of your head because you don't want to face up to what a coward you are (too scared to sit down and put words on a page). The psychology book quoted a poem that characterized this kind of anxiety.

> *I saw a man upon the stair.*
> *The little man who wasn't there.*
> *He wasn't there again today.*
> *I wish the hell he'd go away.*

Maybe he'll go away on his own, but we can't afford to wait around gambling that he will. We have to find a way to get rid of him. But we need to finish with our examination of blocking first.

LAND OF LUNACY

Some common notions: Artists and writers are a little crazy. You have to be loose in the head, detached, unhinged to create. You need a special sensitivity, perception, and self-awareness to be creative. None of it happens to be true. Your personal psychology has nothing to do with it. You can be plenty wacky and be a good writer. On the other hand, sanity is no disadvantage. Writing is apart from all that. Writing is an act of discovery. You write not because you have awareness, but to achieve awareness.

That doesn't mean that the state of mind you get into when you create is the same as what's needed to function in everyday reality. It also doesn't mean that it won't feel crazy or drive you nuts at times. To create, you must go to a place in yourself that you must avoid in order to survive and function in everyday life. It's looser. It's wilder. It's open to anything and everything. You draw on it briefly, now and then, in normal activity, but it's not a place where you can dwell and fulfill normal, everyday responsibilities.

For example, it might strike you, in a tense conversation with your boss, how much he reminds you of a squat, jowly little bulldog you saw on the street that morning. In that situation, you would have to scramble to keep your mind on what he's saying and to push the idea out of your head before you smile or even crack up and get into trouble. But, if you were writing, you would explore that idea—how he looked, your smiling and telling him what he looks like, and walking out. You also can't be open to anything and everything that presents itself when you're walking along the street. If you were, you wouldn't last long.

The creative state of mind is unusual. You're not in your right mind by normal standards. And to get there you have to let go of the normal defenses, protections, and controls that you must maintain to function everywhere else. Giving up your defenses, going from secure to insecure, is never comfortable. Once you get there, it's never so bad, but crossing over is always a problem. One explanation for the resistance is that in order to create you have to **let go of your mind** and implicit in the letting go is the fear that if you let go of your mind you could **lose your mind.** That may be the extreme case, but I think some version of that worry is what makes it difficult to let go.

You can feel good about yourself, your life, your talent, your writing. You can know what you're going to write, know exactly where you're going and what you're going to do and feel good about all of it. But, even with all that in your favor, even with everything as good as it possibly can be, **there's always resistance to putting down those first few words.** That's because you must move from security to insecurity, because you're letting go of defenses, barriers, protections and opening yourself up to the unknown. Such resistance is not only natural, but constitutes self-preservation in the normal world. But then we're not going to the normal world. We're going to the land of vulnerability, of maximum exposure.

This chronic resistance is not the kind of death grip that's got you with an acute block, but it can lead to one if you don't watch out. You could easily start thinking, *If everything's great and I'm still having trouble, how am I ever going to do this? Maybe I don't have what it takes.* Again, everything that happens to you is right. You're OK. It's not you. It's the craziness of the process. You're fine.

You're fine, but what can you.*do* about the resistance? Well, let me tell you my routine. I have a little ritual I go through each morning. I have a cup of coffee and a doughnut and I play the Jumble (scrambled word) game in the paper. What I used to do when I sat down at my desk and started tensing up was to tell myself, "Relax. Take it easy. You don't have to write yet. You get these treats first." That was a relief. I didn't have to face it yet.

But the longer those few things took and the closer I got to having to write, the more my resistance and dread began rising and the more I dragged out finishing my coffee-doughnut-Jumble. And the longer I put it off, the more the resistance increased. OK, but, hey, didn't I have a right to my coffee, doughnut, Jumble? Yes, I did, and I didn't need to deny myself. But I did need to find a way to prevent the resistance and avoidance from building while I had them.

What I learned to do was **write an instant line.** Now, as soon as I sit down, I set my coffee, doughnut, and Jumble puzzle to the side and tell myself, "It's OK. Just do this little bit, then you can have your treats." (Big baby!) Then I immediately write a line or two or a paragraph of what I'm working on. Doing an instant line or two (more if they come easily) as soon as you sit down, *before* you do anything else, breaks the resistance. One line is enough. Don't start pushing for more, but if more come, put them down.

The instant line accomplishes a couple of things. It breaks the resistance, connects you to your subconscious, and helps you feel, *Now that wasn't so bad, was it?* It also starts things (your story) moving on the deeper levels of your mind. Often when you get back to your work (now you have a line or so to look over), ideas triggered by your instant line will be there waiting for you. (See chapter 12 for a full explanation of this.) And because I've started things moving, ideas often start coming to me in the middle of the treats. The writing is drawing me in. That's the best.

I know a lot of this seems pretty silly and wimpy and infantile. That's because it is. We're all big babies when it comes to opening up in this way. We're going to the baby in ourselves, as we must. I've seen macho, body-builder tough guys sweat and shake when I was about to read their writing to the class, even though I wasn't going to give their names. Silly, yes. But these are the kinds of games we have to play with ourselves if we're going to avoid getting hung up, doing nothing for long periods of time.

The old "Just do it!" is lousy advice. It may be OK for sports, where you can power your way through, but it's worthless for creating. If you can power your way through, good luck to you. Most writers, most of the greatest, had to play nursemaid to this kind of "silliness." Creativity requires that you go where lunacy dwells.

A quick footnote about putting things off. When it's time to write, you will often start seeing all kinds of little things that need doing, little housekeeping tasks or calls to make or bills to pay—things that once they're out of the way, you just know, you'll be able to really get going. The answer at that moment is to tell yourself, "OK. Fine, you can do all of that—right *after you finish writing*." Write first. Save those attractive little tasks as your reward for writing. The strange thing is that after you've written those things are never as important as they were before.

THE ROOT OF ALL EVIL

We've looked at the condition of being blocked and what we do to contribute to it, but not at the root cause. For that we have to look at the creative process itself and uncover what it is that brings on these attacks. The problem is that the very skills we have to master in order to create a story can also cripple us. A carpenter's best tool may be his saw, but not if it's used the wrong way, slips off the table, and cuts into his leg.

There are two processes that you must master in order to create anything. The first is the **flow process.** The flow process is what happens when you open up and let whatever is in you flow onto the page. It's what you must do to get something to work with. This part of the process is quick, fluid, messy, emotional, and most of all **nonjudgmental.** If you're lucky, this flow will go on for several pages; if you're very lucky, it will go on for an entire draft.

But there's more to it than getting loose and pouring something onto the page. Eventually the momentum (flow) stops, and you have to go back and look at what you've got and decide what to do with it—decide what stays, what goes, and what gets redone. That going back

and that evaluating are the **editing process.** The editing process is slow, deliberate, organized, intellectual, and, most of all, **judgmental.**

Now, when things are going well, you can switch back and forth from flow to edit in an instant. You write a stretch (flow). It's not quite what you want (edit). You cut some (edit), then dash off some more (flow). It's better, but it's not there yet (edit). You work it again (flow). Ah, that's it (edit). You have a feel for what you want, and you keep working until you get it. So, flow and edit work together—two parts that make up the creative process. Neither one is better or more valuable than the other.

So, what happens when you get blocked? What happens, and this is all that's happening (it's enough), is this: **you're editing when you should be going with flow.** Being blocked is editing run amuck. At its worst, you edit yourself out of the picture entirely—*I have no talent. I'll never publish, I'm wasting my time. I might as well give up.* Or you may be editing ideas in your head—discounting them, telling yourself they're lousy—before they even get to the page, before you get a good look at them and give yourself a chance to turn them into something that works.

Remember: **Nothing counts until it's on the page.** Do not work in your head. Unless you have a special genius for it, **never, never edit in your head.** Get it out on the page where you can get a good look at it.

OK, that's all fine and good, but no matter what I say, you will edit in your head, you will turn against yourself, you will get blocked. We all will. What can we do about it?

TREATMENT

You're blocked. What do you do? Well, I once had an inspiration that got me out of a block. I was feeling, *This is crazy? Why torture yourself?*

Life would be so much easier without writing. But I had a bit of perspective and realized that I was in the dumps and that it was no time to be making a serious decision (which means it wasn't a severe block). So, I said to myself, "I'm going to write until it gets good again, and if I still want to quit, I will." And that got me back, plugging away, *not trying* to be good. Not only did it get me back to work, but it felt like the solution to getting unblocked. So, I made a little sign and hung it on the wall I was facing. NEVER QUIT ON A BAD DAY, the sign read.

Now, the next time it was my turn to get blocked, I did. But now I had my sign, and I looked up at it. What do you think happened? Did it get me back to work the way it had the last time? Did I start writing instantly? Had I truly found the single key to unblocking myself? No. In fact, my reaction was more like, "Yeah, yeah. B.S. Not this time."

As time passed, I looked for more solutions. Each time I figured something out, I made notations on my sign. "Never trust your emotions when they're negative," worked—*once.* "Everything that happens is right" was another. It reminded me that a writer is blocked because of the process and that it has nothing to do with his or her talent or anything else. That realization *might* work. It did for me a couple of times. But these are ideas—idea solutions. They're in the head. Just as you don't write or edit in your head, you rarely get unblocked in your head. No, **you will never think or talk your way out of a block.** To get unblocked **you must do** something. **You must act.** Just as action is what moves a story, taking action is what will move you back onto the page, which is where you need to go.

IDEAS THAT HELP

That doesn't mean ideas are worthless. They can work sometimes—especially with a mild case. (I'm contradicting myself, I know.) But you can't count on them to do the job. Stronger medicine is needed for a severe block. But ideas can help. They can loosen you up and make it easier to act. Here are some ideas that I've found helpful.

The Muse: What about the Muse? You know, the spirit or goddess who inspires writers and artists, the source of inspiration, a magical presence that pours wonderful ideas into your head. When ideas are flowing out of you as fast as you can think, when you can just barely keep up, when it feels like a voice is dictating to you, that's the experience of being in touch with the Muse. If you write enough, you will experience her, sometimes for brief periods, sometimes for long stints. It's a thrill. It's the kind of energy and surprise, in one form or another, that keeps us writing. But it's not something you can count on, something you wait around for, or something you need before you can start writing, or something you need to write well. Just as you don't wait until you *feel* like writing to do so.

The best way to connect with the Muse is to start writing, because **the Muse is you.** It's all a matter of getting in touch with what's inside of you and letting it out. Easier said than done. One reason this is difficult that I haven't touched on is that our culture, with its strict puritanical ethic, does not help or encourage us to get into that place in ourselves, because doing so requires letting go, giving up, being empty.

In our culture, we're taught to think things through first, to plan ahead, to outline, to know where we're going, to prepare, to be ready, and then to pay close attention to what we're doing and to be in **control** at all times. Actually, we are the worst for *not* letting go, for *not* valuing emptiness, randomness, for *not* seeing the value of *not knowing*. Control is your enemy for creating, for getting into the flow, for letting it happen. In fact, I would go so far as to say that if you're in control, you're in trouble. Einstein said that all his great ideas "just came to him" when his mind was empty. Eastern culture values emptiness as the state of mind out of which all things come, especially ideas.

Our belief is that we must think in order to write well. We think in order to find our writing mind. That's the exact opposite of the way it works. We don't think in order to write, **we write in order to think.** We don't get in the mood to write. **We write to get in the mood.** We start writing to get our mind going, to uncover our ideas. We don't wait around for a feeling or an idea or anything else. We **start with nothing.** Your mind is full. You have volumes and volumes inside you, waiting to be uncovered (enough for twenty novels). Think about it. How much of you, of what you know and who you are, is in your conscious mind at any one time? One-tenth of 1 percent? Not much. Plus, your mind is never empty. It goes at 150 to 300 words a minute every waking hour. You always have ideas in your head. They may not be ideas you like, but your mind never stops. But if you're only trying for good ideas, you will have problems, because:

You Must Write Badly First: Expect to be bad. Scientists have studied successfully creative people and found that they had a lot more good ideas than everyone else and a lot more . . . what? Can you guess? A lot more *bad* ideas. They had a lot more ideas to chose from, because they let all their ideas out and didn't try to pick and choose between the good and the bad. The beginning writer looks at his first draft and says, "This is garbage. I'm screwed." The experienced writer looks at his first draft and says, "This is garbage. I'm on my way!" Unrealistic expectations and trying to do it right the first time are a major cause of blocking. Hemingway said, "The first draft is shit." So, don't expect to do better than Hemingway. Get busy and write some shit.

Falling Apart: Another thing that can bring on blocking is the falling apart that takes place when you're creating a story. At some point you lose track of where you are and don't know what to do next with the tangled mess in front of you. Not only is this falling apart painful, but for almost all writers it's a necessary step in the process. Yes. **Falling apart is good.** It's discouraging. It's maddening. But it's good. So, when it happens, pat yourself on the back. You've gotten to exactly where you need to go. You've gotten loose enough and produced enough material to lose your way.

Falling apart is inevitable, because you can't be open and loose enough to create and, at the same time, keep track and control of what's coming out of you and how it all fits together. Art comes from error. Uncertainty is good.

OK, but it's going to feel like a crisis. In crisis, we're open to trying anything and everything to survive. We're willing to try anything. Finding the order, putting it back together, is when good things happen. So, you're suffering, you're miserable, you're doing great. Once you get used to it, you'll be able to accept it and relax.

Organization: **Organization is the last thing you need to worry about—ever.** Why? Because you will find order in your story instinctively. That's what our species does. Human beings impose order on every damn thing they see. We have philosophy, religion, psychology, sociology, anthropology, biology, etc., etc. We label, categorize, examine, measure, define everything. Ordering is our nature. That's why we get so nervous when we don't have it. The solution is to just keep working your material and **let the order find you.** You will organize your story whether you want to or not. You have no choice. So, it's a false issue. The real issues are always want, obstacle, action, resolution. The plan. Keeping your eye on the ball.

First Things When? Another thing that contributes to blocking is the feeling that you have to write your story in some sensible order (beginning first, etc.). It's fine to write the end or the middle first. You might write from the middle toward both ends, or inside out, upside down, or backwards. If when you sit down, you're not sure how to start, but you have a strong sense of the first big scene and are dying to do it, go there and do it. Respect your impulses. **Go where your energy takes you, always.** In the end, you will have to shape your writing into some meaningful form, but that's in the end—never in the beginning.

That's for most writers. A few are detailed planners. If that's your nature, do it. Remember, all of this has to be tempered with who you are and how you work best. This is art, not science. If it works, do it. And "do it" is where we're at. What do you *do* to get unblocked? Just thinking is seldom enough. Thinking might give you the edge on a minor block, but you will never think your way out of a severe attack.

Three things can block you: **Story/craft:** You have an idea for a story, but you don't know how to make the first move, or you're into a story but don't know where to go or what to do next or how to find the answer. **Emotions:** You get into a funk about yourself, your skill, your progress, the quality of your writing. **Work methods:** You're stumped because you can't figure out how to approach your story, where to take hold of it, how to organize it, or if there's some other way you should be going about the whole thing.

Simple, right? Well, not always. You don't always know what's blocking you. Even if you do, you may not know what to do about it. The problem may be one or all three of these things at once. You may know that, or you may just feel numb. Any of these problems can make you feel that way. It's not easy to know what's at the bottom of it. But you don't have to. All you have to do is treat them one at a time.

So, let's take work methods first. I've just addressed some of the work method troubles you may experience and given you some possible solutions (organization doesn't matter, plan or don't, etc.), but **work methods** are addressed in chapter 9, so if you're blocked in that way, review that chapter. If once you've figured out how to approach your work, things get moving, fine. But if you're still stuck, it just means that more than one thing was troubling you or that your problem has shifted. No matter. Just move on to the next solution.

Emotion: All blocks have a large emotional component. They all feel bad. Also, any problem can turn into an emotional block without warning, especially if you drift into thinking, *What's wrong with me now?* But what I'm calling an emotional block is a problem between you and you, how you feel about yourself and your ability, your self and your work, not about some specific work method or story craft problem. This is the most disabling and prolonged kind of block. You can either treat it directly (I will show you how later), or you can *turn it into an issue of craft,* which is the best way if it works. This is also the same thing you do if you have a craft problem, which means this is the **solution for story craft problems** also.

With this method, you ignore the emotional issues, set them aside as much as you can. They're still going to nag at you, but that doesn't have to stop you from acting. Remember, you can't control your feelings, but you can control your actions. (You don't get into the mood to write. You write to get into the mood.) Then you turn your emotional block into a problem of story craft. You do that by using some story material that you're working on or would like to work on. If you don't have any, pick one of the scene or full-story exercises from the course. You need a piece of writing to work on. It doesn't matter what it is as long as you have something. Then apply the story craft to it. You know the formula: want + obstacle + action + resolution + emotion + showing. The plan. Keep your eye on the ball.

Fine, but how? You might feel that you know, or you might not. Either way, I'm going to give you specific directions. All you need to do is to go to chapter 8, on rewriting. Go to the place several pages in where WANT, OBSTACLE, ACTION first appear in large type. Follow it step-by-step. It's all laid out. If everything goes right, it will take you into a story and unblock you in the process. If everything goes right. But what if it doesn't? What if you're still stuck? Well, then you're in the midst of a stubborn emotional block, and you have to treat it directly. How? Read on. That's what the next set of remedies is for.

The first four points make up one remedy and are designed to ease you back into yourself and then into your story (even if you don't have one). Do them first, in this order, and don't stop until you've done all four or you get unblocked and move into working a story. This is the one time to do as you're told, whether you want to or not. That's because when you're seriously blocked, you're in no condition to be thinking for yourself or trying to judge what to do next.

REMEDIES

1. **Wake Up**. The first thing to do is to recognize that you're blocked. It's possible to be wandering around avoiding the idea of writing without realizing you're doing it. It's like when you feel sluggish, lazy, or depressed, before you realize that you're getting sick. You must realize it's got you—the writer's affliction. Now the way you

acknowledge it is key. You acknowledge it by **acting,** by sitting down to your desk and writing, "I'M BLOCKED." Remember that nothing counts until it's on the page. Writing, "I'M BLOCKED," is just the beginning. Next, you continue writing everything that's going on in your head.

In judo, you use the enemy's strength against him. So, not only do you write what's in your head, but you join in the attack. "I have no talent. I have no ideas. I'll never publish. I don't know what to do next in this story." You're already attacking yourself, so do it, all-out, full force. Get it all out there. Put it all down—just how stupid, unimaginative, and gutless you really are. Continue with that until you've drained it all out onto the page, where you can get a good look at it. Often, just reading it and seeing how excessive it is will give you *some* perspective, a bit of an edge on the problem.

Your relationship to an idea on the page is different from your relationship to an idea in your head. You're committing it to print, fixing it, putting it out there, outside yourself, so you can examine it and respond to it. Also, writing something down activates three times more nerve centers in your brain than you use just thinking about it. So, you engage more of yourself and of your awareness. Many people who don't normally write start writing things down when they're in a crisis in order to figure out what's going on, how they feel, and what to do about it. Also, going on record in this way can help you focus and limit your sense of the trouble. In your head, ideas float around, hide out, attack, take cover, etc.

2. **Vent.** Now do some ventilating—ranting and raving, bitching and moaning, howling, purging yourself with what's wrong with this stupid, lousy, asinine process, etc. What you dislike, hate, despise about writing. How it makes you feel. What a waste of time it is. Why only a fool would waste time doing it, etc.

3. **The Good.** You did what's bad. Now write down what's good about writing. What you like or have liked about it in the past. Then, write **what you want to happen right now.** Then, write down what you would like to happen in the long run.

4. **Back Door.** The thought of sitting down and committing yourself to writing an actual story or even a scene may be too intimidating. But that doesn't mean you can't make some progress without actually laying it on the line and tackling the whole thing head-on. In this method, you don't start writing the actual story, but you write down what you'd like to write about once you get going again. You're just exploring the kind of story you *might* write, *possible* characters that *might* be in it, and the direction that the plot *could* take, *maybe*—once you get back to really writing again. Because there's no pressure to commit yourself or pin anything down, characters often start emerging, snatches of dialogue pop up, or full scenes begin taking place and larger portions of story start unfolding. So, by *not trying*, not committing, by just tossing it around on the page, the real thing often starts taking shape.

These first four steps are a unit. If at this point you're ready to work on a story, but still feel stiff, go to chapter 8, on rewriting, and follow the steps that start with WANT, OBSTACLE, ACTION.

If that's too much to face, apply the following solutions until you've recovered.

5. **Burn It.** Write as if no one will ever see your work but you. I call this the *write it, burn it* technique. You're going to write a few pages of a story, then destroy them.

6. **Distraction.** Write distracted. Write with the TV on. Write on the bus, in a crowd. Go to a busy restaurant and write. Now, you can't really watch TV or watch the crowd and write at the same time. In order to write, you have to close out the distraction. To close out

distraction, you have to engage your organized, intellectual, calcu-
lating mind. Sound familiar? The editor, the one who's attacking,
disabling, blocking you, is the part of your mind you use to close
things out. So, you're preoccupying the editor (this lunatic that's
run amuck) by giving him something else to do so you can get
some peace and do some writing.

I worked with a journalist who used to go down to her busy office to write fiction, because she needed the hustle and bustle going on around her to help her keep her mind on her work.

7. *Write Wrong.* Since you're such an awful, untalented, uncreative
writer, **write a terrible story.** Intentionally write the worst story
imaginable. That should relieve the pressure to write well. Also,
you cannot write beneath yourself. You're going to write the way
you write. To write below your ability will take a lot of work—
work you don't have to go through. The idea is to just get the flow
going, to get yourself unblocked. In the course of writing this terrible story, you'll find yourself turning up ideas that aren't terrible,
that have some potential. You can go with them if you want, or,
now that you've made contact with your skills, you can go on to
something else.

8. *Piggyback.* A Greek essayist and biographer named Plutarch who
lived around A.D. 46 whom you probably haven't heard of wrote
The Parallel Lives, which you probably haven't heard of either. His
works were handed down through the years. In the 1500s a young
playwright took many of Plutarch's story ideas and transformed
them into his own plays. The plays were *Romeo and Juliet, Julius
Caesar, Coriolanus, Timon of Athens,* and *Antony and Cleopatra.* Yes,
Shakespeare "stole" the plots for these plays. In the broad sense,
there's no copyright on plot—unless you do the exact same story.
Older stories, classics, are fair game. You're free to retell them any-

way you like. *The Wide Sargasso Sea* retells *Jane Eyre* from the point of view of the wife who was locked in the attic. *Wuthering Heights* has been retold from the point of view of Heathcliff. *Great Expectations* was retold in a modern setting. *Ahab's Wife* is a retelling of *Moby-Dick* from the point of view of Ahab's wife. *Rosencranz and Gildenstern* is a play based on two minor characters from *Hamlet*. Hemingway was told the story of a man alone in a small boat catching a giant fish, and he put a man he knew personally in as the character and wrote *The Old Man and the Sea*. Bernard Sabath, my friend and mentor, wrote a play in which Tom Sawyer and Huckleberry Finn meet again in old age. (It was produced on Broadway, with George C. Scott and John Cullum as the stars.) Many stories have been written using God, the Devil, Christ, or other biblical characters *(The Inferno, Paradise Lost)*. When you use the classics, you have the originals—the Bible, Shakespeare, the Brontës, Melville, Twain—working for you.

Now, the goal here is to get unblocked. So, you might fool around with putting Woody Allen in as Rambo or your uncle in as King Lear or your aunt as Madame Bovary or combining characters from different classics (Hamlet meets Gatsby). Remember *Abbott and Costello Meet Frankenstein*? Once you're unblocked, you can get back to what you were working on before you were disabled or continue with this or one of the other remedies that could turn into a full-blown project. If they do, then all the better.

9. ***Editing Your Way Back.*** With this approach, you get one of those cheap novels you find in a dime store or drugstore. They used to call them dime novels. They're often romance novels, and they're very poorly written. Get the worst one you can find, take it home, and edit it. You'll find plenty to do, cleaning things up, rewriting dialogue to make it more believable, and working conflict (want +

obstacle) and action into every scene. Now, again, the goal is just to get unblocked, but if you really get absorbed in this task and find new dimensions for the characters and drama for the plot and go all the way through, it won't be the author's novel, it'll be *your* novel. You won't have to worry about plagiarism, and you'll be unblocked.

10. ***Quit!*** If it's so bad, so painful, so miserable, why not quit? I bring this up because I did it once. I'd only been writing for a few years, but I was quite serious about it. I wasn't writing much. My life was a mess, and I had little or no time to write, and I was agonizing about it. In the middle of it I thought, *Why bother? Why torture myself like this? Who cares? Why not just quit?* So I did, for about a day and a half. For the first day, even though I wouldn't have written anyway, I felt something was missing in me and in my life. Just the *idea* that writing was no longer a part of my life made me feel empty and adrift. Writing was my rudder, even though I wasn't doing it. But I didn't want to go through the punishment anymore.

About halfway through the second day I thought, *Well, maybe I'll just do it for the fun of it.* The fun of it? Fun, the reason I got into it in the first place when I took my first writing class and loved it. It was *fun.*

So, I didn't need to quit. I just needed to get back to the fun of it—to write what I felt like writing, the way I felt like writing it, and the hell with the rest of the world. And that must be true for you also. You must have experienced some pleasure in writing at one time. So, you need to remind yourself that it's OK to enjoy it, to play around, goof off, on the page—*just for the fun of it.* Not only will it be fun, but that's often when you do your best writing. Which brings us to an important point.

The less you care, the better you write. The harder you try, the worse it gets. It sounds strange, but the more you care, the harder you try to make your writing really good, the worse you write. So, don't be surprised if the writing you work your hardest to make really good turns out to be stiff and dull, while the writing you dash off on the spur of the moment and don't have time to think about or put a lot of effort into will be more alive and exciting. When you try hard, you're too conscious, too aware of what you're doing, trying for too much control. You're preoccupied with judging every move you make and that tends to make you tense up.

So, what's the solution? Stop caring? No, that won't work. Trying to force the tension away will only make it worse. You can't control your feelings, but you can control your actions. The solution is to just keep writing and writing and writing. If you write enough, you'll get past that tension and loosen up. The problem will solve itself. You'll be able to *let go*, to *get out of the way* and let it happen. Remember, **you don't do it. It does you.**

Ray Bradbury's solution, in his neat little book *Zen and the Art of Writing*, is to work, relax, and don't think. The way you learn to relax is to work and work and work. You tire yourself out so that you loosen your controlling grip on everything. You tire yourself out so you don't have the energy to keep fussing with your work, and you just knock it out to get it over with. The way you learn to not think (to not think the kind of thoughts that get you blocked) is to work, work, work. You help yourself by working, relaxing, and not caring. *The less you care, the better you write. The harder you try, the worse it gets.* So relax—you don't have to take it or yourself so seriously.

11. *Sleeping Giant.* When you're blocked, you are of two minds. One part of you wants to write, while the other wants none of it. You

experience a tug-of-war within yourself. Two minds at least, maybe more. Sometimes it's more like a riot than a tug-of-war. Our concern here is with two minds—conscious and subconscious—and connecting the two. The subconscious is where most of our mind, our knowledge and our experience, resides—where imagination dwells. Only a small amount of who we are and what we know is in our conscious minds at any one time. We are and we know a lot more than what we are consciously aware of.

The subconscious is endlessly creative and full of great ideas, but it often acts more like an ingenious tease than the creative powerhouse that it is. The subconscious is capable of enormous work, but it's not waiting on the doorstep to be let in and put to the task. No, it's hiding out. It may be endlessly inventive, but it's also inherently lazy. If it's not made to work, it won't. The good news is, it's quite trainable. The techniques you use to train it are an excellent way of getting unblocked. In fact, much blocking happens because of this subconscious resistance.

You must do two things in order to train your subconscious. First you must get its attention, then you must condition it to be ready to go when called upon. The first, getting its attention, is accomplished by getting in touch with it. The best time to do that seems to be first thing in the morning, before you talk to anyone or read anything. Some call this *morning pages* or *flow writing*.

The first step is to begin writing as soon after you awaken as possible. Sit up and begin writing while still in bed, or go directly to your desk. The reason you do it when you have just awakened is that you're closer to your subconscious in that state. What you write is totally irrelevant as long as you write complete sentences and don't write the same sentence over and over. You can write about a dream, your plans for the day, what happened yesterday, your hopes for the future, your worries about the future, how much you hate doing these morning pages, and how stupid it is. Whatever's in your head is fine. Your thoughts can skip around. They don't need to have any particular focus or transitions to tie them together. Just write. Go steadily for 15 minutes or until you fill one page. (If you're not able to do this first thing in the morning because of your lifestyle or the way your mind works, then do it the first chance you get—before setting off in the car, on the train or bus, before getting out of your car in the parking lot, or get to work early and get a cup of coffee and do 15 minutes hiding out in a back booth of a coffee shop.)

Do this kind of flow writing until you can fill a page or more easily in 15 minutes. If you can spare the time, write until you can fill two pages in 20 to 30 minutes. If not, the one page is fine as long as you can start as soon as you sit down and continue through to the end without stopping, editing, or criticizing. When you finish these pages, do not reread or reexamine them in any way. Put them away and leave them alone until you've completed the second phase of the training.

The next step is to train your subconscious to be available, any time, any place, at the drop of a hat. This is the critical part of all of this. Morning pages and flow writing are popular, but those methods alone will not give you the kind of access you need to be fully creative. The way you do that is to schedule a 15-minute writing period during the day. So, if you know you're going to be free from 7:00 to 7:15 this evening for sure, make a date with yourself. When 7:00 comes, sit down and flow write for 15 minutes. If you get involved, you can write more, but the timing is the important thing in this phase of the training. Tomorrow, you will do the same thing, but it must be **at a different time.** It doesn't matter when you do it as long as it's at a different time. The farther away from yesterday's time, the better—at least two hours' difference, if possible.

The main thing is that you plan carefully so that your time will be free and, come hell or high water, you sit down and begin writing on the dot. Do not put it off for one second. You must never negotiate. If you negotiate, you're giving the subconscious the message that maybe you're not all that serious, maybe there's a way out. That's a bad message to give to an unruly child. If you give it the slightest opening, it will use all its genius to sidetrack you. You cannot afford to waver. That's why it's critical that you set the time when you're certain you can make it. Then, at the appointed moment, you must sit and begin writing immediately. Write anything you want, just as you did before. You can complain about how difficult this is, how much you hate it, how stupid it is, etc. You might write out orders to your subconscious to just shut up and get busy, etc.

Remember, the resistance is coming from your subconscious, which does not want to let go of its defenses and give itself over to the process. But the more you do this, the easier it gets. Taking the plunge will become easier and easier. Eventually your subconscious will be your partner rather than your adversary. Continue with this second part until you are able to do it without resistance. Then you can go on to whatever project you choose. You may want to go through all the pages you've filled in these exercises and see what you've got, or go onto something else.

12. *The Invisible Enemy.* Often when you're blocked, what's blocking you isn't visible. "I don't know what's wrong. I just can't get started." There's a problem or unanswered question that you're not aware of that's holding you back. I was once writing about a character who was getting off work and heading home from down-

town. He was going to take the subway. At that point, I stopped and began staring at the wall. I didn't know what to do next, but I wasn't aware that I didn't know. I knew what was going to happen when he got home, but how did I get him there? It was a simple transition problem, getting from here to there on the subway, but how did I make the subway ride eventful and meaningful? That's what was blocking me, *but* I wasn't aware of it. So, I sat there, feeling stumped, not knowing what to do next.

After a half hour in the fog, I realized what was going on, that the ride on the subway was the problem, that I didn't know how to make the subway ride eventful, worthwhile. Once I was aware of the problem, I was able to solve it quickly. How do you imagine I got the character home? Well, I had him finish work, head for the door, and then I wrote: "When he got home . . ."

I eliminated the subway ride completely, along with the walk home from the subway, climbing the stairs to his apartment, fumbling for keys, opening the door, etc.—all of which might have been meaningful in another story, but not in this one—not for this character. At that time, as I saw it, I didn't need any of it. He went from his work to home, inside his apartment, in one short sentence. I could just as well have said, "After dinner that evening," skipping even more and getting away with it. Fiction is selective. In this case, something I didn't need to do but thought I did, something I was actually able to do easily (that's not always the case), had me stumped, simply because I hadn't made myself put the problem in focus, hadn't asked myself directly, "What's the problem here? What's holding me back?" My problem was that I wasn't aware of the problem.

Thinking that the subway ride was necessary was the first level of my problem. Thinking that I *needed* to make it eventful when I had no idea how and no interest in doing it was the other level. I sat there, unable to move, with a vague notion that I should do something even though I had no ideas and no desire to do it, *and* **I wasn't fully aware of any of it.** I wasn't aware because I hadn't said, "Exactly what is the problem here?"

Now, another writer might have done wonderful things with the subway ride. I might have also—in a different story with a different character. And even in this story, I might, in later drafts, have decided to use the subway ride. Nothing is final in this game, until you decide it is. The important thing here is that I couldn't see what was in my way, because I hadn't asked myself, "How do I get him home? What happens on the way?" And I especially hadn't realized that my problem was that I didn't know how to make this el ride worthwhile. And I hadn't asked, "Do I need it?" Once I did, I saw what the problem was and solved it easily.

13. *Ask and You Shall Receive.* Often we don't have an answer to what's in the way simply because we don't ask ourselves. The most common unanswered question is "What's my problem?" Just asking and answering that *on the page* will put you on the trail of the solution. You can't solve a problem unless you know what it is. Now, if you ask, "What's the problem?" and the answer is "I don't know," the answer to that is "My problem is that I don't know what's wrong." The next step is to work on solving that problem— in this case by figuring out, defining, what the problem is.

But what if you can't figure out what the problem is? What do you do then? Well, no matter how bewildered you feel, there's always a way to move toward a solution. When you are unable to define the problem, *guess.* Guessing is a wonderful tool. After all, guessing is a major part of creating fiction. Fiction is a game of wondering and guessing and imagining. So, when you can't figure out the problem, ask yourself, "What might it be? What are the possibilities?"

ANECDOTES

Here are some anecdotes that make some good points about all of this.

When Tom Wolfe had his first major assignment as a reporter, he did all of the legwork and got all the information ready and then became totally blocked. He went to his boss, the editor, and told him that he couldn't do it. The editor said, "OK, get all your material together, put it down so someone can make sense out of it, and I'll have George do it." Wolfe went home, wrote, "Dear George, this is what I have," at the top of the page, then laid out all the information for him. When he took it in the next day and handed it to his boss, his boss took it, scratched out "Dear George" and told him to give it to the printer. (When the pressure is off, you write better. You may have to trick yourself into it.)

In another anecdote, Wolfe says that he goes to write at a studio away from his home so he won't be distracted. He says that he first gave himself so many hours to put in before he could leave and go home. But he found that he could waste 4, 5, or 6 hours doing nothing just as easily as he could waste 2 or 3. His solution was to force himself to write 1 page per half hour until he wrote 4 pages, and then he could quit. He says that he's always able to force out 1 page every half hour even when it seems awful. On bad days he does his 4 pages and quits. The strange thing, he says, is that later on when he looks back over what he's written, he can't tell the difference between the pages he forced out and the ones he wrote when he felt inspired. (You can't trust your emotions when they're negative. No writer can judge his own work.)

A little girl asked her father what he did at the school where he worked. "I teach people how to draw pictures," he said. "You mean they forgot?" she said. (You have what you need already. You just have to learn [remember] how to use it.)

A mother asked her little boy what he was drawing. "I'm drawing a picture of God," he said. "But no one knows what God looks like," she said. "They will when I get done," he said.

The teacher divided her pottery class into two groups. The first group was told they would be graded only on quality. They would make only one pot that semester, but spend the entire time making the perfect pot. The second group was told that they would be graded on quantity alone. The more pots they made, the higher their grades. At the end of the semester, which group do you think made the better pots? The quantity group had produced far better pots than the quality group. (Quantity leads to quality. You cannot learn on one pot—or one story.)

Write the way you talk. The language of fiction is simple, emotional, direct. Don't send the reader to the dictionary. Use small words.

DAILY PREP LIST

These are things we need to remind ourselves of over and over. This list is worth going over on a regular basis to help prevent blocking.

There is always resistance to writing the first line. Write an instant line as soon as you sit down.

You must write badly first.

You don't think in order to write. You write in order to think. You don't get into the mood to write. You write to get into the mood. Write first. Think second.

You don't do it. It does you. Open up, and *let* it happen. Get out of the way.

Negative emotions (attacks on your work or yourself) are *always* wrong and beside the point. Whatever is happening is OK. It's the process, not you.

The story already exists. You're just writing to uncover the pieces and fit them together.

You are as good as your best writing. If you stick to it, no matter how deeply you slump, you will return to your best level and exceed it. Then you will fall away again. It's up and down just like the rest of your life (good days and bad days). You will always fall away, but you will always come back and exceed yourself—if you stick to it. Bad days are as important as good ones.

CONCLUSION

Now you have thirteen remedies plus some other ways of looking at blocking to help you when you get blocked. When you find yourself blocked, follow the procedure I've laid out for you in this chapter. It's no time to get into a discussion with yourself. First, put your feelings aside as best you can and practice your craft (chapter 8). If you're not unblocked after that, do the first four remedies in the list as part of one approach. Then, if you're not unblocked, start doing the others in whatever order appeals to you. If you do that, you will be unblocked long before you do them all.

All the techniques in this chapter and in the entire course are merely tools designed to help you uncover the energy and drama you have in you. Tools are neutral. You can use them to write anything you want any way you want to write it.

EXERCISES

Two people competing for the love of a third person.

Having to be nice to someone who's treating you badly.

Being in a place where you don't belong—physically or psychologically.

16

Stage and Screen

This chapter may seem too short to cover both screenwriting and playwriting. But it's not, because the story form (conflict, action, resolution) is identical whether it's on the page, stage, or screen. There is no difference. So, what you've learned about story up to here has given you everything you need to create a story for the screen or stage. Also, because stories for stage or screen don't get into the mind the way the written story does, they're actually easier to write.

It's important to realize that **books and courses on writing screenplays or stage plays are 95 percent story and 5 percent format.** That tells us two things. One, story is the all-important ingredient. Two, there isn't that much to the format. What you get in this chapter is all you need to sell your play or screenplay—*if* you have a strong story. Have I said it often enough? It's the story, the whole story, and nothing but the story.

I don't recommend any stage play or screenplay books (or any other books) on story craft. All the books I've read on story (over two hundred) are either too vague or too complicated or give misleading advice. I wrote this book to provide what I couldn't find in any of the books I read.

So, the story form moves comfortably from one medium to the other. Novels become movies. Stage plays become movies. Novels become stage plays and then movies *(Of Mice and Men)*. Once in a while a movie is made into a novel, rarely successfully. Stage plays often lose something when made into movies, since they are created for a confined space. Opening them up without interfering with the flow of the story is tricky. Also, the chemistry between live actors and the audience is lost on the screen.

But novels tend to lose the most when translated onto the screen, with a few exceptions. *Midnight Cowboy* was a weak novel that was made into an excellent movie. A novel is almost always too hefty to get into a single movie, so we only get part of it. *Lonesome Dove* was made into a multipart TV movie that had pretty much the whole story. They did an excellent job—about as good as possible. But was it as good as the book? No. If it was as good as it could have been, but still was not as strong as the book, what was the problem?

That brings us to the important difference between the written story and the performed story. The written story, as I've said before, gets into the mind. It gets into the secret life, the secret thoughts, of the character—the things the character will tell no one. So, by definition, you can't express such thoughts on stage or screen, since you only have speech. The stage uses asides or soliloquies, but unless you're Shakespeare or deliberately writing in an antique style, it doesn't work with modern audiences. Movies sometimes use voice-over, but a little of it goes a long way. It works best in comedy *(Alfie)* and as used in the soaps is often unintentionally comic or heavy-handed. *American Beauty* used it well, but sparingly. In contrast, novels are full of thoughts presented word for word on the page as they occur in the character's mind.

You can get close to the character's thoughts, and you *must*, you *must* find a way for your character to express his deeper feelings, often by forcing him to reveal them. That's the tricky part of doing a stage play or screenplay. So, on the one hand, we could say that what's easier about a stage play or screenplay is that everything is spoken, it's all dialogue, and you *don't have to* get into the character's mind. On the other hand, we could say that what's trickier about a stage play or screenplay is that everything *must* be spoken. It's all dialogue. You *cannot* get into the character's mind. However you put it, you can never go as deeply into the character on stage or screen as you can in the written story.

So, the screenplay, because it's all dialogue (doesn't get into the mind) and is not confined by setting, is the easiest to write. It is, however, because of the nature of the film industry, a lot harder to market. A lot of people have to agree, have to come together, to work together and put out a huge amount of money to produce a film. All of these are obstacles. Stage plays are similar in that, again, a lot of people have to agree and cooperate to put them together. (More on stage play and screenplay marketing later.)

The story form is identical, but the format for screenplays and stage plays are quite different from the written story and from each other.

SCREENPLAY

What you need to sell a screenplay, besides a good story, is a *spec script*. A spec script is not what is used to shoot a movie. That's called a *shooting script* and has all the technical directions for shooting the movie. It's not the best way to showcase your story. You want your story to be as readable as possible. So, you should only put in enough shooting directions to allow the reader to understand the story, and no more. If you're not a filmmaker, you shouldn't get into them, because you'll look like an amateur. If you are a filmmaker, you should know better already. Both spec and shooting scripts use the same format. Screenplays are from 90 to 120 pages long.

The screenplay for *Basic Instinct*, bought for three million dollars, contained only dialogue, scene headings, and description. That's what we'll concentrate on here. That's all you need.

Remember, you should only be putting down what can be seen or heard. Don't describe how the character feels. "He was furious. He could stand it no longer. He had to strike out" should not be in a script. Those feelings are what the character is supposed to be expressing through actions—what can be filmed.

> "You having a good time?" Marlo said, pushing away from the card table. "A great time," said Eddie. "That's my money you got in front of you," said Marlo. "Not anymore." "Money ain't gonna help you where you're going." Marlo raised his pistol. "Say good-bye to your last pot."

Although this isn't in script form, it's all visual.

There's really nothing tricky about the screenplay form. It's all perfectly logical, just another way of doing the same old thing—telling a story, another way of showing what's going on with language—**the language of film.** Instead of describing a setting, you say:

INT. LARGE KITCHEN—DAY
Outside the window over the sink, a DIRTY, BEARDED FACE appears. The face bobs back and forth, looking down into the kitchen sink.

("INT." stands for interior.) It's a simple matter of giving us what we need to *see*. In an early chapter, I said that fiction is a most visual medium. I was talking about the *written* story. **The written story is at least as visual as film.** If the reader doesn't have a picture in his head, your story is in trouble. So, in that sense, this is nothing new. It's just slightly different language for telling a story. The main thing is that **you don't have to know how to make a film to write a good screenplay.** You don't have to know how to use a camera, light a scene, edit film, etc. The professionals who read your screenplay see things in cinematic terms and will have their own ideas on how to film it. You don't want to get in the way of their expertise.

Don't get me wrong. You need to learn the form and know how to put your story into it. But in the end, it's your story that does the job—that sells your screenplay. If you can tell a strong story, the world (Hollywood included) will beat a path to your door.

Basically there are three elements: **1** Headings. **2** Description. **3** Dialogue.

Here's how it's done:

1   EXT. WHEAT FIELD—DAY

2   A WOMAN is running through the wheat pursued by a
     MAN on horseback

3   WOMAN
             The Lord is my shepherd. I shall not want.
             He leadeth me to green pastures.

2   She turns and looks at the horseman bearing down on her.

3   WOMAN
             Bastard. Son of a bitch. Jesus, please. Just
             this once.

Those are the fundamentals of the screenplay form. There are a lot more things that you can do. Just think about it. A close-up of the rider's face. An over-the-shoulder shot as he bears down on the woman. You might come in from an aerial shot of the two characters from high above. The thing is not to get bogged down in these particulars unless you have a sense for them. Get your story out first, with scene headings, dialogue, and description, then go back and put in as many shooting directions as you think you can get away with. But be careful not to overdo it. Check out books by Syd Field and *The Screenwriter's Bible* by David Trotter. They both have different ways of presenting the same material and are both worth looking at if you want to get into more specifics. But you don't have to. If you're not sure that something is needed, leave it out. Both books do a good job on format, but I don't recommend them or any others for story.

In terms of type style, the standard is twelve-point Courier. You won't go wrong with that. You might go wrong with others. Don't get fancy with any of this—no pictures, no fancy paper, fancy cover, fancy binding, or fancy title page. The only thing that you have to sell is your story. Stick to that. To bind your screenplay, use a heavy, solid-color cover and bind it together with a three-hole, round-head fastener. It should be typed only on one side, on white, 8½ x 11 paper. The title page should have the title in the middle of the page with "a screenplay by [your name]" under it. In the lower right-hand corner, put your address and phone number. That's all. Your screenplay begins on the next page with "FADE IN:" at the left-hand margin. It ends with "FADE OUT." Do *not* number your scenes.

The next thing that you need to do before you try to market your screenplay is to protect it. You can do that by copyrighting it and by registering it with the Writers Guild of America.

Copyrighting is easy. All you have to do is get the forms and fill them out. They're very simple. For screenplays you need the Class PA (performing arts) forms. They're free. You can get them by writing to: Information and Publications Section, Copyright Office, Library of Congress, Washington, DC 20559. Request the "Application for Copyright Registration." Or you can call 202-707-3000 and order the forms over the phone. Internet: *www.loc.gov/copyright*.

To register with the Writers Guild, contact the Writers Guild of America, 555 West 57th St., New York, NY 10019. Phone: 212-757-4360. Internet: *www.wga.org*.

You do not have to include copyright or registration information on your screenplay, but it's important to copyright it.

You've written your screenplay. You've protected it. Now it's time to market it. The screenplay game is the most cutthroat of all. There's a wide range of advice. The advice covers the gamut from saying that you must move to L.A. where the action is to saying that you can market your screenplay just as easily from Peoria, Illinois. To cover the different strategies would take another one to two hundred pages, so I'm going to have to cop out by referring you elsewhere. *Selling Scripts to Hollywood* by Katherine Atwell Herbert is worth looking at. *Writer's Market* also has a section on marketing screenplays. These books will also tell you how to enter **screenplay contests** and will give you a list of them. The contest prizes range from $250 to $25,000. In addition, they're judged by professionals who are on the lookout for new material. Even if you don't win, you'll get exposure and have a chance of selling your screenplay that way.

A good reference guide in all of this is *Writer's Guide to Hollywood Producers, Directors and Screenwriter's Agents* by Jeff Herman, from Skip Press. This book also gives you the ins and outs of marketing your screenplay.

Another thing to consider is that it may well be easier to break into movies by writing your story as a novel. As I said in an earlier chapter, the mystery is the easiest kind of novel to write and the easiest to sell. Also, you can write a solid mystery thriller without having to get so deeply into your character's mind (the hardest part). Literary agents and publishers are well aware of movie rights that are part of many book deals. Pay attention, when you see a movie, to the screenplay credits and see how many say, "From the novel by _____." A huge number of novels are turned into movies. Also, there's nothing stopping you from writing the novel and then the screenplay and marketing them together. But don't force yourself. If your heart's not in it, chances are it won't work.

STAGE PLAY

Once again, I remind you, story is story, no matter where you find it. The form is the same in a stage play (conflict + action + resolution) as in any other kind of story. Traditionally it's Act One: conflict, Act Two: action, Act Three: resolution. The difference is that it's all dialogue (no thoughts) and a confined space. As a beginning playwright, don't write anything that requires elaborate staging. Keep it simple and inexpensive to stage, with as few set changes as possible. Pay attention to the plays you see. Also, check out *A Streetcar Named Desire* and *The Glass Menagerie* by Tennessee Williams, *Death of a Salesman* by Arthur Miller, *Who's Afraid of Virginia Woolf* by Edward Albee.

Just like the screenplay form, the stage play form is totally logical. It's even simpler, since you can't get distracted worrying about camera angles, etc. Use white, 8½ x 11 paper. You can't go wrong with twelve-point Courier type. Use a solid-color cover and bind it with a sturdy binder. Left margin is 1½ inches. Right margin is 1 inch. Stage plays are eighty to one hundred pages long.

The first page inside the cover is the title page. The title should be centered 3 inches from the top of the page, underlined, in capitals.

Two spaces below is the description (e.g., "A Play in Three Acts"). Single-spaced below that is the word "by." Single-spaced below "by" is the author's name.

THE CASE AGAINST MY WIFE
A Play in Three Acts
by
Bill William

The copyright notice goes in the lower left-hand corner. Author's address and phone go in the lower right-hand corner.

On the page following the title page you list the characters. Type the word "CHARACTERS" in the center. The character list starts two spaces below, with the name at the far left and the description several spaces to the right. The description is single-spaced.

George Longman: A big, ham-handed, potbellied, tiny-footed
                   yet graceful, maternal man.
Fred Fredrick: A thin, pale, fragile, yet vicious policeman.

If you have space, put the time and place on this page.

Time: The present.
Place: Chicago.

Page numbers are typed in the upper right-hand corner. The numbers start with the first page in the first scene. In one-act plays the page numbers appear alone. In multiple-act plays the act appears as a Roman numeral, followed by the page. Act One, page one is "I-1." If you have multiple scenes in an act, the scene number appears between the act and the page number. Act One, Scene Two, page 22 is "I-2-22." The page numbers are consecutive throughout. Don't start numbers over with a new scene or a new act.

We have the time and place, but we need to know the exact setting and what's taking place as the curtain rises. This is how to do it:

<u>ACT I</u>
<u>Scene 1</u>

SETTING: Lunch counter with booths along the sides. Pay phone near the door. Cash register on counter at right.

AT RISE: Manager, GEORGE, is standing at the cash register.

The lines of dialogue are single-spaced and run from the left margin to the right. Double-spacing is used between character's speeches. The characters are identified by their names in capitals in the middle of the page.

GEORGE
(singing sweetly to self)
I hate this job. I hate myself. I hate the world and everybody in it. This place is going down the drain, down the drain, down the drain, and I'm going with it.

If the stage direction (such as "singing sweetly to self" above) is more than one word, it goes on a separate line. If it's one word, it goes on the same line.

FRANK (sadly)

If two characters are talking at once, the format runs like this:

GEORGE   FRED
Don't start with me today.   You want me to leave? I'll go.

A scene ends with:

(BLACKOUT)
(END OF SCENE)

At the end of the play it's:

THE END

Those are the basics. Check out a few scripts and see how play-wrights do it. There's nothing tricky about it. The main thing is that what's going on needs to be clear.

You copyright a play the same way as you do a screenplay (see above).

The procedure for marketing plays is different from that for other story forms—especially short stories and novels. With plays, it's about production, not publication. You want to get your play performed. You submit your play to 1. Theater and production companies, 2. Special programs, 3. Contests, and 4. Agents. The best way to find out how to do that is to check *The Playwright's Companion,* published by Feedback Theatrebooks. They do an excellent job of laying it all out. There's much more than we can do justice to here. A second book to look at is *The Playwright's Handbook* by Frank Pike and Thomas G.

Dunn. *Writer's Digest* and *The Writer* magazines also regularly list upcoming play contests.

One thing to remember when marketing your material is to send it out, then *get busy writing something else*. Don't wait around for a reply.

Speaking of getting busy, let's do it. Here are some exercises. You also have lots of others from before. Pick something, anything, and write.

EXERCISES

Trying to get fired.

Do Cinderella from the point of view of the stepmother and make her sympathetic.

Do Little Red Riding Hood from the point of view of the wolf and make him sympathetic.

17

To Market to Market

WHEN TO SUBMIT, HOW, AND WHY

OK, so you've worked your heart out and finished a short story or a novel. What's next? I've said that writing is art, not science. Well, marketing your work is business, not art. Although there is some art to the business of marketing.

When: OK, so how do you know when you're ready to submit your work? You probably won't, but it doesn't matter. There's no set time. And you have nothing to lose beyond some self-esteem if you get rejected. You can't hurt yourself by submitting early. My advice is that you submit early and submit often. Get used to rejection. It goes with the territory. *Gone With the Wind* was rejected twenty-six times. "There's no interest in the Civil War," the editors said. The thing to keep in mind in all of this is that the editor or reader at the other end, who reads your story, is just a person with prejudices, personal tastes, and skewed judgment like everyone else, and not some literary god, applying infallible rules of editing and marketing.

Also, if you get rejected by a magazine or a publisher, you haven't blown your chances for that story at that magazine. In fact, if you sent it back by return mail, chances are you'd get a different reader. That reader might have a different reaction, or he might not. I don't advise resubmitting that fast. It's better to wait a month and retitle your story.

You **don't need a perfect story** in order to submit. If you have a story that has some real strengths beyond its weaknesses, send it out. If you work it too much, trying to make it perfect, you run the risk of weakening the strong points. Also, it doesn't have to be perfect to get published. As long as it gives the reader enough, it has a chance. Even if they don't accept it, the editors may like the strong parts so much that they'll ask you to rewrite the story according to their suggestions and resubmit it.

Why: So, you're always hoping to get published, but you also submit just to **get their attention,** to create some interest in you and your writing. Also, editors do a lot of rewriting and correcting themselves. I would advise letting them do anything they want to your writing if it means getting into print. That's your choice. But realize that if they do rewrite your work, you may not like or may even hate the changes they make.

The short story market is not good. The *New Yorker,* the flagship of short stories, used to publish two short stories a week. They cut it down to one or none. That was a blow. To make matters worse, when this reshuffling took place, short stories got some bad press. At least one negative article appeared in a major national publication, claiming research had shown that even though readers said they really liked the fiction, they couldn't name the last story they read or the author. Not remembering the title or author is a common problem in my experience, but the researchers used that to prove stories didn't justify the costly space they took to publish. That idea seemed to catch on. So, it was a double hit.

All this means that you could be writing publishable stories and not getting published because there's so much competition for so few spots. Magazines tend to publish the big names first, even if it's poor quality material, since they increase sales. Several years ago, when the market was decent, one study claimed that the average story that got published had been rejected twenty-eight times before it was accepted. Now, I don't know what went into that average and what magazines were studied, but I think it's a rough gauge of the market, even now.

How: OK, so you're going to submit a short story. (We'll get to novels next.) What should you do? First, let me tell you what you should *not* do. Do not go to the store and buy two manila envelopes, one for the submission and one for self-addressed stamped envelope (SASE) for the return, and then take them to the post office and then go home and sit down and wait for a reply. It'll take one to six months to get a response, so you need to get writing again right away. That's the first thing. Get going on something else.

Now, if you've gone through the procedure I've described above, when your story comes back with a rejection slip, which is a downer, you have to start all over and go out and buy two more envelopes and go to the post office to get them weighed and mailed to the next magazine. Not only is that a drag, but there's a good chance that you will put it off and not do it for a while or ever.

So, what do you do? Well, I'm assuming that you're going to keep writing stories and submitting them. In that case, go to an office supply store and buy a whole box of manila envelopes. They come in boxes of one hundred, and they're a lot cheaper that way. While you're there, buy yourself a postal scale. They go for about eight to fifty dollars. A basic one will do. Then go to the post office and buy lots of stamps. One hundred dollars' worth or more. So, now you're fully equipped and don't have to go running around to send out a story.

The next thing to do is make a list of 20 or more magazines you want to submit to. I'll tell you how to choose the magazines later. After you make your list, address all twenty envelopes and the twenty return (SASE) envelopes. After you've done that, it's time to send them out. The problem is that if you submit to 1 magazine at a time, it'll take two years or more to make the rounds to 20 magazines. I recommend submitting to 5 magazines at one time. Submitting to more than 1 magazine at a time is called *simultaneous submission*.

Writer's Market, a publication that's updated regularly and is in any good library, is the standard reference for how and where to submit short fiction to magazines. It has a complete list of all the magazines you would want to submit to and what their editorial policy is. *Writer's Market* will tell you the basics that you need to know. But there are some other issues that you need to consider when submitting.

Some magazines don't want simultaneous submissions. Others say that it's OK, but want you to tell them if you're submitting elsewhere. This brings us to an important and perhaps sticky point of strategy in this whole game.

Do you do simultaneous submissions to magazines that don't want them? Their policy may say no, but they have no way of knowing what you've done. And if you submit to magazines that take simultaneous submissions, do you tell them as they ask you to? I'm not going to tell you what to do, but I'll tell you what I've found works best. I submit to at least 5 magazines at a time regardless of their submission policy. Of course, if they don't want simultaneous submissions, I'm not telling them I'm doing it. But even if they accept simultaneous submissions, I don't tell them. I see no advantage in telling them and some possible disadvantages.

Think about it. A first-level reader at the magazine opens an envelope with a story from an unknown, unpublished author and a note that says, "I've submitted this to these 3 other magazines," etc. What's he going to say—"I'd better hurry up and read this unknown, unpublished author's story before someone else gets it"? How is telling the magazine going to help you? It isn't. Plus, the chances of 2 magazines wanting your story are extremely remote. And, if you do get an acceptance from 1 magazine, all you do is shoot letters off to the others and ask them to withdraw your story. Apologies. "I hope this won't hurt our future relationship," etc., etc., etc.

This has been my practice, and I've never had any trouble. The main reason to do it is to avoid wasting two years waiting for a single story to make the rounds.

There are magazines that publish fiction but do not take unsolicited manuscripts. That means you must write, query, them first and tell them what you'd like to send them. Or it may mean that they will only respond to agents. Sending them an unsolicited manuscript is a very long shot. Chances are that you'll get it back fast with a note saying that they do not take unsolicited manuscripts. But there's always the very slim chance that someone will open it and see that it's unsolicited but be curious enough to read it anyway. You have nothing to lose but postage.

Also, it may be worth a try if you think that you have just the kind of story the editors are looking for. You can send it cold and let it fend for itself, or you can get tricky and address it to one of the fiction editors and say, "Here's the story I told you about. Thank you so much for reading it." Or you might say, "I know you don't take unsolicited manuscripts, but I'm taking a chance because I think this is your kind of story. It belongs in your magazine." Or you may think of another strategy.

I once sent a short story to *Harper's* magazine, not realizing that they weren't even publishing fiction at that time. I got it back with a long personal letter from the senior editor, saying that he regretted that *Harper's* was not publishing fiction, especially since he'd had such a great time reading my story. It was a fine story, and he was sure it would be published elsewhere. Did I regret sending that story? Of course not. That kind of confirmation from someone at the very top meant a lot to me as a young writer. And it taught me something else. If *Harper's* didn't print fiction, how did my fiction make it all the way up to the desk of the senior editor? Surely it wasn't his policy to have every piece of fiction mistakenly submitted routed to him. It had to be a fluke. And if *Harper's* had been publishing fiction but *not* taking unsolicited manuscripts, that fluke could have meant publication.

Where do you submit? You're a beginning writer, so you should start at the bottom, submitting to the small literary magazines, and work your way up, right? Wrong. Where do you start? At the very top—the *New Yorker,* the *Atlantic Monthly, Harper's, Esquire, Redbook,* etc. Why? Because your chances are just as good with those magazines as with literary magazines, especially with the prestigious literary magazines, whose standards are just as high as those of the *New Yorker,* the *Atlantic Monthly,* et al. The *Atlantic Monthly* is especially receptive to unknown writers. They claim to have over six hundred unpublished writers they're encouraging to keep submitting. Also, the bigger magazines are much more efficient at reading and returning your story no matter what the response. They usually report in 4 to 8 weeks, sometimes in 2 or 3 weeks. Some of the literary magazines take 3 to 6 months. So, the big magazines report sooner, treat you better, are just as prestigious, and pay a lot *more money.* Some of the top literary magazines only pay $100 or $200 plus 5 or 10 free copies of the magazine your story runs in. The big magazines often pay $2,000 and up for a story. So, in 1 month or 2 you can hit all the big magazines and get a yes or a no. Then what? If you've been rejected, *then* you go to the small magazines.

Which small magazines do you submit to, and how do you decide? You choose on the basis of two elements—prestige and prize/anthology opportunity. If you're going to let a story go for $200, you want to have a chance of getting picked for one of the anthologies of top stories for the year. Go to the bookstore, and see what short-story anthologies are on the shelf—*The Best Short Stories of 1999, The Best of the Pushcart Press,* etc. There are several. They come and go. Ask the bookstore people or a librarian which are considered the best.

Next, look at what magazines the stories in the anthology first appeared in. If any of them are from literary magazines or other magazines that you failed to submit to, those are the ones you should submit to next. In the back of the anthology will be a list of all the magazines the editors looked at for stories. There might be a couple hundred. Pick the best of those. Some, like *Story, Paris Review, Tri Quarterly, Partisan Review, Mother Jones,* and *Fiction,* have been around for a long time and are well-thought-of. Many are connected to universities. Again, the bookstore people or a librarian should be able to help you pick the better ones. *Writer's Market* will also have information on them.

The books I've mentioned above will tell you how to prepare your manuscript. Another useful book is *Manuscript Submission* by Scott Edelstein. The whole idea is to make your manuscript as readable as possible and have it formatted (margins, spacing, etc.) so that it can be used in preparation for publication. For that reason, you put the title halfway down the first page with the name that you want to appear below it. That way you're leaving space for any notes the editor may want to make. Also, leave a one-inch margin all around. Use decent white paper, but nothing fancy. Never try to make a statement with your paper. It's the sign of an amateur. At the top left-hand corner of the first page, put your name, address, and phone number. At the top right-hand corner goes the number of words. On the following pages, put your last name on the top left-hand corner and the page number in the top right-hand corner. Always double-space.

I would advise using Courier font. It used to be the standard. Use ten-point type. If you use Times New Roman, which is popular, I would use twelve-point type. Readability is the issue. I never send a cover letter with a short story. Some people think you should to make it less impersonal. I think it's just giving the reader something unnecessary to read. If you have any publishing credits, I would attach a note saying, "I've published fiction in . . ." etc. That's the only thing it makes sense to include, and it could help you get a close reading. It's not going to have any effect on whether or not you get published. Don't staple the pages. Put a paper clip on the upper left-hand corner. That way, the reader can compare pages, etc. In the end, use your own judgment. But check out the sources I've given you, and learn enough so that you'll know what you're doing no matter what you try.

What about agents? Well, you won't get an agent for a short story. An agent gets a percentage of what you get. The amount of money paid for a short story doesn't justify an agent getting involved. Even if you have a collection of unpublished short stories, you won't get an agent, because story anthologies are made up of stories that have already been published, with a few unpublished ones thrown in. Even then, there isn't a lot of money in anthologies, and you might not be able to get an agent, although there's no harm in trying. For an anthology of previously published short stories, you would usually have to go directly to the publisher. Some publishers have a desire to promote good writing and might publish a story collection for that reason. Chances are that you won't get much money for it, and neither will the publishers.

Publishers and agents are looking for prolific authors. The questions they often ask are "What are you working on now? What's your next book?" They want someone who will write a number of novels. So, if they like your writing and you're working on a novel, it could help in getting an anthology published. For publishers and the agents, the novel is the thing.

Marketing the novel is a different game. The first move you make with a novel is to try to get an agent. An agent knows the marketplace and how the game is played. With an agent, you'll wind up with more money in your pocket than you would if you went to the publisher on your own and didn't pay an agent. A good way to find agents is to go to the standard reference book, *Writer's Guide to Book Editors, Publishers and Literary Agents* by Jeff Herman, which you can find at any decent library and which is updated regularly like *Writer's Market,* which also has lists of agents. In them, you'll find a list of literary agents nationwide, along with instructions for submitting your work to agents. Each has about fifty pages worth reading.

My personal preference, or prejudice perhaps, is for New York agents who are members of A.A.R. (Association of Authors' Representatives). Local agents tend not to have the contacts or the clout you want to have going for you. New York is where publishing all happens, just as movies happen in Hollywood. Agents, editors, and publishers are right around the corner from each other. My personal feeling is that if, after a thorough beating of the bushes (fifteen to twenty submissions), you can't get a New York agent, there's a good chance that there are problems with your novel and that you need to work on it. A.A.R. membership is the best assurance you have that an agent is ethical. For a list of agents in the A.A.R., check their Web site at *www.AAR-online.org*.

Besides what I'm going to tell you, you should see what *Writer's Market* and *Writer's Guide to Book Editors, Publishers and Literary*

Agents have to say about getting an agent. One other book worth checking out is *Literary Agents* by Michael Larsen.

The two big issues, as I see it, are the query letter and the synopsis/outline. The query letter is what you write to get the agent interested in reading your novel. Some agents will take a synopsis and fifty to one hundred pages unsolicited. If so, the query letter is not necessary. They may want a cover letter, however. A cover letter tells them about your novel and yourself—the gist of your novel and any credits you have.

The sources that I've given you will tell you how to go about writing cover letters. My advice is to keep them short and to the point. Never tell an agent or editor how good your writing is. That's their business. They don't need or want you giving them an evaluation of your writing. Give them the facts of the story. You can tell them why you think it will sell as long as it's about the marketplace and not about what a great writer you are. As always, show, don't tell. In the end, your story has to sell itself.

The synopsis/outline is another issue. Editors want a quick overview so that they can see what your novel is about and form some idea of how it could be marketed. The big problem, as I see it, is that you may have written a great novel but a lousy synopsis. Boiling your novel down into five to thirty pages is an art in itself. My feeling is that it's better to keep the synopsis as short as possible and hit the high points so that the editors can see the potential and read the novel. The main thing is to do no damage. Create some interest, and shut up. If you go on too long, they may read things into it that aren't there, things that may work against you. You could also write a short synopsis of several pages and a long one and send them both with hopes of hooking them with the short one so that they skip the long one and get into the novel.

For agents I would use the same guidelines I laid out for submitting to magazines: submit to twenty, five or more at a time.

One important thing is that you, the author, should never put up any money to get your work published. You've already put in hundreds of hours of labor writing the book. That's your contribution. Don't get sucked into paying publishing costs. The agent can legitimately ask you to pay some copying, messenger, or express mail fees. Those are the only costs it makes sense to pay. If your writing is good enough, you don't need to pay reading fees (fee to read and evaluate your manuscript) or any of the publishing costs.

There are two kinds of agents you'll be contacting: those who take unsolicited manuscripts (a synopsis and fifty to one hundred pages), and those who want you to query (send a letter telling them about your book and yourself) first.

The rules for the query are the same as for short stories. Check out the reference books I've noted.

If you're submitting a whole novel, you put it in a manuscript box with a cover page and mail it. The cover page will be like the first page of a short story, but with nothing below your name. The novel will start on the next page, with "Chapter One" about one third down the page. Manuscript boxes can be bought at office supply stores. They're a two-piece box that holds five hundred pages. The same kind that paper often comes in, but blank. Don't try to make a statement with your box.

OK, so you've done agents and gotten no bites. What next? You can be your own agent and go directly to the publishers. They're listed in the books whose titles I've given you. Those books will tell you how to submit to them. It's basically the same as submitting to agents.

What do you do if a publisher sends you a letter saying that he wants to publish your book and will pay you x amount of dollars? You can go ahead on your own and accept the deal or try to get more money, but my advice would be to get an agent. You should have no trouble getting an agent for a book that already has a publisher interested. The agent should be able to get you more money than you would get on your own, plus he'll know how to negotiate for paperback and movie rights.

Remember, they're only people at the other end. You're a person too, right? So, learn how the system works, then use your own judgment.

If your novel is accepted, you will get an advance. The advance is the money that the publisher pays you as their part in this business partnership they're willing to enter with you. They're saying that they can make your book work as a saleable item in bookstores. The publisher is the middleman in all of this. Once they've printed your book, they're the ones who have to convince the bookstores to carry it. They have a whole sales staff to do just that. Keep in mind that the advance is not your paycheck for writing the novel. It's simply the publisher's way of sealing the deal and giving you something for going with them. In a sense, both sides are taking a chance. If your book takes off and brings in a fortune, you will clean up also. If your book goes nowhere, the publisher loses what they put into publishing and selling the book, plus the advance, which you get to keep even if the book fails. The publisher has just as much to gain or lose as you do.

Huge advances come when you have a hot, saleable story and an agent who knows how to get the bid up. That's why it can pay to try to get an agent first. Agents know how to play the game and what to ask for and what *not* to ask for. An excellent reference book for all this is *How to Get Happily Published*, by Judith Applebaum.

Contests are another way of getting published. Fiction contests pay as much as $5,000 for a short story and $10,000 for novels. Publication is usually a part of the prize also. The Nelson Algren Awards is a contest run by the *Chicago Tribune* and requires no entry fee. It pays a $5,000 first prize for a short story. You can reach the contest by contacting the newspaper. *Writer's Market* also has a listing of short story, novel, screenplay, stage play, and poetry contests. Some charge a fee, $5 to $30, to enter. That's how they get some or all of the prize money. There's nothing wrong with paying to enter. The writing magazines, *The Writer* and *Writer's Digest,* also publish the contests several times a year. You can buy them at the newsstand or get them from a library.

Even though the subject of this chapter is marketing, you need to keep writing. So, here's the writing material for this chapter.

EXERCISES

A character who is a psychological vampire.

A character being tempted to cheat on his or her lover, coming very close, but not doing it. A close call.

A character looking back on what he or she thought life would be like and how it really turned out. It can be about life in general, marriage, love, children, career, etc.

Conclusion

The single most important thing to keep in mind is that your biggest problem is yourself. Managing yourself so that you keep writing no matter how you feel is the critical issue. Your emotions play a major part in all of this. They are your best guide, your trusted friend. You must depend on them, because without them you're nothing. But no friendship is perfect. The trouble starts when your emotions start suggesting that maybe your ideas aren't so good today, that maybe they're a little silly or foolish or empty or stupid and that perhaps you're wasting your time trying to be a writer, that you really don't have what it takes, that you never did and never will. How do you defend yourself against such a friend?

The one thing you don't do is sit staring at the wall punishing yourself. What you do is catch yourself, remind yourself that you are not in your right mind, that you've been blindsided once again (it happens many times), and that you can never trust your emotions when they're on such a rampage. Then you must act. You must go to your tools immediately. And how do you do that? As soon as you get stuck, ask yourself, "What's the problem exactly? Is it me? Do I feel that I'm no good, that I don't have it? Am I blocked? Or has something in the story got me stumped—something I might or might not be aware of?"

The first step is to define the problem. Then go to the course. It's all there. But it won't help you if you don't use it. Find the place in the course that addresses the issue that's got you stumped. If you're blocked, go to chapter 15, on blocking and unblocking. If it's story that's got you stumped or blocked, go to chapter 8, on rewriting. Follow it step-by-step and do what it tells you. Apply that to whatever is giving you trouble on the page at the time. Also, that's not just for when you're stuck or blocked. You must apply it to every scene, every chapter, and your overall story—with each draft or until you're certain it's there on the page. That is the entire story craft in a nutshell—the source of all drama. These are your tools. They will lead you back into the drama and energy of your story and yourself—everytime.

For every writing problem there's a simple solution. The problem may not feel simple, but your job is to make it simple. You do that not by getting sucked into some extreme emotional judgment of your story or your ability or your character, but instead by stepping back, defining exactly what's in your way, and then finding the solution in the course. Writing can be a lonely, isolating experience. But you're not in this alone. The course is your partner. Keep in touch with it. It's important to keep in touch with the course in two ways: first, by going to it when you're in trouble, but also by going to it on a regular basis. It's part of your training. All the while you're writing or doing your five minutes a day, you need to be reading the course. Two pages every day if possible, one page or half a page if that's all you can do. Don't pressure yourself. Just go to it daily and let it sink in. Keep doing that until you've gone through it at least ten times—particularly chapters 4 through 10 and chapter 14. Different things will impress you at different times as you develop. It won't all register at once.

Keeping in touch in this way is your ongoing training, your way of getting the support and coaching you need. I go over this thirty times a year as I teach. Stories are as complex as life itself. You can't keep it all in your head at once so you need to be reminded regularly what goes into it, how it all fits together, and how and why it works.

A lot, if not all, of this is new. The ideas are new, and what I'm asking you to do is new. Changing your behavior is never comfortable. It takes time to get used to it and to be able to use the tools effectively. But you can do it, and it will work. You have what it takes already. It's in you. You just have to learn how to use it. That's the craft. If you stick with it, eventually it will become a part of you. You will internalize it, and it will start to happen for you. It will be not so much that you do it, but that it does you. When that happens, you will find it's a different and much more exciting game. Believe me, it's worth working for.

For information about *Immediate Fiction*'s online course, turn the page.

About the Author

Jerry Cleaver is the creator of The Writers' Loft—Chicago's most successful independent writers' workshop for the last 20 years. He studied writing at the University of Illinois and Northwestern, where he taught fiction for 10 years. Cleaver has also given special story seminars for Barnes and Noble and *Writer's Digest* and created the "Write Your Novel Now" Internet course. Published in various magazines and ghostwriter of several books, Cleaver has spent the last 30 years studying the creative process and uncovering the fundamentals that make every story and every writer work. He lives in Chicago with his wife. Contact the author at *jerry@immediatefiction.com*.

Index

A.A.R. (Association of Authors' Repre-
    sentatives), 268
Absolute Power (Baldacci), 203
acquired skill
    writing as an, *xix*
action
    conflict and resolution, 25–28
    fine-tuning, 47
    See ALSO conflict
adventure
    example of, 14
agents, 268–69
Albee, Edward, 255
Alfie (film), 79
American Beauty (film), 79
Animal Farm (Orwell), 13–14
Applebaum, Judith, 271
Aristotle, 112, 147
awards
    talent and, *xix*

bad writing
    at first, 2
    technique as a way to fix, 3

Baldacci, David, 203
beginning
    working from, 140
beginning, middle, and end
    necessity of, 187–88
Billy Bathgate (Doctorow), 93
blocks, 211–47
    exercises, 247
    daily prep list, 245–46
    remedies, 232–45
Boys in Autumn, The (Sabath), *xvi*
Bradbury, Ray, 238
Brave New World (Huxley), 15
Brothers Karamazov, The (Dostoyevsky),
    15, 207
Brown, Elizabeth, 28–29, 103

Caldwell, Erskine, 140
Catch-22 (Heller), 4, 5, 216
Catcher in the Rye, The (Salinger),
    205
character
    histories and biographies, 142–43
    as point of view, 155–58

character development, necessity of, 188
characters
  making sympathetic, 259
  sympathy for, 91–92
  worries, fears, hopes of, 88–89
Christie, Agatha, 209
conflict, 20–21, 22–24, 24, 25–28, 32–33
  and action and resolution, 25–28
  fine-tuning, 47, 48–54
Connors, Jimmy, 59
Conrad, Joseph, 105
contests, 271–72
copyrighting, 253–54
craft, 13–15
cutting, 133

dead weight, 186–90
Death of a Salesman (Miller), 255
dialogue
  rewriting, 129–32
discovery
  mistakes leading to, 2
Doctorow, E. L., 93
Dunn, Thomas G., 258–59

Edelstein, Scott, 266
emotion, 28, 57–58, 72–99
  characters, sympathy for, 90–91
  exercises, 96–99
  thought, 78, 79–88, 96
  vulnerability and identification, 92–93
  worries, fears, hopes of characters,
    88–89
exercises, 144–45, 272
  characters, making sympathetic, 259
  fine-tuning, 61–63
  making time to work, 185
  method, 144–45
  mystery writing, 209–10
  plots, 149–51
  point of view, 160

self-editing, 69–71
showing, 108–9
story, 21–22
  rewriting, 134–36
writers block, 247

fantasy
  examples of, 13–14
Faulkner, William, 207
fears
  of characters, 88–89
Field, Syd, 253
Fielding, Henry, 158–59
fine-tuning, 43–63
  action, 47
  the active ingredient, 96–99
  building drama, 56–58
  conflict, 47, 48–54
  exercises, 61–63
  happiness, uses of, 55
  resolution, 47
  showing, 58–61
first draft, finishing, 140
Fitzgerald, F. Scott, 49, 105, 106, 114,
  158–59
flashbacks, 125–28
Flaubert, Gustave, 3–4, 216
Fowles, John, 105, 113–14, 158
French Lieutenant's Wife, The (Fowles),
  105, 113, 158

Geranium, The (O'Connor), 114
Gone With the Wind (Mitchell), 49, 50,
  149, 260
Goodbye, Mr. Chips (Hilton), 4–5, 217
Great Gatsby, The (Fitzgerald), 49, 50, 54,
  155–56

"Haircut" (Lardner), 153–54
Hamlet (Shakespeare), 52–53
happiness, uses of, 55

Harper's magazine, *xv*, 265
Harrison, Rex, 211
Heller, Joseph, 4, 5, 216, 217
Hemingway, Ernest, 146, 210, 229, 236
Herbert, Katherine Atwell, 254
Herman, Jeff, 254
Hilton, James, 4–5
hopes
    of characters, 88–89
How to Get Happily Published
    (Applebaum), 271

identification, 15–16, 19–20
    vulnerability and, 92–93
importance, unimportance of, 3–4
interesting story
    necessity of, 189–90
Intruder in the Dust (Faulkner), 207
Invasion of the Body Snatchers (film), 76

Johnson, Lyndon, 89
Jordan, Michael, 43
Judgement Day (O'Connor), 114

Kazinski, Ted, 13
King, Stephen, 209

Lardner, Ring, 153–54
Larsen, Michael, 269
Last Tycoon, The (Fitzgerald), 114
le Carré, John, 86
Liddy, G. Gordon, 87
likeable character
    necessity of, 189
Literary Agents (Larsen), 269
Lolita (Nabokov), 4
Lonesome Dove (McMurtry), 149, 157

McBain, Ed, 207
"Macintosh" (Maugham), 149
McMurtry, Larry, 149, 157, 200

Madame Bovary (Flaubert), 14
Magus, The (Fowles), 113–14, 158
Man in Full, A (Wolfe), 4, 216
Mann, Thomas, 105
Manuscript Submission (Edelstein),
    266
marketing, 260–72
    agents, 268–69
    contests, 271–72
    literary magazine, 265–66
    magazines, 265–66
    screenplay, 254
    short-story anthologies, 266
    stage play, 258–59
Maugham, Somerset, 149, 176, 205,
    210
Melville, Herman, 49
mess, inevitability of, 1–2
method, 138–45
    beginning, working from, 140
    character histories and biographies,
        142–43
    exercises, 144–45
    first draft, finishing, 140
    multiple stories, working on, 143
    not finishing, 143–44
    planning, 139–40
    premise, writing from, 141
    research, importance of, 141–42
    story, never talking about, 140
Miller, Arthur, 255
Milton, John, 166–67
Misery (King), 209
mistakes
    leading to discovery, 2
Mitchell, Margaret, 49, 149
Moby-Dick (Melville), 14, 45, 155–56,
    236
multiple points of view, 157–58
multiple stories
    working on, 143

mystery writing, 206–9
    example of, 14
    exercises, 209–10

Nabokov, Vladimir, 4
narrator
    nonparticipating, 159–60
    omniscient, 158–59
Nelson Algren Awards (*Chicago Tribune*), 271–72
Nietzsche, 86–87
nonparticipating narrator
    point of view from, 159–60
not finishing, 143–44
novel versus short story, 191–210

obstacle, 38–40
    and conflict, 32–33
Occam's razor, 186
O'Connor, Flannery, 114, 149
Odd Couple, The (Simon), 176
Of Human Bondage (Maugham), 205
Olivier, Laurence, 211
omniscient narrator
    point of view from, 158–59
outlining, necessity of, 189
"Outstation, The" (Maugham), 149, 176
overwriting, 132–33

page (rules of), 1–6
    discovery, mistakes leading to, 2
    importance, unimportance of, 3–4
    mess, inevitability of, 1–2
    technique, 3
    uneven progress, 4–6
    writing badly at first, 2
payoff, 16–17
Perkins, Maxwell, *xiv*
person as point of view, 152–55
Pike, Frank, 258

planning
    importance of, 139–40
Playboy magazine, *xvii–xviii*
Playwright's Companion, The, 258
Playwright's Handbook, The (Pike/Dunn), 258–59
plots, 146–51
    retelling, 235–36
Plutarch, 235
point of view, 152–60
    character, 155–57
    exercises, 160
    multiple, 157–58
    nonparticipating narrator, 159–60
    omniscient narrator, 158–59
    person, 152–55
practice
    importance of, 3–4
premise
    writing from, 141
process, 8–9

rejection letters, *xv–xvi*
research
    importance of, 141–42
resolution, 40–42
    action and conflict and, 25–28
    fine-tuning, 47, 54–55
rewriting, 110–37
    cutting, 133–34
    dialogue, 129–31
    double duty, triple duty, 123–24
    exercises, 134–37
    flashbacks, 125–28
    overwriting, 131–32
    the why technique, 131–32
    writing as, 3, 111–12
romance, example of, 14
Romeo and Juliet (Shakespeare), 49, 56, 118–19
Roosevelt, Franklin Delano, 110

Sabath, Bernard, *xvi–xvii*, 236
"sadistic licence," 49, 120
Salinger, J. D., 205
Schulze, Hugh, 31, 42
science fiction, example of, 13
screen (writing for), 248–50
    copyrighting, 253–54
    marketing, 254
    screenplay, 250–55
Screenwriter's Bible, The (Trotter), 253
self-editing, 64–71
Selling Scripts to Hollywood (Herbert),
    254
sensitivity, 204–5
Shakespeare, William, 118–19, 134–35,
    235
Shaw, George Bernard, 141
"Short Life of Francis Macomber, The"
    (Hemingway), 149
short story versus novel, 191–210
showing, 28–30, 100–9
    as basic weapon, 58–61
    exercises, 108–9
    scene as, 35–38
Silence of the Lambs, 204
Simon, Neil, 176
social interaction
    story as essential to, 11, 11–13
stage (writing for)
    exercises, 259
    marketing, 258–59
    stage play, 255–58
story, 19–42
    cause and effect, 17–18
    the complete story, 15
    conflict, 20–21, 22–24, 24, 25–28,
        32– 33
    craft, 13–15
    emotion, 28
    as essential to social interaction, 11,
        11–13

exercises, 21–22, 38–42
identification, 15–16, 19–20
as need, 9–11
never talking about, 137
obstacle, 38–40
payoff, 16–17
resolution, 40–42
showing, 28–30
showing, scene as, 35–38
as a visual medium, 31–32
story work list, 169, 175–78, 178–80
Streetcar Named Desire, A (Williams),
    255
Streets of Laredo (McMurtry), 149, 157
Sunset Boulevard (film), 79

teachers of writing
    writers as, *xiv–xv*
Teresa, Mother, 72
theory, 7–18
    cause and effect, 17–18
    the complete story, 15
    craft, 13–15
    identification, 15–16, 19–20
    payoff, 16–17
    process, 8–9
    social interaction, story as essential to,
        11, 11–13
    story as need, 9–11
Thirty-Six Dramatic Situations, The, 147
This Boy's Life (Wolfe), 149
thought
    as active ingredient, 78, 79–88, 96
time
    wasting, *xv*
time (for writing), 161–85
    exercises, 185
    feeling it, 183
    five for thirty-day trial period, 165–80
    leaping and looking, 184
    nothing is something, 182

time (for writing) (*cont.*)
  output, 182
  skipping the 5 minutes, 181–82
  slop, 183–84
  story work list, 169, 175–78, 178–80
  30 to 365, 180–81
Tolstoy, Leo, 112
Tom Jones (Fielding), 158–59
Trotter, David, 253
Trump, Donald, 72
Twenty Master Plots, 147

unimportance of importance, 3–4
universal plots, 146–51
  retelling, 235–36

voice and style
  necessity of, 188
vulnerability
  and identification, 92–93

want and conflict, 32–33, 48–54
War and Peace (Tolstoy), 112
Watergate, 87
Watership Down (Adams), 14
Who's Afraid of Virginia Woolf (Albee), 255
"why" technique, 131–32
Wilde, Oscar, 4, 216
Williams, Tennessee, 143, 255

Wilson, Edmund, 114
Wolfe, Tobias, 149
Wolfe, Tom, 4, 105, 216, 217, 245
worries
  of characters, 88–89
Writer magazine, 259, 272
Writer's Digest, 259
*Writer's Guide to Book Editors, Publishers
    and Literary Agents* (Herman), 268,
    268–69
*Writer's Guide to Hollywood Producers,
    Directors and Screenwriter's Agents*
    (Herman), 254
Writer's Market, 254, 263, 266, 268, 272
writers
  as writing teachers, *xiv–xv*
writers block, 211–47
  exercises, 247
  daily prep list, 245–46
  remedies, 232–44
Writers Guild of America, 253, 254
writing
  as an acquired skill, *xix*
  as rewriting, 3
writing teachers
  writers as, *xiv–xv*

Zen and the Art of Writing (Bradbury),
    238